Finance for the general manager

THE HENLEY MANAGEMENT SERIES

Series Adviser: Professor Bernard Taylor

Also available in the McGraw-Hill Henley Management Series:

MANAGING INFORMATION
Information systems for today's general manager
A V Knight and D J Silk   ISBN 0-07-707086-0

THE NEW GENERAL MANAGER
Confronting the key challenge of today's organization
Paul Thorne   ISBN 0-07-707083-6

THE COMPETITIVE ORGANIZATION
Managing for organizational excellence
Gordon Pearson   ISBN 0-07-707480-7

TOTAL CAREER MANAGEMENT
Strategies for creating management careers
Frances A Clark   ISBN 0-07-707558-7

CREATING THE GLOBAL COMPANY
Successful internationalization
Colin Coulson-Thomas   ISBN 0-07-707599-4

THE HANDBOOK OF PROJECT-BASED MANAGEMENT
Improving the processes for achieving strategic objectives
Rodney Turner   ISBN 0-07-707656-7

CREATING EXCELLENCE IN THE BOARDROOM
A guide to shaping directorial competence and board effectiveness
Colin Coulson-Thomas   ISBN 0-07-707796-2

Details of these and other titles in the series are available from:

The Product Manager, Professional Books, McGraw-Hill Book Company
Europe, Shoppenhangers Road, Maidenhead, Berkshire SL6 2QL
Telephone 0628 23432   Fax 0628 770224

Finance for the general manager

A four-step approach to the key financial techniques

Roger Mills and Jan Stiles

McGRAW-HILL BOOK COMPANY

London · New York · St Louis · San Francisco · Auckland
Bogotá · Caracas · Lisbon · Madrid · Mexico · Milan
Montreal · New Delhi · Panama · Paris · San Juan
São Paulo · Singapore · Sydney · Tokyo · Toronto

Published by
McGRAW-HILL Book Company Europe
Shoppenhangers Road, Maidenhead, Berkshire, SL6 2QL, England
Telephone 0628 23432
Fax 0628 770224

British Library Cataloguing in Publication Data
Mills, Roger W.
  Finance for the General Manager: A four-step
  approach to the key financial techniques
  – (Henley Management Series)
  I. Title   II. Stiles, Janine   III. Series
  657

  ISBN 0-07-707960-4

Library of Congress Cataloging-in-Publication Data
Mills R.W. (Roger W.)
  Finance for the general manager: a four-step approach to the key
  financial techniques/R.W. Mills and J. Stiles.
     p. cm. – (The Henley management series)
  Includes bibliographical references and index.
  ISBN 0-07-707960-4
  1. Corporations–Finance.   2. Corporations–Accounting.
  I. Stiles, J. (Jan).   II. Title.   III. Series.
  HG4026.M56   1994
  658.15–dc20   93-44836

12345 CUP 97654

Typeset by BookEns Limited, Baldock, Herts.
and printed and bound in Great Britain at the University Press, Cambridge.

Contents

Preface

Everything I know about this subject would fit into a nutshell and still leave plenty of room for the nut.

LORD MANCROFT

How many of you perceive your understanding of financial matters in this way? Many general managers recognize the need to know more about the financial aspects of their business, but cannot afford the time involved in becoming a financial specialist. The purpose of this book is to help you to fill this gap and to provide you with a practical understanding of those areas of finance essential for those intent on a career in general management.

Traditionally, general management was considered to refer only to those at the very top of an organization but this has changed over time to include those responsible for taking an integrative, holistic and strategic approach to the management of their organizations. Today, such managers are to be found in several functions and levels in organizations, not only at the top.

What do such individuals look like today? Paul Thorne in *The New General Manager*, the first book in this series, provides an apt description:

> a person who takes a piece of business, and accepts the responsibility for producing a profit from it. The general manager cannot raise capital on the free market and he is constrained by corporate policies concerning the nature and direction of growth. Otherwise, it is as if the business is his own. There may be as little as £1 million or as much as £500 million in turnover.

These general managers are almost all under 45. They are ambitious, work-driven, capable and, for the most part, highly analytical. They are often left very much to their own devices, with limited specialist advice and (for several reasons, including cost and distance) little supervision. Their appointment may well mark the first time that they have had to consider managing as a heavily people-focused activity.

What the book covers and how to use it

The book has been written to develop a chronology of accounting and finance for the general manager as distinct from the financial specialist. In recognition of the limited formal exposure you may have had to accounting and finance the book begins simply, with a review of basic principles in Part One. The following parts are designed to build on this basic framework and to introduce more complex issues as you progress through the book. In this way, we believe it deals with financial matters particularly relevant for those focusing upon general management in a structured and applicable fashion.

The book has been divided into four main parts, these are:

- Part One: Financial Principles and Practices
- Part Two: Financial Awareness
- Part Three: Financial Management
- Part Four: Financial Direction.

The contents of these parts are outlined below:

Part One

Chapters 1 to 6 deal with *financial principles and practices*. They provide a review of the basic principles and language of accounting, together with a discussion of the main financial statements and basic ratio analysis. These chapters are intended to provide a review of accounting for those who have a limited knowledge of basic accounting principles and techniques.

Part Two

Chapters 7 to 11 cover issues associated with published annual reports and accounts such as what information is provided, what influences the amount and quality of information produced, how to analyse such information, how it is possible to manipulate it, and how it differs between various countries.

Very simply, these five chapters can be thought of as dealing with *financial awareness*, an important issue for all managers including general managers.

Part Three

Chapters 12 to 17 cover issues associated with *financial management* for which general managers are typically ultimately responsible. These include: managing cash, working capital, business costs, capital expenditure and risk.

Part Four

Chapters 18 to 20 are concerned with issues relating to *financial direction* and, in particular, the measurement and management of business value. Somehow all facets of the business have to be drawn together and considered in financial terms to permit sound financial direction.

What is the book's focus of attention?

Many general managers will have developed an understanding of accounting and finance based upon what can be termed the conventional wisdom, which focuses upon profit analysis over a relatively short-term horizon. This conventional wisdom represents the language of accounting within most of the organizations of which we have experience and cannot, therefore, be completely ignored. It is our view that such wisdom has many shortcomings and that an alternative approach is required to meet the needs of general management. However, because most businesses operate within a profit-oriented short-term framework, we will not only review the conventional practices but also develop them to include a longer-term perspective relevant to the needs of the general manager.

This corresponds with our view that the financial management of any business is extremely difficult for a general manager without the use of an appropriate framework, specifically one which is integrative, holistic and strategic. As we will demonstrate, such a framework can be developed using various principles, tools and techniques of accounting and finance.

We can use Fig. 0.1 to help clarify matters. It concerns motorists, their level of awareness and how they overtake. Those with high and low levels of awareness but who seldom overtake (boxes 1 and 2) may cause considerable frustration but are less of a danger on the roads than those with a low level

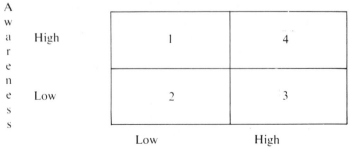

Figure 0.1 Awareness/overtaking matrix

of awareness who are keen to overtake (box 3). They are a real menace because they take unnecessary risks which will almost inevitably lead to disaster. The situation is different from those with a high level of awareness who overtake frequently (box 4) but only when it is safe to do so.

This analogy can be seen to have some relevance to general management. Ultimately, those general managers responsible for directing the enterprise have to ensure that they satisfy the requirements of shareholders, together with other stakeholders. In common with the driving analogy this responsibility means not driving recklessly by overtaking when it is unsafe to do so, and also that safe opportunities for overtaking should not be missed.

Of course, the real challenge is to ensure that the cause and effect relationship between the driving of the car and the resulting performance is clearly understood. Without this it will be impossible to guarantee results. So it is for the general manager(s) responsible for directing the business. While for a car the relevant controls that have to be operated to achieve a given result are well known, those for a business are far less clear-cut.

For many years there has been a heavy reliance by those directing the business upon accounting-based measures of performance. These measures have been strongly criticized because of their tendency to encourage short-termism. This is an issue that has received extensive media coverage in recent times, and a major contribution to understanding it has been provided by Paul Marsh, Professor of Management and Finance at the London Business School. In his publication *Short-termism on Trial* he reviewed the evidence relating to the short-termism debate. In particular he considered the notion that the competitive edge of Britain and America has been dulled by their failure to emphasize long-term investment and this, in turn, is the fault of their financial markets.

Marsh found no support for the stock market's pricing behaviour being the cause of short-termism. His research showed that shares are not mispriced and the markets do not give too much weight to current and near-term earnings and dividends. Furthermore, a substantial body of research has revealed that company announcements about capital expenditure, research and development and new investments are often treated as plus and not minus factors by the market.

In contrast, management often takes short-term measures in the corporate sector. For example, businesses are milked and research and development is neglected because of pressures which are felt to be real, such as the following perceived needs:

– To enlarge the dividend.
– To increase the share price.

– To respond to fund managers and to owners who are speculators rather than investors.
– To ward-off the takeover threat.

In fact Marsh identified management as being a major source of the short-termism problem. This is illustrated by his concluding paragraph which has significant implications for the general manager: 'In short, the message is simple, if trite. The way ahead for both City and industry is for UK managers to get on with managing as if tomorrow mattered.'

What support is there for Marsh's view of a short-term perspective being taken by UK management? Well, for example, a study undertaken by MORI on behalf of Coopers and Lybrand Deloitte in 1991 found that three out of four senior managers believe profit to be the most important measure of corporate performance, compared with only one in three analysts and fund managers and the City which judges business less by reference to accounting profits than to sustainable cash flows. The survey concluded that businesses and investors should adopt measures of performance that concentrate on the present value of future cash flows which have a distinct advantage over more traditional approaches which may often be subject to accounting distortions.

This message has also been conveyed by others like UBS Phillips and Drew (now UBS) in its publication *Accounting for Growth*, which observed that ultimately all accounting comes back to cash. Cash flow is the most difficult parameter to adjust in a company's accounts and, equally important, the tracing of cash movements in a company can lead to the identification of unusual accounting practices. This is quite unlike profits which are relatively easy to influence and, as a consequence, there should be less emphasis placed on the reported progression of earnings per share and more attention paid to balance sheet movements, dividend potential and, most importantly of all, cash. This is a significant observation, particularly in light of the traditionally held importance of accounting-based measures of performance.

We will show how, in principle, it is possible 'to manage as if tomorrow mattered' by adopting an approach where the focus of attention is placed upon cash flow, or money, rather than profit. Just as cash is important in our private lives, it is also important in business. Indeed, comments as to its importance have been forthcoming particularly in light of the incidence of corporate failures in the early 1990s.

In fact, the importance of cash and a focus upon cash-related issues is a significant feature of this book. This is because a considerable amount of empirical research has demonstrated that there is a significant relationship between cash flow and share prices. This is particularly so when cash flow is measured in terms of those cash flows to and from long-term lenders and shareholders.

As well as research confirming the superiority of cash flow measures over conventional accounting measures, specific accounting-based measures of performance have been found in recent UK studies to fare poorly as indicators of what shareholders expect to receive by way of dividends and capital appreciation. For example, in a study reported in 1988, Michael Barron and John Lawless found that there is, overall, only a modest statistical relationship between shareholder return and earnings per share growth and virtually no relationship at all with return on equity, both popular accounting-based measures of performance. This has been confirmed more recently by Dennis Henry and Geoff Smith of P-E International. In their work, based upon a sample of the 250 largest UK industrial and commercial companies over a five-year period, they found no correlation at all between earnings per share and shareholder return.

How can it be that there is such a poor relationship between earnings per share and shareholder return? A major source of the problem as far as the United Kingdom is concerned can be attributed to what is known as creative accounting practices – an issue we will discuss in a later chapter.

Summary

As we indicated at the outset of this preface, the concern of the book is to provide a review of accounting and financial matters relevant to the needs of the general manager of the 1990s.

We have identified the need to manage as if tomorrow mattered and hence the importance of a cash flow perspective, as distinct from the conventional wisdom of accounting and finance. However, general management will demand the ability to be able to work within conventional wisdom, quite simply because this is the accepted *modus operandi* in most organizations. As a consequence we will provide a comprehensive review of such conventional wisdom, but we also take you beyond by reviewing the application of discounted cash flow analysis in the measurement of business value which has become so important in viewing restructuring opportunities for organizations in the form of acquisitions and divestments.

In short, the book has been written to tell a story which goes from the basic principles encapsulated in the conventional wisdom through to contemporary value-oriented approaches. Many of you will not need the whole story, certain parts may be too basic for you. But, hopefully, you will find the manner in which the book has been written allows you to work with it in a manner which suits your needs.

Acknowledgements

The authors would like to acknowledge the contributions of Christopher Reilly of S. G. Warburg Securities, Graham Quick of Extel Financial Ltd and Derek Bonham of Hanson PLC who spared their valuable time to provide information for this text. Many thanks also to David Parker for his helpful comments and advice.

PART ONE
FINANCIAL PRINCIPLES AND PRACTICES

If you find the language of accounting or the way financial information is presented to be a mystery, and if you have heard of the balance sheet, profit and loss account and cash flow statement, but you do not have a clue what they really mean, read on! Part One has been written for you.

You may find Part One very simplistic and we recognize that many of you will be able to skip through it quite quickly. Nevertheless it is important because issues covered here form the building blocks for what follows.

What are the issues we cover here? They can be summarized as:

1. A review of the differences between the three main financial statements.
2. The distinction between profit and cash flow.
3. How to form a view of the business using the three main financial statements.
4. The principles applied in preparing financial statements.
5. Ratios to assess profitability and the use of business assets.

Without a sound grasp of these key financial principles and practices it really is very difficult to come to terms with financial matters, even from a general management perspective.

1
The balance sheet

The trouble with facts is that there are so many of them
SAMUEL McCHORD CROTHERS

The world of accounting and finance can often seem full of mystique, and nowhere is this more apparent than with the financial statements produced to convey the financial performance of a business. In fact, there are three such statements and in this chapter we will pay attention to one of them – the balance sheet. This statement is particularly useful for providing an understanding of how those involved with finance as a specialism view the world. If you are able to come to terms with the balance sheet with regard to both its content and the principles involved, you will have overcome a major barrier encountered by many general managers.

In this chapter, we will show that the principles underlying the balance sheet are very straightforward. If you understand some very basic arithmetic equations, then you can go a long way to understanding the balance sheets produced by businesses operating in very different countries. This understanding is essential for the general manager. It is also important to have an insight into how those involved with preparing financial statements like the balance sheet interpret the rules for their production. We will review the rules in a later chapter, but for now we will turn our attention to the balance sheet itself.

1.1 What is the balance sheet?

The balance sheet is not really complicated in principle; it is quite simply a snapshot of a business's assets and liabilities at a particular point in time. It is reliant upon the simple notion that the total money value of the assets or possessions of a business equals, or balances with, the financial claims on the business; that is:

```
+-----------------------------------+
|                                   |
|            ASSETS                 |
|                                   |
+-----------------------------------+

              equal

+-----------------------------------+
|                                   |
|          LIABILITIES              |
|                                   |
+-----------------------------------+
```

In a balance sheet you will find far more than just two totals, or balances, one corresponding with the assets, or possessions of the business, and the other the liabilities, or the financial claims, against them. Businesses typically have many different types of assets like land and buildings, plant and machinery, vehicles and stocks of raw materials, partly finished and finished goods. Equally they may have many different types of liabilities, for example, long-term loans and bank overdrafts. Each of these different types of assets and liabilities can be identified individually to show how the totals or 'balances' of assets and liabilities are made up. Let us examine the composition of the balances a little further by looking at liabilities. These are typically divided between the owners who have an equity stake – known as owners' equity – or shareholders' funds, and those who have no equity stake but who simply lend to the business as a commercial proposition. Such lenders agree to be rewarded typically by way of interest payments to be made irrespective of the performance of the business, unlike the owners whose returns will be related to business performance.

This distinction between owners' equity and external liabilities means that the balance sheet can be rewritten as:

```
+-----------------------------------+
|                                   |
|            ASSETS                 |
|                                   |
+-----------------------------------+

              equal

+-----------------------------------+
|                                   |
|        LIABILITIES +              |
|        OWNERS' EQUITY             |
|                                   |
+-----------------------------------+
```

In most organizations a balance sheet is typically produced as a result of a process of which you will doubtless have heard – 'double-entry book-keeping'. This process involves two bookkeeping entries for every transaction and while it can become very complex, it is basically very straightforward. Consider, for example, the purchase of a factory to be funded by a commercial loan of £1 million. In double-entry bookkeeping terms there would be an entry recorded against both a factory (asset) and a commercial loan (liability). Very simply, with just this transaction, the balance sheet would end up as follows after receipt of £1 million cash from the commercial lender and the payment of £1 million to the seller of the asset:

```
┌──────────────────────────────────┐
│                                  │
│            ASSET                 │
│        Factory £1 million        │
│                                  │
└──────────────────────────────────┘

               equal

┌──────────────────────────────────┐
│                                  │
│          LIABILITY               │
│        Commercial loan           │
│          £1 million              │
│                                  │
└──────────────────────────────────┘
```

The double-entry bookkeeping process ensures that both parts of the balance sheet are equal (i.e. that they balance) – provided of course that the bookkeeper makes no errors! At the end of a trading period, it is the practice in many businesses to sum assets and all of the liabilities in what is known as a trial balance. If both are equal then this provides a reasonable, but not perfect, indication that the financial records of the business are accurate.

A useful way of looking at a balance sheet for the general manager is as a mathematical equation in which there are two equal sides and items can be moved from one side of the equation to the other quite simply by changing signs.

This is such an important point that it is worthy of further illustration. Consider the following business with assets, owners' equity and external obligations:

	£ million
Assets	2
	2
Owners' equity	1
External obligations	1
	2

By moving external obligations and changing their sign such that they are grouped with assets, the balance sheet totals change significantly, although they still equal one another:

	£ million
Assets	2
Less External obligations	1
	1
Owners' equity	1
	−1

This simple illustration is important because it serves to explain how the same information can be portrayed so as to appear to produce very different results. You will also find it useful in understanding the differences between UK balance sheets and those produced in other countries.

1.2 What does a balance sheet look like?

Typically, a balance sheet will reflect the individual sources of finance and the assets they have been used to acquire. However, the amount of detail will depend upon circumstances such that, for internal purposes, a considerable amount of information may be provided, in stark contrast to what will often be found in published accounts. There is a further distinction between the format of internal balance sheets and those for publication. While those produced internally vary from organization to organization according to specific requirements, published balance sheets in the United Kingdom are constrained in format by legal requirements as you will discover in Chapter 7.

While you may find balance sheets vary considerably in terms of layout and presentation, the underlying principle used in drafting them is identical from business to business and from country to country – there *must* be two equal parts. To illustrate this, consider the following balance sheet, which bears a resemblance in format to that likely to be encountered in the published accounts of UK public limited companies. This is known as the vertical format, where one part of the balance sheet sits above, rather than alongside, the other.

Balance sheet at year end

	£ million	£ million
Fixed assets		
Land and buildings	20	
Plant and machinery	100	
Vehicles	<u>10</u>	130
Current assets		
Stocks	38	
Debtors	40	
Bank balances and cash	<u>2</u>	
	80	
Less Creditors: amounts falling due within one year	<u>40</u>	
Net current assets		<u>40</u>
Total assets less current liabilities		90
Less Creditors: amounts falling due after one year		<u>30</u>
		<u><u>60</u></u>
Capital and reserves		
Owners' equity:		
Share capital		20
Reserves		<u>40</u>
		<u><u>60</u></u>

The grouping of certain items within the balance sheet is important to note. 'Current assets' and 'Creditors: amounts falling due within one year' are grouped together, the difference between them showing 'net current assets' otherwise known as working capital.

1.3 Sources of business finance

Sources of business finance can be divided into

- Owners' equity (in the example above £60 million).
- External obligations (£70 million).

Each of these can be subdivided such that owners' equity comprises:

- Share capital (£20 million).
- Reserves (£40 million).

External obligations comprise:

- Long-term liabilities (creditors falling due after one year) (£30 million).
- Short-term or current liabilities (creditors falling due within one year) (£40 million).

Let us now look at these sources of finance individually.

Share capital

The owners of share capital are usually only liable for the debts of the company up to the value of their share investment because of the principle of limited liability. In other words, unless personal assets have been secured against a business loan, the maximum loss a shareholder can suffer in the event of failure is the share capital invested. This is quite unlike organizations, such as sole traders and partnerships, where individuals are personally liable for all debts incurred by the business.

Share capital may consist of different types of shares, each carrying particular rights, preferences and priorities. The two main types of share capital are 'preference shares', which give rights to a preferential or predetermined dividend, and 'ordinary shares' (sometimes referred to as equity shares), the holders of which are entitled to the residual profits from the business after all other claims have been met. While the ordinary shareholders take more risk than the preference shareholders, they do stand to make greater gains or greater losses. This is because they forgo a fixed dividend in favour of one contingent upon the fortunes of the business.

Long-term liabilities

These are liabilities typically with more than one year to maturity which are often incurred because there is no desire to divide the ownership further, or because such sources are cheaper. One often-used source is a commercial loan from an institution like a bank, where, for a mature company, loans will be given against the security of company assets. The security takes the form of a 'charge on assets' which gives the lender priority in terms of recovering the loan should the business fail.

Short-term or current liabilities

These are liabilities in the form of moneys owed and payable by the business within the normal trading cycle, but you will often find them being classified in the annual accounts published by businesses as items due and payable within one year. Examples include bank overdrafts, creditors and taxation. The cost of such liabilities may be obvious, such as the interest payable on a bank overdraft, but on other sources like trade creditors, the annual cost of such finance may be far less apparent. Delaying the payment of trade creditors or paying them more quickly will have cash flow implications. At its simplest, delaying the payment of creditors may well reduce the need for a bank overdraft. Paying them more quickly may have the opposite effect. In either case, there will be an effect on the amount of interest payable to the bank as a result of having a higher or lower overdraft.

Reserves

These are created by accumulating funds from internally generated profits which have been retained in the business. In a profit-making business, after tax and interest have been accounted for, any profit which remains belongs to the shareholders. This remaining profit may either be paid out to shareholders as dividends, or kept in the business to fund future growth. Typically, some is paid out and some is retained, that which is retained being known as a 'reserve'.

The term 'reserve' is one of the most commonly misunderstood financial terms. It is often incorrectly assumed that a reserve represents a cash sum held by a company in case of emergencies. However, this is rarely the case. Often reserves have been, or will be, reinvested in the assets of the business and do not exist as cash.

1.4 How are funds deployed?

Broadly speaking, funds raised can be used for three purposes:

1. To purchase fixed assets (in the case of our earlier example £130 million).
2. To fund working capital (of £40 million).
3. To make one or more external investment(s) (none in the case of our example).

Fixed assets

These are possessions the business uses to carry out the activities from which it hopes to generate profit. The term 'fixed' is used because they are not for sale in the normal course of business. They include such items as land, buildings, plant and machinery, office equipment, motor vehicles and computers. These are called the 'tangible' fixed assets of the business because they can be seen and touched. In a later chapter you will encounter another type of fixed asset known as the 'intangible' fixed asset, one of the most common of which is 'goodwill'. Goodwill arises when a business is purchased for a sum greater than the value of its net assets acquired (tangible assets *less* any liabilities). In other words, the business has a value to an outsider which is greater than its tangible value.

One final point worth noting about fixed assets is that money spent upon fixed assets is known as 'capital expenditure', a subject we will discuss more fully later in Chapters 15 and 16.

Working capital

All businesses need finance to provide funds for use in the everyday operation of the business. In order to operate efficiently and effectively, businesses will often incur expenditure on making the operations and the processes of the business better. Such expenditure may be for the bulk purchase of raw materials to obtain discounts and to ensure that sufficient is available to guarantee smooth production. Other finance may be needed to support credit sales and to provide stocks of finished goods so that immediate deliveries can be made to customers.

At any point in time, a business is likely to have finance tied up in the following items, which are known as 'current assets'. In terms of the earlier example, current assets amount to £80 million consisting of the following:

- Stocks of raw materials and components, partly finished goods or work-in-progress (WIP), and finished goods of £38 million.
- Trade debtors, that is, the money owed by customers of £40 million.
- Liquid funds in the form of surplus cash of £2 million.

Items of working capital may change in value. For example, stocks of raw materials, components or finished goods may fall in value in the following circumstances:

- When they have deteriorated over time and are now not fit for use.
- When they are held for a product no longer manufactured or no longer sold.
- When they are held but have been superseded by others that are better or cheaper.

In each of these cases the value of the stock may fall but, of course, there are also situations in which the opposite might happen. For example, every time the price of a product goes up, stocks of finished goods become more valuable. We saw a classic example of this in the latter months of 1990 when oil prices increased. This resulted in an increase in the price of petrol charged by the oil companies and an increase in the value of the stock of petrol held by filling stations.

Even the debtors' value shown in the balance sheet may not necessarily be an accurate reflection of the money that can be collected. Some customers may undergo financial difficulties and others may dispute the quality and/or the quantity of the goods or the services provided. Such circumstances may make it impossible to collect 100 per cent of the figure invoiced.

Holding too many current assets is not desirable. In effect, holding too many represents a lost financial opportunity in terms of the returns that could be obtained from investing in areas of the business which provide growth like fixed assets. As a consequence, it is vital to keep current assets as lean as possible.

Any discussion of current assets is incomplete without considering current liabilities, such as trade creditors and bank overdrafts which are £40 million in our earlier example. The difference between current assets and liabilities (£80 million − £40 million) is known as 'working capital' or 'net current assets'. Most businesses monitor their working capital position very carefully and you will often find current assets and current liabilities grouped together for this reason. The composition of net current assets can change from day to day, which means that the balance sheet for any given day may differ substantially from that on another − a point clearly to be borne in mind when interpreting financial statements.

Good working capital management is vital to the success of the business and is worthy of particular managerial attention. For this reason we consider this issue in greater detail in later chapters.

Investments

In the event that there is a short-term money surplus (that is, the money will be required by the business again in the near future), short-term investments will be made which can easily be reconverted back to cash as the need arises. If the surplus continues and is seen to be long term, then long-term investments will be sought to ensure the highest possible return on investment. Alternatively, established companies may reach a situation where it is not profitable to invest more finance in the business as it stands. In such circumstances the directors may well look outside the business for profitable investment opportunities. Investments considered might include:

- Making long-term loans
- Investing in government stocks
- Buying shares in other companies
- Purchasing other companies outright.

As regards the inclusion of investments in the balance sheet, the investment of money for short periods of time is typically classified as a current asset, whereas long-term investments are usually accorded separate status.

1.5 Conclusion

The balance sheet represents a useful starting point for understanding financial matters.

– It provides a snapshot of the financial position of a business.
– It provides an insight into the sources of business finance.
– It illustrates what the sources of business finance have been used for.

The same general principles underpin a balance sheet despite differences in format and language. One useful way of understanding balance sheet layouts is in terms of a mathematical equation in which items can be readily moved from one side to the other providing the sign is changed.

There will not necessarily be consistency in the way that assets and liabilities are grouped together. To make sense of a balance sheet with which you are not familiar you may find it necessary to redraft it and regroup items which is a relatively straightforward task.

2
An introduction to profit and cash flow

The chief value of money lies in the fact that one lives in a world in which it is overestimated

HENRY LOUIS MENCKEN

The value of money should never be underestimated, but in the world of finance other indicators of performance are also important. The balance sheet serves as a starting point for understanding financial matters, but you will not get very far without also having a good grasp of profit and cash flow, and how they relate to the balance sheet.

In this chapter we will consider profit and cash flow with reference to the financial statements used to produce information about each of them – the profit and loss account and the cash flow statement. But first let us consider an important question.

2.1 Why produce more than one financial statement?

We will illustrate the reason for producing more than just one financial statement, i.e. the balance sheet, using an example of two general managers. Both hold similar positions in the same multinational company, earn identical incomes and their spending pattern is almost the same, apart from the fact that one, Steve, is buying a house while the other, Terri, rents similar accommodation. Their income and expenditure are as follows:

Monthly income and expenditure

	Steve £	Terri £
Income		
Net salary	3000	3000
Expenditure		
Property costs, food, car, clothes, social, etc	3000	2700
Surplus	–	300

In an average year Terri will generate a surplus of 12 × £300 = £3600 which she invests, while Steve, who generates no surplus, is unable to save anything.

From the information it appears that, of the two, Terri is better off. However, when additional data are included, the picture changes:

Assets owned at the present time

	Steve £	£	Terri £
Car		11,250	11,250
Cash (invested)			3,600
Property	131,250		
Owing on mortgage	108,750	22,500	
		33,750	14,850

The additional information throws a slightly different light on the financial picture. Terri certainly does appear to be wealthier than Steve in terms of monthly surpluses generated, but when their assets are taken into consideration the picture is not as clear. Steve has £33,750 of net assets (total assets *less* the mortgage liability), while Terri has assets of only £14,850. According to this measurement Steve is wealthier than Terri! Of course we cannot overlook the fact that in terms of realising the assets quickly Terri may be far better off. The slump in UK property prices in the early 1990s has served to show this only too well.

The point of this example is to show that there are different facets of the financial picture about which a balanced view must be taken. To focus upon any one is not sound practice. From one perspective, assets, Steve is 'better off' than Terri, and vice versa from the other.

To illustrate the importance of understanding different business perspectives, in a recession many apparently profitable companies find themselves in severe financial difficulties because of a shortage of cash. As a consequence, companies rely on profit and cash information from two separate financial statements together with information about assets (and liabilities) from a third.

2.2 The profit and loss account

While the balance sheet provides a snapshot of the financial position of a business at a specific point in time, the profit and loss account reveals what has happened to business fortunes over time. Just like a balance sheet, there is no single layout used for a profit and loss account, but a common one you will encounter is shown in the example below:

Profit and loss account for the current financial year

	£ million	£ million	
Sales turnover		100	A
Cost of sales		40	B
Gross profit (A−B)		60	C
Distribution costs	8		
Administrative costs	7	15	D
Operating profit (C−D)		45	E
Interest payable		5	F
Net profit before tax (E−F)		40	G
Taxation		10	H
Net profit after tax (G−H)		30	I
Dividends		5	J
Retained profit (I−J)		25	

This profit and loss account starts with the sales turnover for the financial year from which successive costs and charges are deducted, revealing the following different measures of profit:

− *Gross profit*   The difference between sales turnover and cost of sales.
− *Operating profit*   Gross profit after the deduction of distribution and administrative costs.
− *Net profit before tax*   Operating profit after the deduction of interest payable.
− *Net profit after tax*   Net profit before tax *less* taxation.
− *Retained profit*   Net profit after tax *less* dividends.

Each of these may be useful, depending on what it is you want to measure, so you need to ensure that you use the most appropriate measure for the task in hand. It is also important to be aware that the measurement of profit is not an exact science. Two companies with identical characteristics could display different profit figures, which, as we will show in a later chapter, is because a good deal of discretion can be exercised in the interpretation and the application of accounting rules.

However, leaving this aside for the time being, let us consider what information value is provided by each layer of profit found within a profit and loss account.

Gross profit

Gross profit is the difference between the sales turnover and the cost of those sales. It is a widely used measure of profit for businesses involved in multiple activities, where a key concern is to relate the revenues generated from specific lines of business to costs that can be directly attributed to them.

Sales from each activity are related directly to the cost of sales used in their generation and expressed in terms of the gross profit, often called the 'gross margin'. Gross margins, expressed as percentages of sales revenue, are widely used by retailers to indicate the relative profitability of their products.

Operating profit

The next layer of profit, known as the operating (sometimes trading) profit, involves the deduction of distribution and administrative costs. This measure is typically used to gauge the profitability of a part of the business as distinct from the services and/or products it provides. It is important to know what profit is generated after the deduction of overheads like distribution and administrative costs but many of these costs are difficult to attribute to products or services. Therefore, there are problems in identifying operating profit at the product level without making a good deal of human judgement.

Net profit before tax

Net profit before tax is calculated by deducting net interest income from the operating profit. As with all of the measures of profit it can be used to evaluate performance, typically by expressing it as a percentage of sales or the funds used in its generation. However, because operating profit is measured before interest and before taxation, it is often preferred as an indicator of profitability when making comparisons. This is because interest payable, which is deducted in calculating net profit, may give a distorted picture as to the real underlying profitability of a business. Why this may be so is easiest to understand if we consider two companies, identical except for their capital structure. One – Company A – is financed by a mixture of owners' equity and external loans and the other – Company B – is financed entirely by external loans.

Profit and loss account

	Company A £ million		Company B £ million	
Sales turnover	100		100	
Cost of sales	40		40	
Gross profit		60		60
Distribution costs	8		8	
Administrative costs	7	15	7	15
Operating profit		45		45
Interest payable		5		10
Net profit before tax		40		35
Taxation 30%		12		10.5
		28		24.5
Dividend payable		5		–
		23		24.5

Balance sheet (extract)

	Company A	Company B
Owners' equity	50	
Long-term loans (10%)	50	100
	100	100

For Company A there are financing costs consisting of a mixture of interest payable and dividends. Its interest payable is £5 million, while for Company B the interest payable is £10 million While each of these two has the same operating profit (£45 million) the net profit before tax differs: that is £40 million for Company A as distinct from £35 million for Company B. The difference in the interest payable could be taken to imply that a distinct difference exists between the two businesses which apart from the capital structure is clearly not the case. Hence the preference for operating profit when comparing performance.

Net profit after tax

This is a useful indicator of the returns to shareholders. Their concern is typically with the return they will derive from the funds they have tied up. This is calculated after both interest and tax are subtracted to provide an indication of the profit that will be received from equity invested.

Retained profit

This is the fifth and final layer of profit. It is the profit after allowing for dividends and constitutes that profit which is ploughed back into the business. It is also reflected in the balance sheet by an increase in reserves (and assets).

In effect this entry from the profit and loss account can be thought of as providing information about what has happened to a business in the trading period since the last balance sheet showing also how assets have grown. While the balance sheet provides a snapshot relevant only at a specific point in time, the profit and loss account provides a picture of what has happened between successive balance sheets. However, the profit and loss account even in conjunction with a balance sheet, does not provide a sufficiently comprehensive picture of a business. For this, we need a third statement, the cash flow statement.

2.3 The cash flow statement

To achieve success businesses must be profitable and generate sufficient liquidity. We have seen how the profit and loss account provides information about the profitability of a business for a given time period. In a similar vein, the cash statement gives important information about the liquidity of a business.

In the United Kingdom and the United States cash flow statements are required to be produced by organizations and are included by public companies in their annual report. Typically these statements show what has happened to the liquidity of the business over a given time period, usually one year. Such statements are also typically produced for internal purposes and more frequently, i.e. monthly, weekly, or even daily. Often they will be in the form of forecasts rather than summaries of historical events.

These internal statements will be our main focus of attention for now, and we will reserve our consideration of those typically produced for inclusion in an annual report until later. The following example demonstrates a fairly typical format:

Cash flow forecast

£ million	Jan.	Feb.	Mar.	Apr.	May	June
Opening balance (*A*)	—	−4.8	−12.0	−17.8	−23.6	−25.4
Receipts						
Sales	4.0	4.6	5.0	7.0	6.0	6.0
Loan	8.0					
Total (*B*)	12.0	4.6	5.0	7.0	6.0	6.0
Payments						
Materials	6.0	6.0	5.0	7.0	2.0	2.0
Wages	3.5	3.5	3.5	3.5	3.5	3.5
Costs						
Direct	1.3	1.3	1.3	1.3	1.3	1.3
Admin.	0.4	0.4	0.4	0.4	0.4	0.4
Distrib.	0.6	0.6	0.6	0.6	0.6	0.6
Fixed assets	5.0					
Total (*C*)	16.8	11.8	10.8	12.8	7.8	7.8
Closing balance (A)+(B)−(C)	−4.8	−12.0	−17.8	−23.6	−25.4	−27.2

The forecast illustrated shows cash inflows and outflows for a six-month period. Section A shows the opening cash balance for each month which, apart from the first month, is negative, implying an overdraft situation. To this opening balance any cash in, by way of receipts from sales or additional funding obtained, is shown in Section B and any cash payments in running the business are shown in Section C. The result of adding the receipts to the opening balance and deducting any payments produces the closing balance at the end of the month. To understand this, let us consider the month of January. There is no opening cash balance and the only cash potentially available for use will arise from receipts from sales of £4 million and a loan of £8 million. From this £12 million cash inflow during January, prospective payments for materials, wages, other costs and fixed assets are estimated to amount to £16.8 million. This £4.8 million excess of cash outflows results in a negative closing balance for January and opening balance for February, which has, by definition, to be financed somehow, assumed in this case to be by bank overdraft. Taken overall, the situation is disastrous, with the negative balance increasing to an overdraft at the end of the six months of £27.2 million. (Incidentally, what is also important to note is that the costs of servicing such an overdraft have been omitted from the forecast!)

What is vital to understand and what cannot be overemphasized, is that such a poor cash flow situation may not correspond with profitability for the same time period, typically because different practices are applied in its measurement. The essential difference between cash flow and profit is timing. Whereas profit takes account of events which have neither caused cash to be generated nor spent, cash flow ignores such events and only recognizes those corresponding with inflows and outflows of cash. The practices responsible for such differences are, in fact, the subject of a later chapter.

2.4 Conclusion

Profit and cash flow are vital indicators of business performance that must be understood to run a business successfully. They are different but unfortunately are not always recognized as such. This means that too much attention may be paid to one at the expense of the other. In fact, there may often be an overemphasis on profit and a relative ignorance of cash flow. This, as we will show, can be a dangerous practice. However, before doing so, it is important to understand what, if any, relationship exists between the two. This we consider in the next chapter. Before we move on it is worth remembering the main points made in this chapter:

- The profit and loss account provides information about the profitability of a business over a given time.
- The cash flow statement provides important information about the liquidity of a business.
- To get a good understanding of financial matters you need to have a good grasp of profit and cash flow and how they relate to the balance sheet.
- There are different facets of the financial picture about which a balanced view must be taken. To focus upon any one is not sound practice.

3
The relationship between financial statements – forming a view of the business

Where profit is, loss is hidden nearby

JAPANESE PROVERB

How often have you heard conflicting views of the financial picture of a company? This can prove to be a major source of difficulty for the general manager trying to form a clear financial picture, a point that may already have become apparent to you from our discussion in the preceding two chapters. In order to form a clear view of the business the three financial statements already mentioned – the cash flow forecast, the profit and loss account and the balance sheet – need to be used together. Each of these three statements contains different information and offers a different perspective of the business. In this chapter we will develop our discussion from the preceding chapters and show why each of these perspectives is important in order to form a clear view about a business.

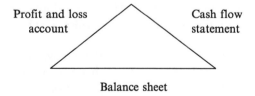

Profit and loss account   Cash flow statement

Balance sheet

Figure 3.1 The financial triangle

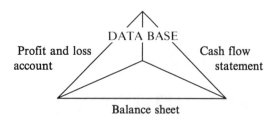

Figure 3.2 The financial pyramid

As illustrated in Fig. 3.1, the financial picture can be crudely likened to a triangle, the sides of which represent the three main financial statements: the balance sheet, the profit and loss account and the cash flow statement. The picture created by a triangle in geometry will be influenced by the length of its sides, an analogy we can apply to the financial picture. Change the length of any of the sides of the triangle and the picture portrayed will be affected and so it is with the three main financial statements. Changes in items found within any of them will typically influence the overall picture.

The financial triangle, as illustrated in Figure 3.2, can be redrawn as a pyramid. The mass within the pyramid can be likened to the database necessary to produce the financial statements – change the database and the cash flow statement, the profit and loss account and/or the balance sheet will change.

The detail of this database (Fig. 3.2) is not the concern of the general manager but rather that of functional specialists, like the management accountant. It is typically used to generate internal management reports or accounts which are of necessity very detailed. A good example of one application of internal management reports to which you will doubtless have been exposed is budgeting. Using the organizational database, together with other projections, budgets can be put together, the final output from the process being a 'master budget' in the form of a cash flow forecast, profit and loss account and balance sheet. This master budget portrays the future financial picture of the business and provides a yardstick against which actual performance can be measured.

The database may also be used in the preparation of the published accounts which record the financial history of the business. Many organizations publish accounts comprising a profit and loss account, cash flow statement and balance sheet that portray the financial picture for the most recent year, with the previous year as a comparison.

3.1 How the main financial statements are related

In this section, using an example we will show how the three main financial statements are related to one another. It draws upon data relating to a 12-month financial plan for a company and will focus upon internal accounting, as distinct from external accounting portrayed in the published accounts. Using these data we will show how internal financial statements in the form of a profit and loss account, a cash flow forecast and a balance sheet can be produced.

3.2 Background information

It is proposed that a new business will be set up under the name HMC Ltd on 1 January. It has been established that £5 million will be required immediately to purchase £5 million of fixed assets, including land valued at £1 million and £4 million of plant and machinery. It has been agreed that this £5 million plus an additional £3 million will be provided by way of a 10-year interest-free loan from its parent Multinat PLC. However, there is some concern about whether such funding will be sufficient. Initial projections for the 12-month period are as follows:

– Sales	£130 million
– Materials used	£48 million
– Materials required to be purchased to allow for closing stock of £4 million	£52 million
– Labour in sales	£42 million
– Other direct costs (including depreciation of £400 000 for the 12-month period)	£16 million
– Administrative costs	£4.8 million
– Distribution costs	£7.2 million

Cash receipts and payments for the 12 months have been estimated. After making an allowance for credit to be allowed to customers and expected to be available from suppliers, the estimates are:

	Cash receipts from sales (£ million)	Cash payments for materials (£ million)
January	4.0	6.0
February	4.6	6.0
March	5.0	5.0
April	7.0	7.0
May	6.0	2.0
June	6.0	2.0

	Cash receipts from sales (£ million)	Cash payments for materials (£ million)
July	8.0	2.0
August	8.0	2.0
September	13.0	2.0
October	13.0	2.0
November	16.0	2.0
December	16.0	2.0
Total for 12 months	106.6	40.0

All expenses other than materials will be paid in equal instalments each month.

Step 1   Preparing the profit and loss account

A number of steps need to be followed to establish the profit or loss for the period. First, cost of sales needs to be calculated and deducted from sales in order to determine the gross profit for the 12-month period. This cost of sales consists of materials, labour and other direct costs and is calculated as follows:

	£ million
Materials	48
Labour	42
Other direct costs	16
Cost of sales	106

Using this information we can complete the following profit and loss account:

	£ million	£ million
Sales turnover		130
Cost of sales		106
Gross profit		24
Distribution costs	7.2	
Administrative costs	4.8	12
Operating profit		12
Interest payable		—
Profit before tax		12
Taxation		—
		12
Dividends		—
		12
Retained profit		12

The profit and loss account is in the same format as that reviewed in Chapter 2. However, because there is no interest payable, taxation or dividends within the plan, the operating profit and the retained profit are identical.

Step 2   Preparing the business cash flow forecast

On the basis of the plan HMC appears to be profitable, but what about the concern expressed about the funding of the business? In order to form a view about this we need to examine the prospective cash flow forecast, which for the first six months of the plan is as follows:

£ million	Jan.	Feb.	Mar.	April	May	June
Opening *balance* (A)	–	−4.8	−12.0	−17.8	−23.6	−25.4
Receipts						
Sales	4.0	4.6	5.0	7.0	6.0	6.0
Loan	8.0					
Total (B)	12.0	4.6	5.0	7.0	6.0	6.0
Payments						
Materials	6.0	6.0	5.0	7.0	2.0	2.0
Wages	3.5	3.5	3.5	3.5	3.5	3.5
Costs:						
Direct	1.3	1.3	1.3	1.3	1.3	1.3
Admin.	0.4	0.4	0.4	0.4	0.4	0.4
Distrib.	0.6	0.6	0.6	0.6	0.6	0.6
Fixed assets	5.0					
Total (C)	16.8	11.8	10.8	12.8	7.8	7.8
Closing balance (A)+(B)−(C)	−4.8	−12.0	−17.8	−23.6	−25.4	−27.2

You may recall that this cash flow forecast for the first six months is the same as that discussed in Chapter 2. It shows that the initial funding to be provided will be inadequate and that at its worst the funding required will be £27.2 million (see Fig. 3.3).

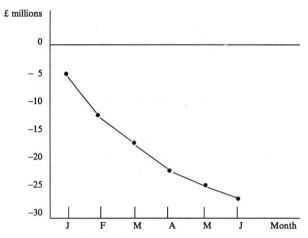

Figure 3.3 Cash flow forecast for first half year

Of course to gauge a complete picture it is necessary to complete the cash flow forecast for the last six months.

£ million	July	Aug.	Sept.	Oct.	Nov.	Dec.
Opening *balance* (A)	−27.2	−27.0	−26.8	−21.6	−16.4	−8.2
Receipts Sales	8.0	8.0	13.0	13.0	16.0	16.0
Total (B)	8.0	8.0	13.0	13.0	16.0	16.0
Payments Materials	2.0	2.0	2.0	2.0	2.0	2.0
Wages	3.5	3.5	3.5	3.5	3.5	3.5
Costs: Direct	1.3	1.3	1.3	1.3	1.3	1.3
Admin.	0.4	0.4	0.4	0.4	0.4	0.4
Distrib.	0.6	0.6	0.6	0.6	0.6	0.6
Total (C)	7.8	7.8	7.8	7.8	7.8	7.8
Closing balance (A) + (B) − (C)	−27.0	−26.8	−21.6	−16.4	−8.2	—

The cash flow forecast for the second six month period reveals that the funding position does not worsen. In fact, by the end of the 12-month period the total cash inflows and outflows are equal – as indicated by there being neither a positive nor a negative closing balance for December (see Fig. 3.4). The implications of this are important. Had the cash flow picture been measured for only the 12-month period and not month by month, no cash flow difficulties would have been evident, as shown by the equality of cash inflows and cash outflows in the last month of the plan. This demonstrates the value of frequent cash flow forecasting and the weakness of statements spanning long periods of time.

Step 3 Preparing the balance sheet

To complete the financial picture we need to prepare the balance sheet. As you will recall from earlier chapters, while the profit and loss account shows the profit or loss that is expected from the plan and the cash flow forecast the cash that will be generated, or the additional funding required, the balance sheet provides a snapshot of the expected financial position at the end of the plan. In fact, information from both the profit and loss account and the cash flow forecast is used in preparing the balance sheet. Retained profit is included within the owners' equity section of the balance sheet and any positive cash or bank balance is included with current assets; any negative balance is included with creditors – amounts falling due within one year. We will now draw the plan together and use the information provided to complete the balance sheet on the last day of the 12-month period.

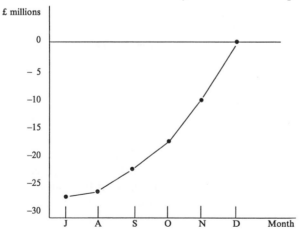

Figure 3.4 Cash flow forecast for second half year

Balance Sheet as at 31 December

	£ million	£ million
Fixed assets		
Land		1.0
Plant and machinery	4.0	
Less: Depreciation	0.4	3.6
		4.6
Current assets		
Stocks	4.0	
Debtors	23.4[1]	
Bank balances and cash	– [2]	
	27.4	
Less Creditors: amounts falling due within one year		
Creditors	12.0[3]	
Net current assets		15.4
Total assets *less* current liabilities		20.0
Less Creditors: amounts falling due after one year		8.0
		12.0
Capital and reserves		
Owners' equity		–
Reserves	[4]	12.0
		12.0

(1) Sales £130 million – cash receipts £106.6 million from sales.
(2) December balance from cash flow forecast.
(3) Materials purchased £52 million – cash payments for materials £40 million.
(4) Retained profit from profit and loss account.

3.3 Changing the Plan

It is quite normal for changes to have to be made to the first draft of a financial plan. In the case of HMC Ltd, the concern about the sufficiency of the funding was well founded, with the cash flow forecast showing that there is a major potential problem associated with this proposed business venture and that there will be a real cash flow crisis if the plan is implemented as it stands. In this case, the level of funding required might well call into question the desirability of the whole venture although it is ultimately profitable.

Is there anything that might be done to alleviate the problem? Clearly any action to increase the cash inflow or to decrease the cash outflow will improve the cash flow position. Areas to consider would be:

- Decreasing the time taken for debtors to pay
- Increasing the time taken to pay creditors
- Deferring payments for capital expenditure
- Obtaining another source of funding.

What is important to understand is that taking any of these courses of action has an impact upon more than just one of the statements. Consider the first, decreasing the time allowed for debtors to pay. Let us consider the impact upon the plan of the rather extreme situation whereby the £23.4 million receivables (debtors) shown to be outstanding on 31 December are assumed to be collected with other cash receipts from sales in six equal monthly instalments from July to December inclusive. In this case the cash flow forecast would be:

£ million	July	Aug.	Sept.	Oct.	Nov.	Dec.
Opening balance	−27.2	−23.1	−19.0	−9.9	−0.8	11.3
Receipts Sales	11.9	11.9	16.9	16.9	19.9	19.9
Payments						
Materials	2.0	2.0	2.0	2.0	2.0	2.0
Wages	3.5	3.5	3.5	3.5	3.5	3.5
Costs:						
Direct	1.3	1.3	1.3	1.3	1.3	1.3
Admin.	0.4	0.4	0.4	0.4	0.4	0.4
Distrib.	0.6	0.6	0.6	0.6	0.6	0.6
	7.8	7.8	7.8	7.8	7.8	7.8
Closing balance	−23.1	−19.0	−9.9	−0.8	11.3	23.4

The earlier receipt of cash is reflected in the cash flow forecast, where now a £23.4 million cash balance is to be found at the end of the six-month period, by comparison with the previous zero balance. This can also be seen in the balance sheet where the former £23.4 million debtors' balance is replaced by bank balances and cash for the same amount.

Balance Sheet as at 31 December

Fixed assets	£ million	£ million
Land		1.0
Plant and machinery	4.0	
Less Depreciation	0.4	3.6
		4.6
Current assets		
Stocks	4.0	
Debtors	– [1]	
Bank balances and cash	23.4 [2]	
	27.4	
Less Creditors: amounts falling due within one year	12.0	
Net current assets		15.4
		20.0
Less Creditors: amounts falling due after one year		8.0
		12.0
Capital and reserves		
Owners' equity		12.0
		12.0

(1) Sales £130 million – cash receipts from sales £130 million.
(2) December balance from cash flow forecast.

It would appear that only two of the three financial statements would be affected, but this is in all likelihood an oversimplification. A comparison of the original and the changed cash flow forecast for the last six months shows a significant reduction in required funding and hence probably a reduction in interest payable which has not been taken into consideration.

For purposes of simplification we have ignored interest payable on the additional funding required, but the truth of the matter is that it represents a cash outflow when paid and is a charge against profits in the profit and loss account. Thus the effect upon cash flow of receiving earlier payments from debtors would be beneficial and any reduction in interest payable would also improve profitability. In other words, the effect of such a change would impact upon all three financial statements.

3.4 Is there a unique financial picture?

The simple answer is no. It is important to realize that a different picture may be perceived by different individuals (Fig. 3.5).

Accounting and finance has characteristics which make it far more like an art than a science and the way profit, assets and wealth are measured can be highly subjective, with resulting values being very dependent upon the view of the person making the measurement. This is best demonstrated by examining how an asset such as a company car might be valued according to different perspectives:

1. *The accountant's view*   An accountant would value a car in terms of its original or 'historical' cost, and for each year owned an amount known as 'depreciation' would be deducted for general wear and tear and loss in value. At any point in time, if asked what the car was worth, the accountant might say that its 'book value' was £5000 – that is the difference between the original cost and the total amounts deducted for depreciation.
2. *The owner manager's view*   An owner manager would be highly likely to value the car in terms of what it would cost to replace should the business

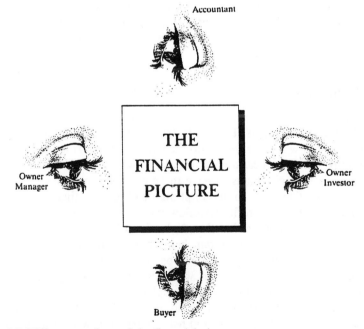

Figure 3.5 Different versions of the financial picture

be deprived of it. This value, its 'replacement' or 'deprival' value, may well be substantially higher than the current net book value.

3. *The buyer's view* The preceding valuations would be unlikely to be used as any source of reference to a buyer such as a secondhand car dealer, whose concern would be with the scrap, or 'net realizable', value. This may well be much lower than the accountant's or the business value.

4. *The owner investor's view* In a situation where the car is one of many assets owned by a business financed from selling shares or borrowing externally, shareholders or investors will be mindful of their total personal investment. They will be concerned not only with cash to be generated to pay dividends but also with the possible increase in value of shares. Consequently, they may wish to know the profit-making capacity of the assets of the business of which the car is a part, taking into account all of its possible cash flows over its life, valued in some way in today's money. This form of valuation is known as 'economic' value.

In short, we have seen with reference to a simple example that there is a variety of methods that can be used in forming a financial picture. Which method is used will depend upon the circumstances and the perspective of the observer.

As a general manager it is important to be aware that there is normally no one unique view of your own or any business – whether it is the whole business or a major part of it. Others outside your business may view it very differently in financial terms.

3.5 Conclusion

We have shown that there is an important relationship between the three main financial statements. The results from both the profit and loss account and the cash flow forecast feed into the balance sheet. This relationship has some important implications, particularly when we consider that it is common for financial plans to have to be changed until they meet express requirements. Changes to assumptions within the financial plan will crucially impact upon profit, cash flow and financial position.

You might be thinking that the production of a financial plan involving three financial statements is extremely mechanical. Indeed, in some respects, it is and in fact the whole process can be, and often is, modelled to operate on computer software. However, while this may be the case, we need to recognize that there are rules and principles that underpin the content and format of financial statements. What these rules and principles are we consider in the next chapter. As you read on try to remember what you have learnt in this chapter, particularly the following points:

- In order to form a clear view of a business the three financial statements – cash flow forecast, profit and loss account and the balance sheet – need to be used together.
- Any changes made in one of these main financial statements will typically influence the overall picture they portray.
- There is no unique financial picture, a different picture may be perceived by different individuals.
- The way profit, assets and wealth are measured can be highly subjective, and resulting values are very dependent upon the view of the person making the measurement.

4

Principles applied in preparing financial statements

Three men apply for a job as an accountant. They are asked one question
'What is two times two?' The first two fellows got it right. The third one replies
'What figure did you have in mind, sir?' He got the job

ANON.

The preparation of financial statements has been made simpler by the
general acceptance of certain accounting principles that can be applied.
What has to be appreciated, however, is that how they are applied is still
open to a fair degree of user interpretation. This means that sometimes they
can be and are applied differently in practice. In many cases they concern
matters of principle which are capable of different interpretation. Nevertheless, there are some important basic principles that are applied in
producing the profit and loss account and the balance sheet. These
principles we discuss in the next section.

4.1 Generally accepted accounting principles

The following represent the generally accepted accounting principles used in
determining profit in the profit and loss account, and financial position in
the balance sheet:

- *Separate identity* An organization is deemed to have a separate existence
  from its owners, which means that personal transactions are excluded
  from business accounts.
- *Going concern* An organization is assumed to continue in operational
  existence for the foreseeable future.

34

- *Money measurement* Accounting only records those events which may be described and measured in money terms.
- *Timing of reports* A time period is fixed as a basis for measuring profit or loss.
- *Realization* Accounting recognizes only those profits that have been realized in an accounting period.
- *Consistency* The accounting treatment of particular items should be the same from period to period; if changed, the difference should be revealed.
- *Prudence/conservatism* Provision should be made for all potential costs whereas profits are not accounted for until realized.
- *Matching* Accounts have to ensure that costs are matched with their associated revenues.
- *Materiality* Non-standard usage in accounting practice is permissible if the effects are not material.

The effect of applying some of these accounting principles can be seen if we compare the difference between the overall cash position and the profit for the 12-month plan for HMC Ltd, the example we introduced in the last chapter. Consider the following:

£million	Cash (Column 1)	Profit (Column 2)	Difference (Column 2−1)
Receipts			
Sales	106.6	130.0	23.4
Loan	8.0		(8.0)
Total (A)	114.6	130.0	15.4
Payments			
Materials	40.0	48.0	8.0
Wages	42.0	42.0	
Costs			
Direct	15.6	16.0	0.4
Administrative	4.8	4.8	
Distribution	7.2	7.2	
Fixed assets	5.0		(5.0)
Total (B)	114.6	118.0	3.4
(A) − (B)		12.0	12.0

The differences between the overall cash flow position and the profit and loss account serve well in illustrating how accounting principles affect the preparation of financial statements. First, in calculating profit, debtors and creditors are recognized. For purposes of measuring profit the total prospective sales revenue of £130 million is the relevant figure, whereas for cash flow it is £106.6 million; that is, £23.4 million are credit sales to debtors as yet unrecognized in the cash flow forecast. In the case of the sums owing to creditors, the difference between columns 1 and 2 relating to materials reveals £8 million. To this must be added £4 million of stock purchased on credit and which has not been counted in measuring profit because of the realization principle. It is, however, included and therefore evident from examining the balance sheet.

The second important difference relates to the treatment of fixed assets. A charge of £400,000 has been made against the profit, by comparison with a £4 million cash outflow for depreciating assets within the £5 million for fixed assets included in the cash flow column (column 1). This £4 million reflects the amount spent on fixed assets and is not affected by accounting principles. By comparison, the £400,000 charge in the profit and loss account reflects the operation of the matching principle whereby the costs of the fixed assets are 'packaged' over their useful economic lives as a series of annual charges, i.e. £4 million of depreciating fixed assets are written off over 10 years = £400,000 per year.

There is no single correct way of 'packaging' such depreciation costs over time and, in practice, as we will illustrate shortly, different depreciation methods are used. Companies can choose different methods, these being evident from disclosures provided in published accounts. The important point to note is that profit disclosures can and do vary because of the depreciation method(s) adopted, unlike cash which is not affected by the depreciation method(s) selected.

One of the accounting principles we identified earlier concerns the realization of profits. Stock, because it has not been sold, has not yet realized profit and therefore should not be included in the measurement of profit in the profit and loss account. Stock is normally shown as an asset in the balance sheet which is expected to release both a future flow of cash and profit.

This example based upon HMC Ltd from the last chapter serves to illustrate how the application of accounting principles may impact upon the financial picture portrayed by financial statements.

4.2 Depreciation and changes in fixed asset value

We have touched upon the matching principle already whereby costs are matched against the revenues they will help to generate. For example, we have illustrated how the costs associated with fixed assets are written off against profit. This issue is important for you to understand, hence we will devote considerable attention to it in this section.

It is generally accepted practice to reduce the value of fixed assets in each successive accounting year to reflect their use in the business and what happens to them during the time that the business possesses them. Consider these examples:

- *Land and buildings* Land owned by a company may well increase in value, but taking a long-term perspective the buildings will deteriorate and require modernization or replacement.
- *Plant and machinery* This may wear out, become obsolete, or just be too expensive to maintain; that is, it is uneconomic. In time, it only has scrap value.
- *Vehicles* These tend to lose value as soon as they are purchased and become increasingly more expensive to operate with time.

The reduction in the value of fixed assets is known as 'depreciation' in the case of tangible assets, and 'amortization' in the case of intangible assets. It is accounted for by making a depreciation or amortization charge for each year over the life of an asset so that the total sum written off is equal to the capital outlay. The easiest way to understand how such a charge is determined is with reference to the following example.

Vehicles are purchased for a total sum of £100,000 and are expected to be put to extremely intensive use for four years. At the end of the four years they are expected to have a value equal to the current value of all of them as scrap which has been estimated as being £2,560.

Two questions which need to be answered are:

1. How can we calculate the depreciation charge?
2. How is this charge shown in the accounts?

The first step is to calculate the total depreciation, that is the value lost during their useful life. This is equal to

Original cost less Residual value

In our example this is

$$£100,000 - £2,560 = £97,440$$

The second step is to spread the total depreciation of £97,440 over the useful life of the asset. A common method of achieving this spread is by dividing the depreciation by the estimated life, that is:

$$\text{Annual depreciation charge} = \frac{\text{Total depreciation}}{\text{Estimated life}}$$

$$= \frac{£97,440}{4 \text{ years}}$$

$$= £24,360$$

Applying this, if we charge £24,360 per annum for four years against profit, we can reduce the value of the vehicles from £100,000 (their original purchase price) to £2,560, their estimated residual value at that time. In this way the value of the vehicles at the end of their estimated working life will be the same as the estimated residual value, and their cost will have been written off annually against profits generated.

In practice, companies often have a preset depreciation life for similar types of assets. For example, plant and equipment may be depreciated over many years, whereas computers with a low estimated life, because of high potential obsolescence, typically attract a high depreciation charge. Assets can be depreciated in a number of ways: the 'straight-line' method which we illustrated earlier is popular but an alternative is the 'reducing balance' method. The reducing balance method involves depreciating an asset by a fixed percentage on the balance outstanding at the start of the period. Using this approach, the value of annual depreciation reduces each year. For assets like motor vehicles this is often a better reflection of what happens to their value over time. Quite simply, they fall in value sharply at the beginning of their working life, but this trails-off with time. By contrast, their maintenance costs increase with the passage of time, often with a totally opposite profile to depreciation charges. When taken together the depreciation and maintenance charges may often produce approximately the same annual sum over the life of the asset.

A comparison of the straight-line and reducing balance methods of depreciation, using a reducing balance percentage of 60 per cent, is illustrated below using our earlier example. The reducing balance method generates a higher depreciation charge in earlier years and a smaller charge in later years than does the straight-line method.

Year	Straight-line	Year end value	Reducing balance	Year end value
	£	£	£	£
1	24,360	75,640	60,000	40,000
2	24,360	51,280	24,000	16,000
3	24,360	26,920	9,600	6,400
4	24,360	2,560	3,840	2,560
Total	97,440		97,440	

Companies in the United Kingdom are relatively free to choose the method of depreciation to be used. This means that two identical companies could report different profits in a given trading period because of the adoption of a different depreciation method. For example, given a profit of £100,000 the annual profits after depreciation according to the two approaches using our earlier example would be as shown in columns 3 and 5 of the following:

Year	Column 1 Profit before depreciation	Column 2 Straight-line depreciation	Column 3 1−2	Column 4 Reducing balance depreciation	Column 5 1−4
	£	£	£	£	£
1	100,000	24,360	75,640	60,000	40,000
2	100,000	24,360	75,640	24,000	76,000
3	100,000	24,360	75,640	9,600	90,400
4	100,000	24,360	75,640	3,840	96,160
Total	400,000	97,440	302,560	97,440	302,560

While the *total* depreciation and the *total* profits reported are the same irrespective of the depreciation method, the depreciation charge year on year differs substantially.

Whereas the annual profit using the straight-line method remains constant at £75,640 for all four years, with the reducing balance method the annual profit is lowest in year 1 when the depreciation charge is highest, and highest in year 4 when the depreciation charge is lowest.

The basis for depreciation charged and, indeed, the total annual depreciation charge is disclosed within company annual reports and accounts. For example, Hanson PLC, one of the largest British companies to which we will refer extensively, gives as the basis for its calculation on page 45 of its 1992 Annual Report:

> No depreciation is provided on freehold land except where mineral reserves are being depleted when amortisation is provided on the basis of tonnage extracted. Timberlands are included at cost and depletion is only provided to the extent that the amount of timber harvested exceeds the estimated growth of standing timber. Reforestation costs are charged to the profit and loss account as incurred. Depreciation of other fixed assets is calculated to write off their cost or valuation over their expected useful lives.

It is usual to show the original cost of fixed assets in the balance sheet and then to deduct from that cost all the depreciation that has so far been incurred, normally known as 'accumulated depreciation'. The difference between the original cost of an asset and its accumulated depreciation is typically known as its 'net book value'. This can best be seen with reference to the following example:

Balance sheet as at 31 December

	Cost £ million	Accumulated depreciation £ million	Net book value £ million
Fixed assets			
Land and buildings	40	—	40
Plant and machinery	100	50	50
Vehicles	50	40	10
	190	90	100

4.3 Revaluing fixed assets

We have seen how fixed assets that fall in value as a consequence of applying a depreciation charge are dealt with. Typically, in practice, all assets other than land are depreciated, however, there have been periods of sharp rises in land and property prices which have resulted in the value of land and property assets in the accounts of companies being considerably out of line with market values. As a consequence, the revaluation of fixed assets periodically became popular practice until the slump in property prices in the late 1980s and early 1990s.

Professional valuers are typically used for asset revaluations. In terms of the effect of such revaluations upon the financial statements, the asset values in the balance sheet are adjusted, being accompanied by a balancing entry to reserves using a specific revaluation (capital) reserve as part of the double-entry bookkeeping process. To demonstrate how this works consider the following example in which the value of land and buildings is shown as £40 million. Let us assume that it has now been revalued at £50 million. The effect upon the balance sheet taking this revaluation into consideration would be as follows:

	£ million
Fixed assets	
Land and buildings	+10
Capital and reserves	
Reserves	+10

4.4 Conclusion

In this chapter we have reviewed a number of generally accepted accounting principles used in preparing financial statements and we have focused in particular upon one of these – depreciation.

A sound understanding of these accounting principles is helpful in understanding why businesses may be profitable and at the same time have very little cash, and vice versa. They may be used for both internal accounting and also for external financial reporting via published accounts. It is important to be quite clear, however, that they are principles which may be interpreted and applied differently, a point which will become all too apparent in Chapter 10. Before continuing it is worth recapping the main points of this chapter.

- The preparation of financial statements has been made simpler by the general acceptance of certain accounting principles. However, these are still open to a fair degree of user interpretation.
- Companies can still use different depreciation methods. As a result profit disclosures can and do vary.
- Assets can be depreciated in a number of ways; the straight-line method, and the reducing balance method are two of the most popular.

5
Business profitability ratios

The rate of unemployment is 100%, if it is you that is unemployed
ANON.

Statistics can often be interpreted differently depending upon a particular viewpoint. Therefore, in addition to understanding the meaning of the contents of financial statements and the principles which underpin each, it is important to be able to interpret the message(s) they convey.

We will demonstrate in the next two chapters that ratios can be calculated for evaluating business performance with regard to both profitability and the utilization of business assets. In this chapter we focus specifically on profitability and we will show how a hierarchy of profitability ratios can be developed by drawing upon the main financial statements. This hierarchy operates by identifying the most important or key ratios and only requires further ratio calculations if the information conveyed is inadequate for useful interpretation and management action. It is a useful diagnostic tool that avoids a frequently encountered problem – the calculation of numerous ratios without any structure in approach and no clear understanding as to their value!

In what follows we will assume the focus of attention to be upon a piece of the total business, where the general manager is responsible for producing a profit within the constraints of corporate policy. As such, he or she will usually have responsibility for some assets, but not usually for their financing unless they form part of the working capital. The concern of such individuals may well be to ensure that the return achieved by the assets for which they are responsible, often known as the 'return on assets' or the 'return on capital employed' meets with corporate requirements. A good example of how this can be applied can be seen with reference to the General Electric Company (GEC) plc. Since 1968 Lord Weinstock, the Managing Director, has been reported as using the following seven key criteria to monitor the performance of the GEC divisions:

1. Profit on capital employed
2. Profit on sales
3. Sales as a multiple of capital employed
4. Sales as a multiple of fixed assets
5. Sales as a multiple of stocks
6. Sales per employee
7. Profits per employee.

These seven ratios can be seen to be related to one another within a framework such that the effects of improving events in any one of them can be traced through and measured for the business as a whole. In what follows we will show how key questions about business unit performance can be reviewed using such a related set of ratios by drawing upon the financial plan for HMC Ltd which we discussed in Chapter 3. You will remember that £8 million were raised by way of a long-term interest-free loan from HMC's parent Multinat PLC. In fact, no equity was raised in this new venture, which is quite unrealistic. Shareholders' funds of an amount at least equal to the loan would be expected to be raised by the lenders, particularly to avert the disastrous cash flow forecast. We shall assume that £16 million were raised to finance part of the cash flow and working capital. Ignoring interest payment effects, a £16 million cash balance will be held at the year end because the net cash flow was zero.

   We are now ready to prepare the balance sheet at the end of the year.

HMC Ltd profit and loss account for the year ended 31 December

	£ million	£ million
Sales turnover	130.0	
Cost of sales	106.0	
Gross profit		24.0
Distribution costs	7.2	
Administrative costs	4.8	12.0
Operating profit		12.0
Interest payable		—
Net and retained profit		12.0

HMC Ltd balance sheet as at 31 December

	£ million	£ million
Fixed assets		
Land		1.0
Plant and machinery	4.0	
Less Depreciation	0.4	3.6
		4.6

	£ million	£ million
Current assets		
Stocks	4.0	
Debtors	23.4	
Bank balances and cash	16.0	
	43.4	
Less Creditors: amounts		
falling due within one year	12.0	
Net current assets		31.4
Total assets *less* current liabilities		36.0
Less Creditors: amounts falling		
due after one year		8.0
		28.0
Capital and reserves		
Owners' equity		16.0
Reserves		12.0
		28.0

We will take the first three GEC ratios and show how they, together with some additional ratios, can be used to evaluate profitability. Further discussion of the ratios in the GEC list we reserve for the next chapter where we focus more specifically upon the use of business assets.

5.1 Profit on capital employed

What is meant by profit on capital employed? Quite simply, this is a ratio which relates the profit generated by a business to the capital employed or the assets used in its generation. However, there are some definitional issues. In Chapter 2 we demonstrated that there are different definitions of profit and the same is true for capital employed. Capital employed in the United Kingdom is typically measured in terms of the net assets of the business. In fact, this is a misleading term because it has more than one meaning. For purposes of ratio analysis, net assets are defined as fixed assets plus working capital (fixed assets + current assets − current liabilities). By comparison if you work for a US corporation you may encounter total assets being used (fixed assets + current assets), for calculating profit on capital employed. This typically means that the denominator used in the profit on capital employed calculation is larger and the resulting ratio calculated lower. The existence of alternative measures means that one must always be quite clear about the definitions applied in measuring both return and capital employed in any profit on capital employed calculation. In what follows we will base our discussion of the profit ratio on capital employed around the following definition:

$$\text{Profit on capital employed per cent} = \frac{\text{Profit before interest and tax}}{\text{Capital employed}} \times 100$$

We have considered the definition of capital employed, but not that for profit. Why is profit before interest and taxation payable used in calculating the ratio? The simple answer is to ensure as far as possible that the definition of profit excludes distortive effects arising from the tax system and those from a particular capital structure which may have nothing at all to do with the intrinsic profitability of the business (which we illustrated in Chapter 2).

Profit and loss account

	Company A £ million		Company B £ million	
Sales turnover	100		100	
Cost of sales	40		40	
Gross profit		60		60
Distribution costs	8		8	
Administrative costs	7	15	7	15
Operating profit		45		45
Interest payable		5		10
Net profit before tax		40		35
Taxation 30%		12		10.5
		28		24.5
Dividend payable		5		—
		23		24.5
Balance sheet (extract)				
Owners' equity		50		
Long-term loans (10%)		50		100
		100		100

But do note that there is no universal standard for profitability ratios. You may find a slightly different definition used in your own organization and you will have to learn to adapt to its use. Remember that by and large there is considerable judgement within accounting and finance.

The possibility of alternative accounting and financial definitions flags up one important point for you always to bear in mind – *in any discussions about ratios you must establish how they have been defined, if their interpretation is to be meaningful.* Do remember that there are very few hard and fast rules about ratio calculations and that the method employed will often depend substantially upon the preference of the analyst.

Let us now calculate profit on capital employed percentage using data extracted from the profit and loss account and balance sheet of HMC Ltd taken from Chapter 3.

The profit before interest and tax is the operating profit of £12 million. It could also have been calculated by adding back the interest payable to net profit before tax, a point worth remembering for its calculation in practice. We will use the UK definition of capital employed which is found from the sum of the fixed assets and the net current assets in the balance sheet; that is £4.6 million + £31.4 million = £36 million. The result is:

$$\text{Profit on capital employed per cent} = \frac{£12 \text{ million}}{£36 \text{ million}} \times 100$$
$$= 33.33 \text{ per cent}$$

A profit on capital employed of 33.33 per cent would be a very good achievement to many businesses but do remember this is planned future and not actual past performance. Many studies of practice have illustrated how optimistic forecasts can be and maybe this illustrates the need to ask some very important questions about the assumptions upon which a plan is based before proceeding. Certainly a recent study of medium sized companies revealed that a profit on capital employed of 33.33 per cent would be a very good achievement. It is also important to remember that this ratio is only one facet of the complete financial picture. You may recall when we first discussed this plan in Chapter 3 that the cash flow position was very poor over the 12-month period, reaching a maximum funding requirement of £27.2 million but corresponding with a profit on capital employed of 60 per cent (£12 million/£20 million). As such, an exceptional profit on capital employed had to be balanced against the projected cash flow situation and you will recall it was considered appropriate to raise £16 million by way of equity. Such action takes care of the cash flow difficulties but has the effect of reducing the profit on capital employed.

Is there any way of examining methodically the proposed profit on capital employed which can be used to question how it is intended to be produced and whether or not it is realistic? The answer is yes. By calculating a number of additional ratios and comparing them with expectations for a business of a similar type/size we can form a better view. In practical terms, we need to divide the profit on capital employed ratio into two ratios, on one of which

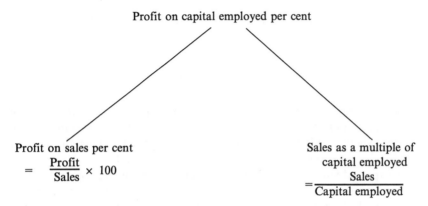

Figure 5.1 Examining the proposed profit on capital employed

we will concentrate in particular. However, to keep the complete picture in mind the two additional ratios are illustrated in Fig. 5.1.

By introducing sales revenue to both parts of the profit on capital employed ratio we can identify two additional ratios which represent ratios 2 and 3 in the GEC list. What is the value of this subdivision of profit on capital employed? It enables different but related questions to be asked, both of which impact on overall performance. First, and for consideration in the remainder of this chapter, what profit is to be generated from the intended sales revenue and is this realistic/achievable by comparing it with other relevant businesses? Second, and for consideration in the next chapter, how efficiently will business assets be used and are the estimates of their use realistic?

5.2 Profit on sales

Like profit on capital employed, the profit on sales ratio is expressed as a percentage and is calculated using the same measure of profit as for profit on capital employed. It gives an indication of the average profit margin achieved by a business across all product lines and/or services, i.e. what percentage or how many pence of profit is on average generated for each £ of sales.

Using the figure for profit before interest and tax used in calculating profit on capital employed and data from the profit and loss account for sales, the profit on sales ratio can be calculated as follows:

$$\text{Profit on sales per cent} \quad = \quad \frac{\text{Profit before interest and tax}}{\text{Sales}} \times 100$$

$$= \quad \frac{£12 \text{ million}}{£130 \text{ million}} \times 100$$

$$= \quad 9.2 \text{ per cent}$$

The above ratio shows that 9.2 per cent or 9.2 pence of profit before taxation plus interest payable will be generated per £ of sales. It is impossible to judge whether this ratio is good or bad without knowing the type of business so that some sort of a comparison can be made.

The expected value of this ratio will differ quite considerably for different types of businesses. A high volume business, such as a retailer, will usually operate with lower margins than a low volume business, such as a contractor.

One means of gauging relative performance is by subscribing to a provider of financial information like Datastream or Extel, or by referring to published studies like that referred to earlier. This study of medium sized businesses revealed return on capital employed and return on sales ratios to be:

	Return on capital employed (%)	Return on sales (%)	Sales as a multiple of capital employed
Business, professional and financial service companies	41.4	19.7	2.1
Retail and distribution companies	11.3	6.9	1.6
Consumer companies	16.1	8.2	2.0
Heavy manufacturing companies	16.7	8.0	2.1
Processing companies	9.0	9.9	0.9

From this study, which was based upon companies of a similar size to our example company, the planned return on sales of 9.2 per cent does not seem to be particularly unrealistic.

It is important to note that, in practice, businesses may have very little ability to influence their profit margin other than by controlling costs. A severe limit to exerting influence upon profit margins is often imposed by the inability of the business to influence prices, the setting of which may be constrained by market forces. For example, retailers operating in a highly competitive market would have to be very brave (or stupid) to increase prices much beyond that which the market will allow. Significantly higher prices are unlikely to have any positive effect upon the profit margin unless the products concerned are viewed as necessities, in which case the price charged will have little influence upon consumer demand.

Analysing and managing costs

Sound cost analysis and cost control can have a marked influence upon profit on sales because the amount of profit made is typically severely constrained by costs incurred. Costs incurred by the business can have a major impact upon business profitability, such that making savings on costs incurred will improve profit on sales and hence, other things being equal, profit on capital employed.

An understanding of the potential benefit from cost control can be seen if we express the contents of the profit and loss account in percentage of sales rather than money terms.

HMC Ltd profit and loss account for the year ended 31 December

	(%)
Sales turnover	100.0
Cost of sales	81.5
Gross profit	18.5
Distribution costs	5.5
Administrative costs	3.7
Operating profit	9.3

Profit on sales percentage can be broken down as shown in Fig. 5.2.

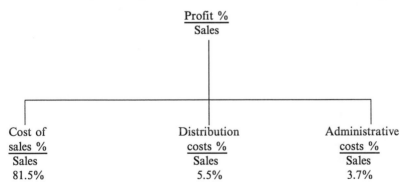

Figure 5.2 Breakdown of profit on sales

Improvements in any of the three cost to sales ratios in Fig. 5.2 must improve profit on sales and hence profit on capital employed. For example, a 10 per cent reduction in cost of sales gives rise to a 53 per cent improvement in profit on sales per cent, other things being equal.

Analysis by cost need not stop at just this subdivision. In fact, for an item like cost of sales which represents a significant area of cost, much more detailed analysis of the specific costs it includes would be typically highly desirable.

5.3 Sales as a multiple of capital employed

Sales as a multiple of capital employed is the third of the ratios in our list of seven for GEC. This ratio together with profit on sales percentage provides information about where profit on capital employed is derived from.

Sales as a multiple of capital employed can be used to understand how business will use its assets to generate sales as indicated by sales as a multiple of capital employed. How is it calculated? Using the information provided in the profit and loss account and balance sheet of HMC Ltd the ratio is:

$$\text{Sales as a multiple of capital employed} = \frac{\text{Sales}}{\text{Capital employed}}$$

$$= \frac{£130 \text{ million}}{£36 \text{ million}}$$

$$= 3.6 \text{ times}$$

The above ratio indicates that the company should generate £3.60 of sales for each £1.00 of capital employed. Of course, whether 3.6 as a multiple is realistic or not is a key consideration. For a venture like this with no track record or history with which to make comparisons a reasonable approach would be to investigate ratios for companies of a similar size. For example, the study we mentioned earlier found the following ratios where, as you can see, the range of multiples was from 0.9 to 2.1:

	Sales as a multiple of capital employed
Business, professional and financial service companies	2.1
Retail and distribution companies	1.6
Consumer companies	2.0
Heavy manufacturing companies	2.1
Processing companies	0.9

In fact, these were averages, nevertheless the highest multiple achieved was 3.4 suggesting that the plan for HMC – 3.6 times – is optimistic to say the least.

Clearly, the higher the multiple the better is the use being made of its asset base for generating sales revenue and, as you will see in the next chapter, we can go yet further to see if we can identify how particular ratios of assets contribute to business performance. In much the same way as we subdivided profit on sales percentage into a number of cost-related ratios, so too can sales as a multiple of capital employed be broken down to see potential areas for improvement.

5.4 Conclusion

In this chapter we have introduced a framework for analysing business profitability using data drawn from the profit and loss account and the balance sheet. It is hierarchical, with profit on capital employed percentage as the key ratio from which profit on sales percentage and sales as a multiple of capital employed are derived, such that:

Profit on capital employed per cent	=	Profit on sales per cent	×	Sales as a multiple of capital employed

$$\frac{\text{PBIT}}{\text{Capital employed}}\% = \frac{\text{PBIT}}{\text{Sales}}\% \times \frac{\text{Sales}}{\text{Capital employed}}$$

If we insert the relevant numbers for HMC Ltd we can see how the profit on capital employed of 60 per cent is derived:

$$\frac{£12 \text{ million}}{£36 \text{ million}}\% = \frac{£12 \text{ million}}{£130 \text{ million}}\% \times \frac{£130 \text{ million}}{£36 \text{ million}}$$

Or, given a rounding error on profit on sales percentage:

$$33.33\% \qquad = \qquad 9.2\% \qquad \times \qquad 3.6 \text{ times}$$

A change in the value of the profit on sales percentage or sales as a multiple of capital employed will clearly impact upon profit on capital employed percentage. In fact, an important objective in managing a business will typically be to increase profitability. As illustrated in Fig. 5.3, this framework offers direction as to ways of potentially achieving such an objective.

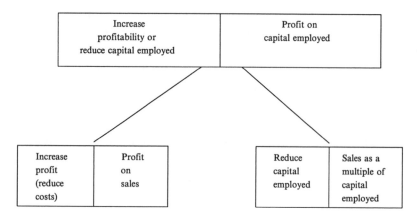

Figure 5.3 Ways of achieving increased profitability

Increasing profit by reducing costs will impact upon profitability. So too will reducing capital employed – quite how we will demonstrate in the next chapter.

The business profitability ratios we have reviewed in this chapter are widely used and represent a good starting point for understanding the interrelationship between various parts of the business, in terms of how their management impacts upon financial performance.

As we will show in a later chapter, such ratios can also be used in analysing published accounts. However, do keep at the back of your mind that they may have some limitations and as we will illustrate there is a more appropriate framework for assessing long-term performance. But before then we need to complete the picture we have started to draw by discussing ratios that can be used to measure how effectively business assets are being employed and if there is any scope for improvement.

Before moving on, however, it is worth reviewing the main points covered in this chapter:

– Business ratios are an invaluable tool in evaluating business performance.
– Seven key criteria to monitor performance are: profit on capital employed, profit on sales, sales as a multiple of capital employed, sales as a multiple of fixed assets, sales as a multiple of stocks, sales per employee, and profits per employee.
– There is no universal standard for profitability ratios and definitions will often vary between companies.
– It is important when using ratios to establish how they have been defined if their interpretation is to be meaningful.

- Sound cost analysis and cost control can have a marked influence upon profit on sales because the amount of profit made is typically severely constrained by costs incurred.
- A useful means of gauging relative business performance is by subscription to a provider of financial information like Datastream or Extel, or by referring to published studies.

6
Ratios to measure the use of business assets

There is a danger in being persuaded before one understands
WOODROW WILSON

In the last chapter we discussed the measurement of profitability using three related ratios from a set of ratios reported as being used for evaluating business performance within GEC. This set is in fact part of a framework developed many years ago by the Dupont Corporation in the United States and which has become a well-established analytical approach for measuring business performance. In this chapter we will look at two further GEC ratios in order to demonstrate how the use of specific business assets can be analysed. We will then consider a number of other working capital ratios.

Whereas for the profitability ratios discussed in the last chapter further analysis focuses upon the breakdown of profit and particularly costs, in this chapter focus is upon the breakdown of capital employed in terms of specific business assets. This can be seen from Fig. 6.1.

Ratios to measure the use of business assets are calculated by dividing sales by the various business assets such as those illustrated in Fig. 6.1 and are referred to as sales/assets multiples. Sales multiple ratios fall into two main categories:

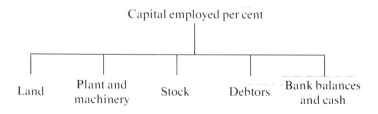

Figure 6.1 Breakdown of capital employed

1. Sales as a multiple of fixed assets.
2. Sales as a multiple of working capital.

In terms of the GEC framework, these sales assets multiples can be illustrated as shown in Fig. 6.2.

As we illustrated in the last chapter, sales as a multiple of capital employed, together with profit on sales percentage affect profit as a percentage of capital employed, such that improvements in either or both will result in a higher figure. Similarly, improvements in sales as a multiple of fixed assets and/or sales as a multiple of working capital will impact upon sales as a multiple of capital employed. In the case of these two ratios an improvement will arise because of a reduction in the fixed assets or working capital employed within the business.

Each of these two ratios gives an indication of what sales value is generated from a specific group of assets. Their values in the case of HMC Ltd are 28.26 times (sales revenue of £130 million divided by fixed assets of £4.6 million) and 4.14 times (sales revenue of £130 million divided by working capital of £31.4 million), respectively.

6.1 Use of fixed assets

The fourth ratio within the GEC framework is sales as a multiple of fixed assets which shows how many £s of costs are generated per £ of fixed assets.

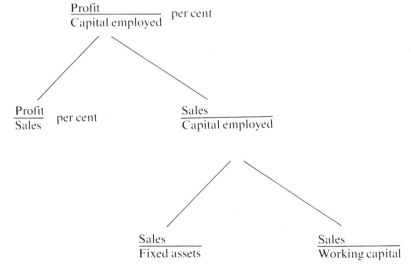

Figure 6.2 Sales assets multiples

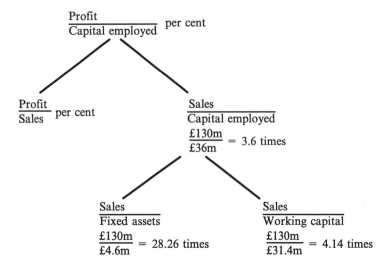

Figure 6.3 Breakdown of sales as a multiple of working capital

In the case of HMC, £28.26 of sales revenue is estimated to be generated from each £ of fixed asset.

In common with other ratios we have discussed, use of fixed assets typically has limited value without further analysis because fixed assets can take a variety of forms like land and buildings, plant and machinery and fixtures and fittings. Breaking down the fixed assets into such groupings can be useful in making comparisons as a recent case we analysed serves to illustrate. Two companies in the same industrial sector were achieving different results which an analysis of the type we have described showed to be a consequence of different degrees of capital intensity. One had invested in new plant and equipment and consequently had a much lower use of assets ratio relative to the other. Nevertheless, it was outperforming overall simply by virtue of a lower cost base through using less manpower.

The efficient and effective use of fixed assets is vital. As you will see in Chapters 15 and 16 on managing capital expenditure, it is not only the subject of retrospective analysis, but also of prospective analysis.

Any reduction in the amount of working capital or fixed assets employed in the business will clearly improve the sales multiple ratio and feed through to produce an improved profit on capital employed. For example, a reduction in the working capital from 31.4 to 21.0 times improves the working capital to sales multiple from 4.14 to 6.5 times. The impact of this upon profit or capital employed is significant as we illustrate opposite:

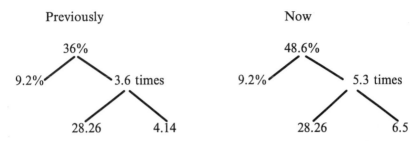

Other things being equal, such a change would result in an even more remarkable sales as a multiple of capital employed of 5.3 and a revised profit on capital employed of 48.6 per cent.

How might such a change in working capital be achieved? As a result of a reduction in stocks and/or debtors and/or cash balances and/or an increase in creditors. Of course, whether this would be feasible from a business perspective is another issue which we will consider shortly. In fact, each of these can be analysed within the framework by breaking down the sales as a multiple of working capital ratio into the components shown in Fig. 6.4. In fact, the middle of these, sales as a multiple of stock ratio, is the fifth ratio used in the GEC framework for monitoring business performance.

In most businesses, the need to control working capital is paramount. Rather than use the 'multiple' approach, it is more commonplace to use a number of working capital ratios. With this in mind and the concern about cash flow for HMC Ltd over the 12-month period we will review a number of working capital ratios.

6.2 Working capital ratios

The multiple ratios we have identified so far may be used in practice, as is the case with GEC, with sales as a multiple of stocks. However, an alternative, and in our experience more popular, form is to express these multiples in terms of a number of days, that is:

$$\frac{\text{Sales}}{\text{Debtors}} \qquad \text{becomes} \qquad \frac{\text{Debtors}}{\text{Sales}} \times 360$$

$$\frac{\text{Sales}}{\text{Creditors}} \qquad \text{becomes} \qquad \frac{\text{Creditors}}{\text{Sales}} \times 360$$

$$\frac{\text{Sales}}{\text{Stocks}} \qquad \text{becomes} \qquad \frac{\text{Stocks}}{\text{Sales}} \times 360$$

In the case of HMC Ltd the working capital ratios in terms of days would be:

For stock: $\dfrac{£4 \text{ million}}{£130 \text{ million}} \times 60 = 11$ days

rather than

$\dfrac{£130 \text{ million}}{£4 \text{ million}} = 32.5x$

For debtors: $\dfrac{£23.4 \text{ million}}{£130 \text{ million}} \times 360 = 65$ days

rather than

$\dfrac{£130 \text{ million}}{£23.4 \text{ million}} = 5.6x$

For creditors: $\dfrac{£12 \text{ million}}{£30 \text{ million}} \times 360 = 33$ days

rather than

$\dfrac{£130 \text{ million}}{£12 \text{ million}} = 10.8x$

Stock ratio

The stock ratio can be calculated in a number of ways depending upon the information available. If calculated internally where information is available about the type of stock, i.e. finished goods, partly finished goods, or raw materials, then a more detailed approach can be taken than we will adopt here. We have calculated it by dividing the closing stock figure by the cost of sales and expressed the result in days. As such, it is a measure of the efficiency of the company's stock control system.

Stock ratio $= \dfrac{\text{Stock}}{\text{Cost of sales}} \times 360$

$= \dfrac{£4 \text{ million}}{£106 \text{ million}} \times 360 = 13.59$ days

The stock ratio illustrates a holding of just over 13 days worth of stock. However, the pros and cons associated with such a stock holding do need to be judged against the type of business. On the one hand, there are some very real costs associated with buying and holding stock connected with insurance, storage and the like, which have to be balanced against the cost to the business of holding inadequate stocks to meet business demands.

Caution also has to be observed in interpreting the ratio because stock can take many forms such as raw materials, partly finished goods, and finished goods. It can also be difficult to interpret meaningfully in diversified groups of companies if there are some subsidiary companies involved in high volume operations and others involved in specialist contract type operations, or where acquisitions have occurred during the period being analysed. Particularly when using published information to calculate stock ratios, considerable attention has to be paid to notes to accounts and other information. Knowing the industry is also essential in drawing meaningful conclusions. For example, some furniture manufacturers have fairly high stock ratios that could be taken to indicate flexibility in responding to sudden market needs. However, what such an observation would omit is that most stock in this case corresponds with a customer order book and is already earmarked.

Debtors' ratio

We have already calculated the debtors' ratio which is typically expressed as a number of weeks or days. In short, the logic of the ratio's calculation is if credit sales in the profit and loss account equal 360 days, how many days do debtors represent? For example, if credit sales for 360 days = £3,600,000 then debtors of £10,000 = 1 day. You will recognize this as being calculated by dividing the debtors by the average weekly sales [£10,000 / (£3,600,000 / 360)]. The ratio indicates the average collection period for debtors, and will reflect the efficiency of a company's credit control system.

For HMC Ltd we calculated the debtors' ratio earlier as being 62 days. This means that according to the plan, the company will take almost nine weeks on average to collect amounts owing from customers. This debtors' ratio is certainly high enough to warrant close scrutiny. Certainly any action to improve this should be highly beneficial to both cash flow and profitability.

One point worth noting is that where ratios are calculated in terms of days, there may be different views about the number of days to use in the calculation. Many businesses use 360 on the basis of there being 30 days to a month, whereas some analysts use 365 days. It does not make a vast difference for this ratio but it does flag up a more important issue – *you must be sure of the definition applied in calculating any ratios you are provided with.*

Creditors' ratio

The creditors' ratio is calculated in much the same way as the debtors' ratio, although it is preferable to use purchases or at least cost of sales rather than sales as we did earlier. This is because creditors exclude any profit element and hence so should that with which they are to be compared. For this reason, you will find the creditors' ratio in this section differs from that discussed earlier. Nevertheless, irrespective of the denominator chosen, the logic of the ratio's calculation is the same as the debtors' ratio. If credit purchases in the profit and loss account equal 360 days, how many days do creditors represent? For example, if cost of sales for 360 days = £360,000, then creditors of £10,000 = 10 days, i.e. creditors divided by average weekly cost of sales [£10,000 / (£360,000 / 360)]. The ratio indicates the average collection period for creditors. For HMC Ltd, the creditors' ratio is:

$$
\begin{aligned}
\text{Creditors' ratio} \quad &= \quad \frac{\text{Creditors}}{\text{Cost of sales}} \quad \times \quad 360 \\[6pt]
&= \quad \frac{\text{£12 million}}{\text{£106 million}} \quad \times \quad 360 \\[6pt]
&= \quad 40.75 \text{ days}
\end{aligned}
$$

There is an imbalance between creditor and debtor days, in so far as suppliers are expected to have to be paid before customers settle their accounts, but whether the creditors' days could genuinely be improved upon would be questionable for a relatively new business like HMC.

What is vital to understand is that these ratios may often vary at different times of the year because of, for example, seasonality in business activities. This has important implications when interpreting working capital ratios. There are two other ratios that can be used to assess the working capital position of a company. They are:

– Current ratio
– Liquid ratio.

The current ratio

The current ratio is calculated by dividing current assets by current liabilities (creditors falling due within one year in the case of published accounts). It attempts to measure the ability of a company to meet its financial obligations within one year.

$$\text{Current ratio} = \frac{\text{Current assets}}{\text{Current liabilities}}$$

$$= \frac{£27.4 \text{ million}}{£12 \text{ million}}$$

$$= 2.28 \text{ to } 1$$

This result means that current liabilities are covered by current assets 2.28 times and many, using conventional interpretive standards, would view such a result very favourably.

For decades, the interpretation of the current ratio has been guided by the unrealistic rule of thumb that current assets should always be double current liabilities for all companies. This is quite unrealistic and should be avoided at all costs because it implies that the proportions of current assets and current liabilities should be the same for all types of businesses. Clearly for a fast food company with small stocks and virtually no debtors the ratio would not normally be the same as for a company undertaking a long-term contract for which substantial stocks, debtors and creditors may well be the norm.

Please also note that you should not interpret a high current ratio as necessarily being a good sign: it can be indicative of idle resources. For example, all other things being equal, the current ratio would increase simply by increasing stocks or debtors, neither of which may necessarily be required for current operations. Also, low current ratios must be interpreted with care. The current ratio would decrease if a company took actions to decrease its stocks or decrease its debtors. We cannot say whether actions to increase or decrease working capital are necessarily good or bad, therefore care should be taken when attempting to interpret both the size of the current ratio and the movements year on year.

Quite simply, when interpreting a current ratio or any other ratio an appropriate comparator ratio should be used in the form of historical performance within that business and comparative performances in other similar businesses, but *not* arbitrary rules of thumb.

The liquid ratio (quick ratio or acid test ratio)

The liquid ratio is defined as current assets *less* stock divided by current liabilities (creditors' amounts falling due within one year in the case of published accounts). It attempts to measure a company's ability to pay its way in the short term without having to liquidate stock. Simply, it is 'the acid test' directed at answering the question: Can we pay our way at very short notice?

$$\text{Liquid ratio} \quad = \quad \frac{\text{Current assets} - \text{Stock}}{\text{Current liabilities}}$$

$$= \quad \frac{\text{Liquid assets}}{\text{Current liabilities}}$$

$$= \quad \frac{\text{£23.4 million}}{\text{£12 million}}$$

$$= \quad 1.95 \text{ to } 1$$

The liquid ratio in this case means that liquid assets are more than sufficient to cover current liabilities, but this may not always be the case. Anyone looking at the liquid ratio for a wide range of different companies would quickly come to the opinion that there is no single value or narrow range of values that operates across all industries. For example, in retail businesses it is not uncommon to find a level of around 0.4 to 1 cover for current liabilities. This is possible through cash trading, a high level of commitment from suppliers and the fact that stock could be liquidated in time to meet maturing debts. Similar to the current ratio, if these companies maintained a higher level of cover for current liabilities, there would be idle facilities within the working capital cycle. This ratio also changes over the course of time. For example, it was estimated that the liquid ratio for all quoted companies (seasonally adjusted) fell to an estimated 1.11 at the end of 1992 from 1.19 at the end of the third quarter of 1992, and 1.21 at the end of 1991. As for large quoted manufacturing companies, the ratios for the same time periods were estimated as being 1.00, 1.09 and 1.18.

Let us pause for a minute to think about the results obtained for HMC. By conventional working capital ratio analysis this business looks sound with its current ratio of 2.28 to 1 and its liquid ratio of 1.95 to 1, even though we know of the cash flow crisis it will face if the plan is implemented. This is a critical point – ratios are typically calculated at a point in time and even though they may be calculated very judiciously a full picture may not be obtained from such a snapshot. This is very much the case here.

6.3 Ratio analysis in a non-manufacturing setting

We have discussed a hierarchy or pyramid of ratios within a manufacturing setting. However, as the Centre for Interfirm Comparison (CIFC) demonstrates, the same principles, but with a different set of ratios, can be used to analyse the performance of any organization, whether it is a private company, a public utility or a professional firm.

In its publications CIFC illustrates how the set of ratios can be extended beyond the confines of the hierarchy, such that the complete analysis of an organization, or a function/part within an organization, can be represented as a set of interlocking ratios, many of which may be unique to that particular type of organization. For example, for a professional firm, like an architects' practice, it may be appropriate to start with the ratio of profit per partner, continue by looking at profit and revenue from each fee-earning department and then go on to explore the reasons behind these figures.

Very often quite different sets of ratios could be chosen to look at particular functions like computing, maintenance or marketing within any large organization. Consider, for example, the distribution function of a retailing business. One approach to analysing its distribution costs would be to isolate the fixed and variable elements of long distance transportation costs, warehousing and local delivery costs, before examining in detail vehicle costs per mile, per tonne, and so on.

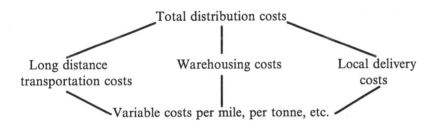

For service industries, voluntary organizations and the public sector, the ratios would again be chosen to relate the resources used to the nature and quality of services provided.

6.4 Interfirm comparison

Organizations like CIFC, undertake interfirm comparisons. Typically this requires cooperation by participating businesses to provide detailed information in absolute confidence to the Centre. More than simply the figures provided in published accounts is required to ensure that performance measures are appropriate. There will normally be a review to determine what information should be included. Furthermore, differences in company practices have to be taken into account so that ratios are properly comparable for all participants within a given sector.

CIFC typically uses about 100 different ratios which are shown in full for each company anonymously by using card letters. The purpose, of course, behind producing such ratios is that comparisons can be made with others in the same sector to assess performance against objective standards to identify areas of relative weakness and strength.

6.5 Conclusion

We have demonstrated how the use of assets can be monitored using ratios and how they fit within an overall framework for understanding the profit generated with the capital employed. While profitability and use of assets ratios have been considered independently, they do influence one another as the last example served to illustrate.

In common with all ratio analysis, it is important to be able to make comparisons which, in this case, reveal that the plan for HMC Ltd may be very optimistic. Our analysis of key business ratios has led us in the direction of having reservations about the plan. In addition, the projected cash position must always be taken into consideration. Certainly we demonstrated earlier with reference to HMC how a truly remarkable profit on assets could be achieved with a quite unrealistic cash flow forecast. By modifying this, more realism was introduced but with a consequently adverse effect on profitability.

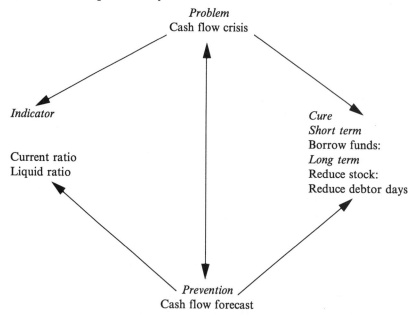

Figure 6.4 Working capital ratio indicator—identification of problems, prevention and cure

It is important to highlight the value of cash flow forecasting as a monitoring device, particularly in conjunction with using ratios to monitor working capital. We have shown how ratios can be used as an indicator of a business illness like insufficient liquidity and how their improvement could serve to redress such a problem.

A number of important issues follow on from our discussion of ratios like the analysis of corporate reports, working capital management and control and the calculation of investment proposals, all of which we will consider in subsequent chapters. You will also find that we will draw upon many of the issues in the chapters in the latter part of the book where this development of a longer-term perspective and an owner's as distinct from a manager's viewpoint is an important consideration.

Main points to remember from this chapter include the following:

- Ratios to measure the use of business assets are calculated by dividing sales by the various business assets and are referred to as sales/assets multiples.
- Sales multiple ratios give an indication of what sales value is generated from a specific group of assets.
- Working capital ratios may often vary at different times of the year due to, e.g. seasonality in business activities, which must be taken into account.
- When interpreting a ratio, an appropriate comparator ratio should be used in the form of historical performance within that business and comparative performance in other similar businesses, but not arbitrary rules of thumb.
- Where ratios are calculated in terms of days, there may be different views about the number of days to use in the calculation.

PART TWO
FINANCIAL AWARENESS

In Part Two we assume that you have come to terms with financial principles and practices and are ready to embark on a journey through what many non-financial specialists seem to regard as a veritable minefield – the published financial information produced by most organizations by way of a corporate report. It is designed to increase your awareness of the influences exerted upon the type of financial information produced by most large organizations, and also the influence over results that can potentially be exercised by the user. If it has a message, it is to be aware of what influences there are upon published financial information because they will surely impact upon perceived performance.

Aspects of Part Two you may find quite challenging, such as the analysis of corporate reports where we have drawn upon the last two chapters of Part One to show how published financial information, like the published accounts, can be analysed using ratio analysis.

7
A review of corporate reports

One cannot walk through a mass-production factory and not feel that one is in Hell

W. H. AUDEN

Many general managers find working with corporate reports a daunting task, particularly the financial statements. To them Auden's comment might well be appropriate to 'walking' through the annual report. However, it contains much valuable information which will allow you to understand the fundamentals of the business reporting process, the key means for conveying financial results within an organization.

Many different types of organizations in both for-profit and not-for-profit businesses are required to publish their financial results. These are typically presented in the form of an annual corporate report. In the commercial sector, companies with shares quoted on the Stock Exchange like Hanson PLC, the industrial management company we will review later, are required to publish annual accounts together with other important financial information. In their case Companies Acts and other influences regulate the information required. The same requirement to produce a corporate report exists outside the commercial sector. A good example is the Civil Aviation Authority (CAA), which is primarily concerned with the safety of all users of UK airspace. It is required by the Civil Aviation Authority (Accounts) Directive of 1987 to produce accounts annually.

Irrespective of the business orientation, corporate reports do play a vital part in conveying an organization's financial results but, unfortunately, they are not well understood without receiving some specific training in their use. Given that such reports are the primary medium by which information about financial performance is conveyed to the outside world, working with them is an important skill for the general manager to have. In recognition of this, and using the Hanson 1992 Annual Report, we will show you what information is typically available from a corporate report. We will also draw upon this annual report in the next chapter for purposes of undertaking financial analysis for shareholders and lenders.

7.1 Influences upon financial reporting practice

All of the principles outlined Chapters 1 to 4 are applied in producing the financial statements to be found in an annual report. However, there are other influences upon the financial statements and parts of the annual report other than simple public relations considerations. These include:

– Legal requirements
– Stock Exchange requirements
– Accounting standards.

Legal requirements

Companies Acts have been a long-standing influence upon the contents of corporate reports and are the principal source of legal requirements for the contents of UK companies' annual reports. Their aim has been to protect shareholders and creditors, however there has been a growing view that companies also owe duties to other groups in society. In 1975 a significant document called 'The Corporate Report' gave the basic aim of the company accounts as being to measure and report on the entity's economic resources and performance. To this end it considered that corporate reports should be 'relevant, understandable, reliable, complete, objective, timely and comparable.'

While 'The Corporate Report' exerted an important influence upon attitudes towards financial reporting, as we will demonstrate, moves towards harmonization within the European Community have been even more significant. In the United Kingdom these moves and earlier influences upon corporate reporting have been reflected in various Companies Acts.

Companies must prepare a profit and loss account and balance sheet each year in one of a number of alternative permitted formats illustrating figures for the latest and preceding year. Furthermore, and of vital importance, such published accounts must show a 'true and fair view' of the profit or loss for the year, and of the company's financial position at the year end. Such a true and fair view does not mean that a balance sheet necessarily discloses the true worth of a company. The balance sheet represents no attempt to value the business, but is merely a statement of those assets and liabilities of a business recognized by the accounting rules we reviewed in Chapter 4. Many significant assets which we will discuss later are excluded, especially intangible assets such as business 'know-how' and the value of people. For such reasons the market value of a business often differs widely from the net book value of its assets illustrated in the published accounts of the annual report.

Stock Exchange

Companies with shares or loan stock quoted on the UK Stock Exchange, known as quoted or listed companies, are subject to a listing agreement, details of which are set out in a document called the Yellow Book for those with a full listing. This specifies, among other things, certain information to be disclosed which may not be required by the Companies Acts. The listing agreement is effected when a company's board of directors passes a resolution binding the company to observe the regulations laid down for listed companies. The effect of the listing agreement is evident in its requirements upon the directors' report in the annual report. The information required to be disclosed by listed companies (some of which is required by law) includes the following:

- The reasons why the trading results shown by the accounts for the period under review differ materially from any published forecast made by the company.
- A statement by the directors of their reasons for any significant failure to comply with Statements of Standard Accounting Practice (SSAPs)/ Financial Reporting Standards (FRSs).
- A geographical analysis of turnover and of contribution to trading results of trading operations carried on outside the United Kingdom.
- The name of the country in which each subsidiary operates.
- Statements of directors' share interests and of other persons' substantial shareholdings.
- Detailed information regarding company borrowings.

Accounting standards

Accounting standards have influenced corporate reporting in the United Kingdom and were initiated as a consequence of such events as the GEC takeover of AEI during the late 1960s which caused major concern about the value of published financial information. In the GEC case, £9.5 million of a £14.5 million difference in reported profits before and after the takeover was the result of different accounting practices. This and other practices fuelled the criticism that, given the same set of underlying facts, two different companies (and for that matter their auditors) might, quite legally, provide a totally different financial picture.

Many accounting standards have been produced covering such matters as stock valuation, depreciation and research and development. They are used in preparing the financial statements of for-profit and not-for-profit organizations and were the subject of considerable criticism during the 1980s. Many of the sources of criticism have been addressed and since 1990 accounting standards have been the responsibility of an Accounting Standards Board (ASB), a body set up following a major review of the framework to support the setting and enforcement of accounting standards. Under the ASB they have legal backing. To add weight to their enforcement, there is also a related body known as the Review Panel to examine and question departures from accounting standards. In the event of there being considered to be a material departure from the accounting standard, the Review Panel can apply to the courts to determine whether a true and fair view is presented. If it is deemed that this is not the case, the company and ultimately the directors, may be required to bear the costs of preparing and circulating revised accounts. *It is important to note that the ASB has introduced some significant changes via financial reporting standards and, indeed, many others are proposed. This means that some changes in financial reporting practices may well have taken place since this book was written.*

7.2 Annual reports

Most annual reports for public limited companies (plcs) contain the following as a minimum:

1. Chairman's statement
2. Directors' report
3. Profit and loss account (and notes)
4. Balance sheets (and notes)
5. Accounting policies
6. Historical financial summaries
7. Auditors' report
8. A cash flow statement.

We will consider each of these and put them in context by drawing upon the information provided in the Annual Report produced by Hanson PLC for 1992, although a full discussion of the published financial statements we reserve for Chapter 8 on analysing corporate reports.

Chairman's statement

This is generally a fairly brief review of progress of the company and its business environment over the past year together with some indications of the proposed direction for the company in the forthcoming year. For example, the one page report from the Chairman, Lord Hanson, in the 1992 annual report for Hanson PLC is reported under the following headings:

– Balance sheet and financing
– Directors, management and employees
– Hanson: the environment and the community
– Shareholder services
– Prospects.

This statement will often highlight major issues and events concerning the company. For example, the 1992 Hanson Report identifies the significance of the tough conditions world-wide and the prospect for even tighter margins in 1993 than were experienced in 1992.

Directors' report

In contrast to the chairman's statement, the content of the directors' report is laid down by statute and by the requirements of the Stock Exchange for listed companies. Auditors are also required to comment in their report if any information given in the directors' report is not, in their opinion, consistent with the company's accounts. A good example of what can be found in the directors' report is illustrated by the following items included in the Hanson 1992 Annual Report:

– Directors interests, i.e. names of the directors and details of their shareholdings
– Associate directors' interests
– Details of service contracts with any directors
– Details of changes in the share capital during the year
– Employment policies
– Charitable and political contributions
– Close company status
– Subsequent events in the form of material post-balance sheet events
– Details of auditors
– Details and notice of the annual general meeting.

A good deal of valuable information may often be found in the directors' report and this part of the annual report can be used to good effect in understanding financial matters underpinning the three main financial statements – the profit and loss account, the balance sheet and the cash flow statement.

Profit and loss account

In the United Kingdom the format of published profit and loss accounts is prescribed by the Companies Acts, but companies do have an element of choice in so far as the Acts provide alternatives.

The general principles applied in producing a profit and loss for inclusion in the annual report are the same as those discussed in Chapters 1 to 3 of this book. What is important to recognize, however, is that this statement and the others produced have been 'consolidated'. This means that all companies making up the group which may operate in very different business environments are pulled together to provide an overall picture. For example, Hanson PLC principally in the United Kingdom and United States operates businesses as diverse as:

– Batteries	– Cement
– Bricks	– Cranes
– Crushed stone products	– Cookware
– Electrical products	– Jacuzzi whirlpool baths and spas
– Chemicals	– Tobacco
– Coal	

This has some real implications for anyone attempting to analyse aspects of business performance using only the annual report. For example, the working capital requirements and characteristics of such diverse businesses would differ substantially and the calculation of a ratio relating to stocks would convey little. This is simply because they would be an amalgam of a diverse range of businesses for which the working capital requirements of each would be highly likely to differ.

A second important feature of the profit and loss account and the other financial statements included in the annual report concerns the detail to be found. Information may have significant commercial value and for this reason companies will reveal no more about some areas, such as costs associated with running the business, than they have to. Even when information is provided it is often to be found buried in the notes to the accounts.

As we will illustrate in the next chapter, the profit and loss account published in an annual report is very much a summarized statement which can only provide a limited indication of how well a business has performed. In working with such a statement you will often want more information than it contains in order to form a more complete view, some of which you may find in supporting notes to the accounts. Do remember, however, that you will rarely find all of the information you wish because companies deliberately restrict what they provide.

Balance sheet

We have already encountered most terms relating to assets and liabilities in a published balance sheet in an annual report. However, as reference below to a part of the consolidated balance sheet for Hanson PLC reveals, there are some items, in particular those included within capital reserves, which we have not as yet considered. We need to explain these in preparation for analysing corporate reports in the next chapter.

Consolidated balance sheet extract – Hanson PLC at 30 September 1992

	Note	1992 (£ million)	1991 (£ million)
Capital and reserves			
Called-up share capital	17	1205	1202
Share premium account	18	1163	1153
Revaluation reserve	18	166	163
Other reserves	18	65	
Profit and loss account	18	1625	807
		4224	3325

Let us consider the new terms. First, the share premium account. This arises when shares are issued at a premium over their nominal, or face, value. For example, where a company issues shares with a nominal value of £1 for say £3, the £2 premium is disclosed separately in the balance sheet under the heading 'share premium account'.

Why might a company issue shares at a premium? The answer is quite simple. A company may issue part of the share capital it is authorized to raise according to its articles of association. Such authorized share capital will have a nominal value which is timeless. Let us imagine it is £1. Ten years ago (say) the company raised half of its authorized share capital at £1 per share. Today the shares are currently trading at £3.50. To issue the remaining authorized share capital in the market for their nominal value of £1 would be foolish because the market will gain the benefit and not the company. Hence the company will typically issue shares just sufficiently below the current market price to make them attractive to shareholders. In bookkeeping terms, the nominal value is included within 'called-up share capital' and any excess is treated as a capital reserve and included in the 'share premium account'.

Second, called-up share capital refers to the nominal value of share capital that has actually been called up from shareholders. In Hanson's case reference to the notes to the accounts shows the company to have 6.6 billion authorized ordinary shares of 25p but has called up 4,820,157,095 of these, all of which have been fully paid.

Third, when a company revalues its assets it reflects that on the other side of the balance sheet by creating a revaluation reserve for the same amount in the capital and reserves section of the balance sheet. In Hanson's case, from the notes to the accounts it can be seen that the £166 million revaluation reserve comprises a balance at 1 October 1991 of £163 million, to which £3 million has been added as a result of disposals during the year.

In common with the consolidated profit and loss account, the consolidated balance sheet contains a limited amount of detail, this being dealt with in the notes to the accounts. As we will demonstrate in the next chapter, these notes can often be of great help in interpreting the results disclosed.

Accounting policies

Companies are required to disclose the various bases on which the accounts have been prepared, that is the interpretation of the rules applied by the company in producing its financial statements. These accounting policies do vary between industries and from company to company. They are important to understand as we demonstrate later in Chapter 10. For now, let us consider what they relate to with reference to those references provided by Hanson PLC which include:

- Accounting conventions
- Basis of consolidation
- Accounting for acquisitions
- Associated undertakings
- Sales turnover
- Tangible fixed assets
- Deferred taxation
- Stocks
- Research and development
- Exploration expenditure
- Foreign currencies.

Accounting policies may often occupy no more than a single page of the annual report and may be very brief. For example, the accounting policy on research and development in the Hanson Annual Report is just 16 words:

Expenditure on research and development is written off in the year in which it is incurred.

However, the importance of even such a brief accounting policy should not be underestimated. Policies like this one can have an important influence upon the results portrayed by a company as we will show in Chapter 10 on the art of accounting.

Historical financial summaries

Historical financial summaries are not a legal requirement, but have been provided by the vast majority of large companies since a request to chairmen of all listed companies for their inclusion by the Chairman of the Stock Exchange in 1964.

The usual period covered by historical summaries is five years and the items included are well illustrated in the Hanson 1992 Annual Report. As regards the profit and loss account, items in the financial summary include sales turnover, profit on ordinary activities, taxation, profit after taxation, earnings per ordinary share – diluted – and dividends. For the balance sheet three main headings are summarized: assets *less* current liabilities; sums financed by shareholders and long-term lenders; and net assets per share. This information is shown for each of the five years from 1988 to 1992 inclusive and a comparison is also provided with results from ten years ago, i.e. 1982.

Historical summaries are a useful source of preliminary information about a company, but do be careful. Changes in accounting practices over a long period may cause an historical summary to be misleading. For example, a decision to capitalize research and development expenditure – that is to carry it forward as an asset whenever the benefits of the expenditure can reasonably be foreseen – will mean that the figures in neither the profit and loss account nor the balance sheet will be comparable with earlier years.

Auditors' report

Every company is required to appoint at each annual general meeting an auditor or auditors to hold office from the conclusion of that meeting until the conclusion of the next AGM. Auditors must report to the shareholders whether in their opinion the profit and loss account, the balance sheet, the cash flow statement and any supporting notes have been properly prepared in accordance with the Companies Acts, and all relevant accounting standards. If they give a true and fair view of the profit and state of affairs of the company or group, and the associated profits and cash flow for the group for the financial year in question, then this might be stated in the auditors' report. For example, see the report of the auditors to the Hanson accounts for 1992.

> Report of the Auditors to the members of Hanson PLC
> 'We have audited the accounts on pages 28 to 45 in accordance with Auditing Standards.
>
> In our opinion the accounts give a true and fair view of the state of affairs of the company and of the group at September 30, 1992 and of the profit and cash flows of the group for the year then ended and have been properly prepared in accordance with the Companies Act 1985'
> ERNST & YOUNG, *Chartered Accountants, Registered Auditor*, Hull, December 3, 1992

A new era?

Although statutory auditors have normally recognized their own role and responsibilities concerning the audit process, the same degree of understanding has not always been attributed to their clients. The purpose, duties and responsibilities of auditors as perceived by clients often tended to differ dramatically from the work actually performed by auditors leading to the creation of what has come to be known as the creation of the 'audit expectations gap'.

In an attempt to bridge this gap the UK Auditing Practices Board (APB) came into existence in 1991 with the purpose of improving the standards of auditing, helping to meet the needs of the users of financial information and enhancing public confidence in the audit process. To help achieve these objectives in May 1993 the APB issued its first Statement of Auditing Standards, 'Auditors' Reports on Financial Statements'. The Standard will apply to all UK companies whose financial statements are intended to give a 'true and fair' view and whose year-end occurs after 30 September 1993. From this date, users of company accounts will notice a substantial change in the length and substance of auditors' reports.

The auditors' report is a key independent link in the accountability and communication process between the owners of the business and those officers who control the corporate resources on a daily basis. However, the auditor's report can be regarded only as the very small tip of a rather large financial iceberg because a substantial amount of the underlying audit work is hidden from users of financial statements.

In the past an auditors' report has consisted of a few lines of narrative which has often been regarded as obscuring more than it revealed. Since many of these users perceived the auditors' report as providing a form of 'financial guarantee' or 'seal of approval', the APB decided to issue its first Standard in an attempt to improve public understanding of reports.

An additional impetus for change has come from a number of large corporate failures over recent years, which have occurred shortly after the issue of an unqualified audit report. By failing to fully appreciate the nature, content and implications of the reports, many investors apportioned blame to the auditors for these collapses. The new standards should in principle help to diminish some of the underlying and commonly held misconceptions.

The Standard provides a detailed exposition of the revised format (see Figure 7.1) and increased content of the new auditors' report. It makes a distinction between the responsibilities of those who prepare financial statements and those who audit them. The report will now emphasize that it is the directors who determine accounting policies and not the auditors. In addition, the respective obligations of the directors and the auditors will be explicitly highlighted. The APB emphasizes that the view given in 'the financial statements is derived from a mixture of fact and judgement, and consequently cannot be categorised as either absolute or correct'. The auditors' report should be seen in this context. As indicated, the Standard provides for two new and significant sections:

---

1 A title identifying the person(s) to whom the report is addressed.
2 An identification of the financial statements that have been audited.
3 Two new and significant sections entitled:
  i) Statement of Responsibility
  ii) Basis of Opinion
  which together clearly indicate:
  – the respective responsibilities of directors and auditors
  – the basis of the auditors' opinion
  – the auditors' opinion on the financial statements.
4 Signature and date.

Figure 7.1

(1) STATEMENT OF RESPONSIBILITY

The Statement of Responsibility must clearly explain the legal and accounting responsibilities of the directors. The Cadbury Report on the Financial Aspects of Corporate Governance (1992) recommends that

STATEMENT OF DIRECTORS' RESPONSIBILITY FOR PREPARING THE ACCOUNTS
Appendix 3

1 In paragraph 4.28 of the report, and in the Code of Best Practice, the Committee recommends that a brief statement of directors' responsibility for preparing the accounts should appear in the report and accounts. The purpose of such a statement is to make clear that responsibility for preparing the accounts rests with the board of directors, and to remove any misconception that the auditors are responsible for the accounts. The directors' statement should be placed immediately before the auditors' report which in future will include a separate statement (currently being developed by the Auditing Practices Board) on the responsibility of the auditors for expressing an opinion on the accounts. Positioning the two statements alongside each other in this way will achieve maximum clarity about respective responsibilities.

2 The explanation of directors' responsibilities will require a relatively formal statement, which should cover the following points:

   (a) the legal requirement for directors to prepare financial statements for each financial year which give a true and fair view of the state of affairs of the company (or group) as at the end of the financial year and of the profit and loss for that period;

   (b) the responsibility of the directors for maintaining adequate accounting records, for safeguarding the assets of the company (or group), and for preventing and detecting fraud and other irregularities;

   (c) confirmation that suitable accounting policies, consistently applied and supported by reasonable and prudent judgements and estimates, have been used in the preparation of the financial statements;

   (d) confirmation that applicable accounting standards have been followed, subject to any material departures disclosed and explained in the notes to the accounts.

3 Boards may also wish to use the above statement as a vehicle for reporting that they have maintained an effective system of internal control, and that the business is a going concern, with supporting assumptions or qualifications as necessary, once the necessary guidance on these subjects has been developed (see paragraphs 5.16 and 5.22 of the main report).

Figure 7.2

companies will provide a detailed description of the directors' responsibilities before the auditors' report so as to provide maximum clarity about respective responsibilities it is intended to cover (see Figure 7.2). However, if this information is not provided in the financial statements it must be shown in the auditors' report.

In highlighting the responsibilities of the directors, specific comment should refer to the need to:

– prepare accounts that give a true and fair view
– keep all necessary accounting records and to select suitable accounting policies and apply them consistently
– make reasonable and prudent judgements
– adhere to Accounting Standards
– prepare the financial statements on a 'going-concern' basis, unless it is inappropriate to do so.

In response to explaining the directors' obligations, the auditors will state that their own responsibility is to form an independent opinion on the financial statements and report this opinion to shareholders.

(2) BASIS OF OPINION

The APB regards it important for auditors to explain why and how they have arrived at their opinion. Therefore, the auditors' report will contain a section entitled 'A Statement of the Basis of Opinion'. In particular it will include:

– a statement that the company has (not) complied with auditing standards
– a statement that the audit process includes an examination, on a test basis, of the evidence which relates to amounts and disclosures in the financial statements
– the assessment of any significant estimates and judgements made by the directors
– a comment that the company's accounting policies are appropriate, consistently applied and adequately disclosed
– a statement that the auditors have planned and performed the audit to obtain a reasonable assurance that the financial statements are free from material misstatement, whether caused through fraud or error.

Finally, the auditor's report must contain a clearly expressed opinion upon the financial statements. Specifically, the auditors are required to comment upon whether these statements provide a 'true and fair' view and have been prepared in accordance with relevant accounting and other requirements. This judgement will include assessing whether:

- the financial statements have been drafted by using consistent and appropriate accounting policies
- they have been properly prepared in accordance with legislation
- there is adequate disclosure of all information that is relevant for a proper understanding of the financial statements.

On occasions the auditors' opinion may be qualified. In the past, financial statements qualified in the former auditors' report were expressed in a form of coded language, and there was a common belief that a large proportion of users simply did not have the necessary skills to understand its significance.

To remedy this situation a qualified opinion in the future will be issued under one of the following clearly defined circumstances:

1. The scope of the auditors' examination has been limited.
2. The auditors disagree with the treatment or disclosure of a matter in the financial statements.

In both these instances the effect of the matter must be so material that the financial statements would not give a 'true and fair' view or comply with other accounting or legal requirements.

Auditors will have to explicitly state that they are giving a qualified opinion and the associated reasons. In most instances a qualified opinion will be clearly prominent and preceded by the phrase 'except for ⋯ ', and then followed by the reason for qualification. The former 'subject to ⋯ ' qualification which was used frequently in the past is no longer acceptable.

The new Standard also requires auditors to give a special explanation of any 'fundamental uncertainties' where, for example, the uncertainty about the outcome of a future event and its potential consequences is regarded as being of such significance in the context of the financial statements. The ultimate sanction of an auditor disclaiming or giving an adverse opinion will, of course, still remain as an option.

Cash flow statement

This statement provides a useful additional perspective to a business's performance over and above that provided by the profit and loss account and balance sheet. How the three statements relate to one another we illustrated in Chapter 3. The cash flow statement provides an historical perspective of the sources of cash and how it has been utilized. As you will see in the next chapter, it analyses cash flows under three types of activity:

- *Investing activities*   These include activities such as purchases and sales of fixed assets and investments and the making of loans.

– *Financial activities*   These include proceeds from share issues and loans, the repayment of loans and finance leases and the payment of dividends.
– *Operating activities*   These are defined as 'all transactions and other events that are not investing and finance activities'.

The cash flows are, generally, those arising from transactions recorded in the profit and loss account. These statements are a relatively new requirement in the United Kingdom and replace what was referred to as the statement of source and application of funds, or the funds statement.

As we indicated in the Preface and in Chapters 1 to 3, information about cash flow may be invaluable in forming a view about a business. It is significant that insolvency (not being able to pay one's way) is the major source of financial distress. Thus information about cash is very important and, while a forecast of future cash flows may be particularly invaluable, historical information like that provided by the cash flow statement can be a useful starting point in building a picture.

7.3 Interim reporting

In addition to the requirement to produce annual reports, listed companies must also produce interim reports for the first six months of each financial year. Items typically to be found in such interim reports include:

– Net turnover
– Profit before tax and extraordinary items
– The taxation charge
– Ordinary profit attributable to shareholders
– Extraordinary items
– Dividends
– Earnings per share
– Comparative figures
– An explanatory statement including information on any events and trends during the period as well as details about future prospects.

The whole interim report must be sent to all shareholders or, alternatively, it must appear in two national newspapers. Such reports are not usually audited and therefore lack the authority and accuracy which annual reports appear to possess.

7.4 Conclusion

Corporate reports play a vital part in conveying the financial results of a business. In this chapter we have tried to explain the various aspects of such reports in order to help you to understand and interpret them more easily. Important factors to consider include the following:

– The annual report is a primary medium by which information about the financial results of a company is communicated to the outside world.
– Financial information may well have significant commercial value and for this reason companies will reveal no more about some areas of their business than they have to.
– Legal and Stock Exchange requirements, and accounting standards all influence the form and contents of corporate reports.
– Published accounts within the corporate report must show a 'true and fair' view of the profit or loss for the year and of the company's financial position at the end of the year.

8

An introduction to analysing corporate reports*

Any figure that looks interesting is probably wrong

ANON.

Are company reports always interpreted in the same way? There are many interested parties in a company who may look at the financial statements differently depending upon their own perspective. In this chapter, with the help of the ratio analysis which we discussed earlier, we will look at how this can be handled.

The principles involved in assessing business profitability and the utilization of business assets from a number of related ratios can be applied in the analysis of published accounts. But, as we will demonstrate, there are some additional ratios that need to be calculated. This is because the perspective of the individual reviewing the financial statements may well be very different. Up to now, we have considered the perspective to be the management of the business but there are other interested parties such as owners and lenders for whom a different set of ratios may be far more appropriate.

Before we begin such analysis let us look again at the main financial statements within the context of the published accounts provided by Hanson PLC.

---

*The authors would like to acknowledge the contribution of Graham Quick from Extel Financial Limited in the writing of this chapter.

8.1 Profit and loss account

Consolidated Profit and Loss Account [Hanson PLC] for the year ended September 30, 1992.

	Note	1992 £ million	1991 £ million
Sales turnover	1		
– continuing operations		7,808	7,555
– acquisitions		903	–
		8,711	7,555
– discontinued operations		87	136
		8,798	7,691
Costs and overheads less other income	3	7,730	6,736
(a*) Operating profit	1		
– continuing operations		978	927
– acquisitions		80	–
		1,058	927
– discontinued operations		10	28
		1,068	955
Continuing operations			
– profit on disposal of fixed asset investments		39	211
– costs of closures		(23)	(57)
Profit on disposal of discontinued operation		156	19
		172	173
Net interest income	5	46	188
(b) Profit on ordinary activities	1	1,286	1,316
Taxation	6	197	258
(c) Profit on ordinary activities after taxation	7	1,089	1,058
Dividends	8	265	529
(d) Retained profit for the year	18	824	529
Earnings per ordinary share	9		
Undiluted		22.6p	22.0p
Diluted		22.2p	21.7p

*Letters (a) to (d) authors' additions.

In common with our earlier discussion of the profit and loss account in Chapter 1, the Hanson consolidated profit and loss account has different 'layers' of profit, prefixed by (a) to (d), many of which are similar to those discussed in Chapter 1. The first operating profit is simply the difference between sales turnover and costs and overheads after deducting other income, but do note that there is a distinction made between continuing operations, acquisitions, and discontinued operations. This distinction reflects the concepts introduced in Financial Reporting Standard 3, 'Reporting Financial Performance', which was published by the Accounting Standards Board in October 1992, only a few weeks before the 1992 Annual Report for Hanson PLC was due for publication. This is essentially a standard dealing with disclosure and presentation of financial information, rather than specifying new ways of treating the numbers. A comparison of the 1992 Annual Report for Hanson with that for 1991 reveals the impact of this new standard.

The second layer of profit includes net interest income (income receivable *less* interest payable) and for many companies, unlike Hanson, this will often be negative. When tax payable is deducted from it, the result is the third layer of profit, profit after tax. Once the proportion of this to be distributed by way of dividends has been determined, we are left with the fourth and final layer, profit retained in the business which, as we demonstrated in Chapter 4, is accumulated in the balance sheet together with the retained profits from earlier years.

The profit and loss account by itself is fairly limited in detail, but a good deal more information about specific items can be found in supporting notes. Exactly where in the notes such information may be found is disclosed in the column headed 'Note'. For example let us consider the last entry in the consolidated profit and loss account, 'Earnings per ordinary share'. This shows how much each of the group's ordinary shares has earned during the year. Reference to Note 9 reveals that it is calculated by dividing the profit after tax during the year by the weighted average number of issued ordinary shares in issue during the year:

9 Earnings per   The calculation was based on the weighted average
share   of 4,813,529,336 ordinary shares in issue during
                  the year and profit after taxation of £1,089 mn.

Where there is another equity share ranking for a dividend in the future, and/or other securities convertible into equity shares in issue, and/or options or warrants exist to subscribe for equity shares what is known as a diluted earnings per share should be disclosed.

Details about any potential dilution are typically disclosed in the notes to the accounts as is revealed further on in Note 9 to the Hanson PLC accounts:

Diluted earnings per ordinary share were calculated on a weighted average of 5,259,164,111 ordinary shares. This allowed for full conversion rights attaching to convertible securities and the allotment of shares under option schemes and warrants, with a corresponding adjustment to income for interest but excluded 553,443,193 shares relating to warrants exercisable at 300p per share as they were not dilutive. The adjusted undiluted calculation for 1991 is based on the weighted average of 4,802,706,150 ordinary shares in issue during 1991 and the restated profit after taxation of £1,058 mn. The adjusted diluted calculation is based on 5,123,225,175 ordinary shares.

Growth in earnings per share is reckoned to be an important indicator of company performance and, as you will see later in this chapter, earnings per share is also used in conjunction with a company's share price in what is known as the 'price earnings', or PE, ratio.

There are many ratios that can be calculated from information contained in the profit and loss account, many of which we introduced in Chapters 5 and 6, but we will defer our discussion of these until after we have looked at the Hanson balance sheet, from which information is required for their calculation. For now, let us look at the consolidated profit and loss account again, where it has been presented in common size terms with all items expressed as a percentage of sales.

Common size analysis of the consolidated profit and loss account – Hanson PLC for the year ended 30 September 1992

	Note	1992	1991
		%	%
Sales turnover	1	100	100
Costs and overheads			
less other income	3	87.86	87.58
Operating profit	1	12.14	12.42
Profit on disposals	1	1.96	2.25
Net interest income	5	0.52	2.44
Profit on ordinary activities		14.62	17.11
Taxation	6	2.24	3.35
Profit on ordinary activities			
after taxation	7	12.38	13.76
Dividends	8	3.01	6.88
Retained profit for the year	18	9.37	6.88

This analysis reveals a decline in profitability. Operating profit and profit on ordinary activities before, and profit after taxation have fallen as a percentage of sales. In the case of operating profit, costs and overheads *less* other income have increased. For profit on ordinary activities, before tax, one noteworthy source of the decrease is net interest income, details of which are provided in Note 5. The following breakdown shows there to have been a significant decrease in interest receivable:

	1992 £ million	1991 £ million
Net interest income		
interest receivable	823	929
interest payable	777	741
	46	188

As regards profit on ordinary activities after taxation, there is a notable decrease in the group tax. This can be related to one other noteworthy feature for 1992 – the significantly lower dividend (3.01 per cent of sales revenue by comparison with 6.88 per cent for 1991).

Quite simply, as is revealed in the notes to the accounts, from 1 July 1992, the company adopted a policy of paying dividends quarterly. This meant that the dividends reflected in the 1992 accounts were approximately one-half of the amount that would be expected in a normal year. This also impacted upon the taxation charge by virtue of tax payable in advance (known as Advance Corporation Tax, or ACT) being £88 million less than would previously have been the case.

Let us stand back from these rather technical issues and place our discussions so far in this chapter in context. First, the principles we reviewed at the start of the book are those applied in published accounts. Second, the format might differ and be subject to other influences like financial reporting standards. Third, a simple to calculate approach in the form of common size analysis can be used to identify significant sources of difference from one year to the next. Fourth, the reasons for such differences will often require digging around in appropriate notes to the accounts.

At this point technical issues and jargon may make further interpretation more difficult for you and it is here that good use should be made of financial expertise available. In common with many parts of the book you will find that there are not always clear cut answers. Where possible we will provide you with these, failing that we will offer you the next best alternative – those questions that need to be asked to form a more complete view. Do take particular note of the common size analysis technique we used for gaining an understanding of areas of change from year to year simply. Remember that its advantage is that all items within the profit and loss account were calculated in relative terms rather than absolute terms making it easier to identify important areas of difference. As you will see, it is an approach that can be used for analysing the balance sheet as well as the profit and loss account.

8.2 Balance sheet

The consolidated balance sheet for Hanson PLC is similar in format to that for HMC Ltd that we discussed in Chapter 3. The only area where there is much more detail is in the capital and reserves section at the bottom, but this was reviewed specifically with reference to Hanson PLC in the last chapter. The only other difference from HMC Ltd is that the company has creditors due after one year which have been grouped in the lower section of the balance sheet.

Consolidated Balance Sheet [Hanson PLC] at September 30, 1992

	Note	1992 £ million	1991 £ million
Fixed assets			
Tangible	24	9,146	6,199
Investments	10	191	429
		9,337	6,628
Current assets			
Stocks	11	1,318	992
Debtors	12	1,441	1,192
Listed investments	13	6	6
Cash at bank		8,439	7,765
		11,204	9,955
Creditors – due within one year	14		
Debenture loans		2,263	1,725
Bank loans and overdrafts		1,881	810
Trade creditors		599	507
Other creditors		1,511	1,332
Dividend		132	377
		6,386	4,751
Net current assets		4,818	5,204
Total assets less current liabilities		14,155	11,832
Creditors – due after one year	15		
Convertible loans		500	500
Debenture loans		1,330	579
Bank loans		3,239	3,801
		5,069	4,880
Provisions for liabilities	16	4,862	3,627
Capital and reserves			
Called up share capital	17	1,205	1,202

	Note	1992 £ million	1991 £ million
Share premium account	18	1,163	1,153
Revaluation reserve	18	166	163
Other reserves	18	65	–
Profit and loss account	18	1,625	807
		4,224	3,325
		14,155	11,832

Approved by the Board of Directors on December 3, 1992

In common with the consolidated profit and loss account, the consolidated balance sheet for Hanson PLC has notes to provide greater detail about specific entries, which are often helpful in interpreting results, but may not always give you all of the information you would ideally like for complete understanding.

The consolidated balance sheet does, at first sight, appear to be very complicated. However, like the consolidated profit and loss account, its interpretation is facilitated by expressing it in common size terms. In fact, a common size balance sheet for Hanson is illustrated below, where each of the items has been expressed as a percentage of the total.

Consolidated Balance Sheet – Hanson PLC at 3 September 1992

	Note	1992 %	1991 %
Fixed assets			
Tangible	24	64.61	52.39
Investments	10	1.35	3.63
(A)		65.96	56.02
Current assets			
Stocks	11	9.3	8.38
Debtors	12	10.18	10.07
Listed investments	13	0.04	0.05
Cash at bank		59.62	65.63
(B)		79.15	84.14
Creditors – due			
within one year	14		
Debenture loans		15.99	14.58
Bank loans and overdrafts		13.29	6.85
Trade creditors		4.23	4.28
Other creditors		10.67	11.26
Dividend		0.93	3.19
(C)		45.11	40.16

	Note	1992 %	1991 %
Net current assets		(D) 34.04	43.98
Total assets less current liabilities		100.00	100.00
Creditors – due after one year	15		
Convertible loans		3.53	4.23
Debenture loans		9.40	4.89
Bank loans		22.88	32.12
		(E) 35.81	41.24
Provisions for liabilities	16	(F) 34.35	30.65
Capital and reserves			
Called up share capital	17	8.51	10.16
Share premium account	18	8.22	9.75
Revaluation reserve	18	1.17	1.38
Other reserves	18	0.46	
Profit and loss account	18	11.48	6.82
		(G) 29.84	28.10
		100.00	100.00

You will recall that the total of the first section is calculated from adding fixed and current assets and deducting creditors due within one year, i.e. (A) + (B) − (C), or 65.96 per cent + 79.15 per cent − 45.11 per cent. (D) simply represents the difference between (B) and (C) and is the net current assets (working capital) expressed in percentage terms.

A comparison of this first section shows the most significant change to have occurred in tangible fixed assets. Unfortunately as is sometimes the case, Note 24 to which the reader is referred does not provide a great deal of useful information. However, as we will demonstrate, further analysis of the notes does provide an indication of appropriate questions to ask.

The second section totals the same as the first, but is made up of the sources of finance for the business assets. There are three main parts to this section: long-term liabilities, or creditors due after one year; provisions for liabilities; and equity and reserves. They are represented by (E), (F) and (G), or 35.81 per cent + 34.35 per cent + 29.84 per cent, which sum 100 per cent. You should take note of these three because we will refer to the relationship between long-term liabilities and equity and reserves in the next chapter when we discuss gearing or leverage.

At this point it is important for us to refer back to the principles which underpin the construction of the balance sheet. Earlier in Chapter 1, we demonstrated how from the same input data it is possible to construct balance sheets with different totals for each side or part, simply because of the way in which items are grouped.

Let us review these principles using the consolidated balance sheet for Hanson PLC 1992 as follows:

	£ million
Total assets	20,541
less	
Current liabilities	£6,386
equals	14,155
Creditors – due after one year	5,069
plus	
Provisions for liabilities	4,862
plus	
Capital and reserves	4,224
	£14,155

While Hanson PLC shows balance sheet totals of £14,155, it is quite feasible to use a balance sheet format which reconciles net assets with owners' equity, a practice not at all uncommon in the United Kingdom. Taking this perspective the results would be:

	£ million
Total assets	20,541
less	
	6,386
Total liabilities	5,069
	4,862
equals	
Owners' equity	£4,224

As illustrated, using the net assets equals owners' equity format would have produced balance sheet totals of £4,224 million rather than the £14,155 million published by Hanson PLC. That different totals can be calculated does not matter, but knowing the basis for their calculation does. This is particularly so when calculating ratios like profit on capital employed, where using £4,224 million as a measure of capital employed would produce a very different result from £14,155 million.

Data sourced from financial databases

With both the consolidated profit and loss account and the consolidated balance sheet plus supporting notes to the accounts from a company's annual and interim reports, the profitability and use of assets ratios we discussed in Chapters 5 and 6 can be calculated. Alternatively, there are many data provision services, like Dunn and Bradstreet, Extel and Datastream, which publish ratios for most companies. To the users of financial information third party databases can prove a valuable tool. Their coverage tends to be wide ranging which means that data will be provided to the user on companies that he or she does not normally follow or is not normally familiar with. This permits the timely and cost effective monitoring of financial statistics and their comparison with alternative organizations.

Because the data taken from the company's reports have been analysed by the data provider it will have been validated and processed through the provider's data quality procedures. Data treatments will normally have been standardized so that report abnormalities can be both highlighted and, when necessary, eliminated. This becomes critical when setting up parameters against which the databases can be searched in order to find a range of suitable target companies. It is also important in ensuring comparability of relationships and definitions when undertaking inter-company or inter-industry comparisons.

Without these quality assessments and standard treatment of data then it becomes at least dangerous and at worst critical to try and compare the performance and status of multiple companies.

When such investigations seek to make comparison across national borders standardization can become even more important. On such occasions reliance must be placed on the data provided attaining a degree of comparability in different national accounting policies and reporting requirements.

In summary, the advantage of using such providers is that they remove much of the effort involved in analysis and (hopefully) have less potential for error, although they may sometimes be difficult to reconcile with your own calculations because of adjustments and fine-tuning which may elude the untrained eye. This difficulty is redressed to some extent because data services do usually provide ratio definitions.

Analysing the report from a management perspective

Notwithstanding the possibility for making adjustments to the data, we have calculated ratios for Hanson PLC using the definitions we discussed in Chapters 4 and 5. These are:

		1992		1991
Profit on capital employed (%)	$\dfrac{1{,}068 + 172 + 777}{14{,}155}$	14.25%	$\dfrac{955 + 173 + 741}{11{,}832}$	15.80%
Profit on sales (%)	$\dfrac{1{,}068 + 172 + 777}{8{,}798}$	22.93%	$\dfrac{955 + 173 + 741}{7{,}691}$	24.30%
Sales as a multiple of capital employed	$\dfrac{8{,}798}{14{,}155}$	0.62 times	$\dfrac{7{,}691}{11{,}832}$	0.65 times
Sales as a multiple of fixed assets	$\dfrac{8{,}798}{9{,}337}$	0.94 times	$\dfrac{7{,}691}{6{,}628}$	1.16 times
Sales as a multiple of working capital	$\dfrac{8{,}798}{4{,}818}$	1.83 times	$\dfrac{7{,}691}{5{,}204}$	1.48 times
Current ratio	$\dfrac{11{,}204}{6{,}386}$	1.76:1	$\dfrac{9{,}955}{4{,}751}$	2.10:1
Liquid ratio	$\dfrac{11{,}204 - 1{,}311}{6{,}386}$	1.55:1	$\dfrac{9{,}955 - 992}{4{,}751}$	1.89:1
Debtors' days [1]	$\dfrac{1{,}314}{8{,}798} \times 360$	54 days	$\dfrac{1{,}112}{7{,}691} \times 360$	52 days
Creditors' days	$\dfrac{599}{8{,}798} \times 360$	24 days	$\dfrac{507}{7{,}691} \times 360$	24 days
Stock days	$\dfrac{1{,}318}{8{,}798} \times 360$	54 days	$\dfrac{992}{7{,}691} \times 360$	46 days

(1) Debtors after one year excluded

Earlier we mentioned that a major difference between the two years reported in the consolidated balance sheet for Hanson PLC related to the increase in fixed assets from 1991 to 1992. This you will recall from our earlier discussion of an interrelated ratio framework impacts upon profit on capital employed and, therefore, profit on sales and sales as a multiple of capital employed. In terms of the ratios for 1992, the relationship between the three can be expressed as follows (allowing for rounding errors):

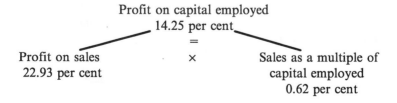

Profit on capital employed
14.25 per cent
=
Profit on sales   ×   Sales as a multiple of
22.93 per cent   capital employed
0.62 per cent

Now the profit on capital employed for the group has fallen from 15.80 per cent to 14.25 per cent, but we can do little to understand what has happened without further analysis. We can achieve a reasonable understanding by looking further into the notes and, particularly, Note 1 which provides a breakdown of the group's activities.

In the following table Note 1 has been reproduced and a common size analysis based upon profit, sales turnover and capital employed has been undertaken. Common size percentages are shown in parentheses:

Note 1 – summarized profit, sales turnover and capital employed

		1992	
By activity	Profit £ million (%)	Sales turnover £ million (%)	Capital employed £ million (%)
Industrial	430 (38.91)	2,720 (30.92)	4,001 (38.86)
Consumer	380 (34.39)	3,631 (41.27)	240 (2.33)
Building products	267 (24.16)	2,360 (26.82)	**5,887 (57.18)**
Trading operations	1,077 (97.47)	8,711 (99.01)	10,128 (98.38)
Other	28 (2.53)	87 (0.99)	167 (1.62)
Total	1,105 (100) (1)	8,798 (100)	10,295 (100) (2)
By geographical location			
UK	461 (41.72)	4,187 (47.59)	1,612 (15.66)
USA	567 (51.31)	4,102 (46.62)	**8,483 (82.40)**
Other	67 (6.06)	422 (4.80)	200 (1.94)
Discontinued	10 (0.91)	87 (0.99)	–
	1,105 (100)	8,798 (100)	10,295 (100)

(1) This is reconciled with profit on ordinary activities in the consolidated profit and loss account as follows:

	£ million
Total profit by activity	1,105
Central expenses less property and other income	(37)
	1,068
Exceptional items (net)	172
Net interest income	46
	1,286

By activity	Profit £ million (%)	1991 Sales turnover £ million (%)	Capital employed £ million (%)
Industrial	451 (44.61)	2,808 (36.51)	4,127 (59.15)
Consumer	319 (31.55)	3,286 (42.73)	243 (3.48)
Building products	195 (19.29)	1,461 (19.00)	**2,424 (34.74)**
Trading operations	965 (95.45)	7,555 (98.23)	6,794 (97.38)
Other	46 (4.55)	136 (1.77)	183 (2.62)
Total	1,011 (100)	7,691 (100)	6,977 (100)
By geographical location			
UK	411 (40.65)	3,730 (48.50)	1,394 (19.98)
USA	494 (48.86)	3,506 (45.59)	**5,368 (76.94)**
Other	78 (7.72)	319 (4.15)	184 (2.64)
Discontinued	28 (2.70)	136 (1.77)	31 (0.44)
	1,011 (100)	7,691 (100)	6,977 (100)

(2) This figure is not reconciled with the capital employed shown in the consolidated balance sheet.

What can be observed from this analysis, albeit with some difficulty, is that there has been a significant increase in the capital employed in building products. In 1991 they represented 34.74 per cent of the capital employed by comparison with 57.18 per cent in 1992. Furthermore, the breakdown by geographical location pin-points this increase to the United States, where the capital employed rose from 76.94 per cent of total capital employed to 82.40 per cent in 1992.

A better gauge of the relative performance of the activities and geographical locations can be obtained if we calculate profit on capital employed per cent, profit on sales per cent, and sales as a multiple of capital employed by activity and by geographical location, i.e.

	Profit on capital employed		Profit on sales		Sales as a multiple of capital employed	
	1992 %	1991 %	1992 %	1991 %	1992 times	1991 times
By activity						
Industrial	10.75	10.93	15.81	16.06	0.68	0.68
Consumer	158.33	131.28	10.47	9.71	15.13	13.52
Building products	4.54	8.04	11.31	13.35	0.40	0.60
Trading operations	10.63	14.20	12.36	12.77	0.86	1.11
By geographical location						
UK	28.60	29.48	11.01	11.01	2.60	2.68
USA	6.7	9.20	13.82	14.09	0.48	0.65
Other	33.5	42.39	15.88	24.45	2.11	1.73
Discontinued	–	90.32	11.49	20.59	–	4.39
Total	10.73	14.49	12.56	13.15	0.86	1.10

These ratios reinforce the point made earlier in Chapter 5 that profit on capital employed, profit on sales and sales as a multiple of capital employed do vary by activity. Highly capital-intensive industries tend to require a much greater investment in capital employed, a feature shown by the Hanson results from comparing the ratios for industrial and building products with consumer activities.

As regards performance by geographical location, the most noticeable feature is the relatively poor results for the United States, but care must be exercised before drawing too hasty conclusions. It is necessary when analysing such ratios to make comparisons with expectations for the type activity. Thus making a comparison between the United Kingdom and United States may not be very meaningful because each has a different portfolio of activities. Trends related to the business cycle should also not be ignored with many of the activities, like building products, being very severely affected.

Last, but by no means least, significant acquisitions should not be overlooked. Details provided in Note 1 (but not reproduced here) show the capital employed for 'Aggregates' within 'Building products' having increased from £797 million in 1991 to £4049 million in 1992. Given the acquisition of the construction/building products company Beazer by Hanson with its extensive US operations, some explanation for the change in the ratio for 'Building products' activity and the US segment can be found.

You may be now reeling from the detail of the analysis, but let us take stock of the purpose of our review of the Hanson corporate report:

1. Similarity in presentation and content between the profit and loss account and balance sheet for publication with those discussed in Chapters 1 and 3 has been reinforced. The principles involved in drafting them are the same but the degree of detail to support published accounts will typically be greater and will be found in notes to the accounts.
2. Where it is difficult to see what changes have occurred by simple observation, common size analysis can be invaluable. By expressing items in the profit and loss account as a percentage of sales and those in the balance sheet as a percentage of total assets *less* current liabilities, the relative significance of complex numbers can be more easily seen.
3. All of the ratios we discussed earlier in Chapters 5 and 6 can be calculated from the published accounts, but in order to get a fuller picture of what has happened further analysis using the notes to the accounts is required, as we just demonstrated with reference to the composition of Hanson's profit on capital employed figures.

You might be feeling that this is all rather complicated and indeed it is. There may be some occasions when you will still wish to draw upon the particular expertise offered by financial specialists rather than undertake this type of analysis personally. However, you should *never* accept any such analysis blindly and it is well worth being aware of the issues we have raised in this chapter.

Finally, what is noteworthy about the ratios for Hanson PLC is their relative consistency between the two years. Hanson has a reputation for management by operating with stringent financial controls in its portfolio of businesses which are generally low risk, mature and cash generative. It cannot also be ignored that businesses with substantial loans may need to achieve prescribed ratio targets as a condition of being granted a loan and continuing for support being provided.

8.3 Cash flow statement

As the recent spate of corporate collapses has served to illustrate only too well, cash is one of the most, if not the most, important indicators of a company's financial health. We have also demonstrated in earlier chapters that it is impossible to form a complete view of performance from the profit and loss account and balance sheet alone. In fact, for many years organizations have been required by an accounting standard to produce a third statement, currently called the cash flow statement. This statement has a standard layout illustrated by that taken from the 1992 accounts of Hanson PLC:

Cash Flow Statement [Hanson PLC] for the year ended September 30, 1992

	Note	1992 £ million	1991 £ million
Operating activities			
Net cash inflow from operating activities	1	1,109	934
Returns on investments and servicing of finance			
Interest received		823	929
Interest paid		(747)	(751)
Dividends received from associated undertakings		6	11
Dividends paid		(510)	(510)
Net outflow from returns on investments and servicing of finance		(428)	(318)
Taxation		(255)	(255)
Net cash inflow before investing and financing		426	361
Investing activities			
Sale of investments		294	843
Sale of businesses	2	135	90
Sale of tangible fixed assets		60	67
Inflow in respect of short-term investments	3	5,987	5,932
Outflow in respect of short-term investments	3	(9,107)	(2,896)
Purchase of subsidiary undertakings (net of cash equivalents)	2	(1,026)	(704)
Purchase of tangible fixed assets		(279)	(266)
Purchase of investments		(12)	(257)
Net cash (outflow) inflow from investing activities		(3,948)	2,809
Net cash (outflow) inflow before financing		(3,522)	3170
Financing			
Issue of ordinary share capital		18	13

Increase in short-term loans		437	1,566
Proceeds of debenture loans		4	92
Repayments of debenture loans		(21)	(75)
Repayments of bank loans		(977)	(350)
Proceeds of bank loans		616	266
New unsecured bonds		900	500
Costs of issue of bonds		(5)	(12)
		972	2,000
Net cash (outflow) inflow after financing	3	(2,550)	5,170

Notes

1. Reconciliation of trading profit to net cash inflow from operating activities

Profit from trading operations	1,077	975
Central expenses less property and other income	(37)	(56)
Depreciation	252	212
Provisions charged	126	147
Profit on sale of tangible fixed assets	(14)	(22)
Decrease (increase) in stocks	(13)	(35)
Decrease (increase) in debtors	93	(35)
Increase (decrease) in creditors	72	(4)
	1,556	1,182
Outflow in respect of provisions, discontinued operations and reorganization costs	(447)	(248)
Net cash inflow from operating activities	1,109	934

The cash flow statement provides the third part of the financial picture, in much the same way as we described earlier in Chapters 2 and 3. There you will recall we demonstrated the link between the three statements which can also be seen with reference to the Hanson results. For example, profit from trading operations for 1992 of £1,077 million (the composition of which was shown earlier in Note 1 to the accounts) is adjusted as shown in Note 1 to the cash flow statement to produce the 'Net cash inflow from operating activities' of £1,109 million. This is then adjusted for 'Returns on investment and servicing of finance' and 'Taxation' to produce 'Net cash inflow before investing activities and financing'. For 1992 this is £426 million which when the outflow from investing activities is taken into consideration produces a deficit of £3,522. However, this deficit is reduced somewhat by the net cash inflow from the company's financing activities. The result is a 'Net cash outflow after financing' of £2,550 million.

This shows the movement in cash flow over the year which, you may recall, would be calculated more frequently for internal purposes. It does not show the cash at bank at any particular point in time. For that we need to refer to the consolidated balance sheet which shows a very substantial balance of £8,439 million. Thus, cash flow statements provide a comparison of the cash flow position as between the last annual reporting date one year ago and today. As you may recognize they do provide valuable overall information but give no indication of what happened at various points in time during the year.

8.4 Conclusion

We have shown how to calculate business specific ratios from published financial statements using the framework outlined in Chapters 4 and 5. It is also possible to analyse the company from an operating perspective using published statements and supporting notes to the accounts, but for this data services may be invaluable in obtaining a fuller picture.

It is also important to consider financial statements from other perspectives. Apart from the management ratios we have discussed so far, there are others that are more relevant to owners and lenders and which can readily be understood by extending the analytical framework that we have developed so far, these we consider in the next chapter.

Useful points to remember from this chapter include:

- The principles involved in drafting the profit and loss account and the balance sheet are the same, but the degree of detail to support published accounts will usually be greater and will be found in the notes to the accounts.
- Where it is difficult to see what changes have occurred year on year, common size analysis can be invaluable. This approach can be used for analysing the balance sheet as well as the profit and loss account.
- Information contained in the profit and loss account can provide the basis for the calculation of important business ratios.
- A knowledge of ratio analysis provides the general manager with a better understanding of how to interpret and, where necessary, challenge financial results.
- Although the profit and loss account is fairly limited in detail, the supporting notes to the accounts will often provide a good deal more information about specific items.
- Cash flow statements provide the third part of the financial picture and provide a comparison of the cash flow position as between the last annual reporting date one year ago and today.

9

Analysing corporate reports – the shareholders' and lender's perspectives

If you don't know where you're going, you will probably end up somewhere else
L. J. PETER

To be an effective general manager it is important to have a good understanding of how different stakeholders interpret corporate information. In Chapters 5 and 6 we introduced you to a number of related ratios that can be used very effectively for analysing financial information from a managerial perspective with profit on capital employed as the key ratio. In this chapter we extend ratio analysis to look at other user perspectives, and how two particular users of the annual report and accounts, shareholders and lenders, might analyse the financial information provided within it.

An understanding of the shareholder's perspective is important to the general manager because of the existence of what is known as the market for 'corporate control'. In addition to paying attention to the market for its goods and services, the most senior general managers in a publicly quoted company and its board of directors have to pay attention to the market for its shares. Shares are priced by the market on the basis of information, an important part of which is provided by a company and its perceptions of potential future performance. This means that the view provided of a company does matter. One key challenge is to avoid a significant discount to the share price arising from, for example, indications of future poor performance and hence the potential for losing corporate control, because the company has become attractive to a buyer who sees it as having a realizable value higher than the cost of acquiring it.

Just what view of a company might be taken by a shareholder we consider with reference to ratios that can be calculated from the published accounts of Hanson PLC.

An understanding of the lender's perspective is also necessary. There are some very real potential advantages to borrowing funds which may make it very attractive. Other than periodic benefits from low interest rates and being able to fix sums payable irrespective of financial performance, interest payable is deductible in the same way as any other business expense, thereby having a distinctive tax advantage over dividends. However, there are some disadvantages, in so far as interest has to be paid and cannot be so readily deferred or avoided as is generally considered to be the case with dividend payments. This means that there is a real risk associated with high levels of borrowed capital. This risk can be measured using a number of ratios that we will review and calculate from Hanson's Annual Report.

9.1 Shareholders

Quite simply, shareholders will hold shares for one or both of the following reasons – the income they provide and their capital growth potential. Regular income will arise for the shareholder by way of dividend payments by the company, and capital growth will come to the shareholder as the market value of shareholdings increase. Shareholders may, therefore, reasonably expect to use financial statements and annual reports to predict future dividend payments, and if possible, the potential for growth in the value of investments.

Shareholders' interests in a company are represented by a number of categories of shareholders. For example, the Hanson Annual Report shows that there are basically two types of shareholders – institutional share-holders, including pension funds and insurance companies, and other shareholders who will typically be private individuals. Institutional shareholders tend to hold more than 50,000 shares each and, although numerically the institutions form only about 23 per cent of the shareholders, they hold about 87 per cent of the total share issue.

All types of shareholder will be interested in past trends of profitability, profit on capital employed and the other ratios we calculated for Hanson PLC in the last chapter. However, there are other important ratios that we will look at:

– Earnings per share (EPS)
– Price–earnings (PE) ratio

- Dividend cover
- Dividend yield
- Return on shareholders' funds
- Gearing
- Interest cover.

In fact, these can be subdivided into three measures which can be seen as providing three important complementary perspectives about a company. These measures are:

1. *Investment measures* They examine the mechanisms by which financial results relate to shareholders' funds and to stock market prices.
   (a) Earnings per share (EPS)
   (b) Price earnings (PE) ratio
   (c) Dividend cover
   (d) Dividend yield.
2. *Operating measures* These are concerned with how profitable the business is and how successfully it is being run.
   (a) Return on shareholders' funds
   (b) Profit on capital employed (discussed in the last chapter).
3. *Financial status measures* These are ratios which are designed to assess the financial status and riskiness of the company.
   (a) Gearing
   (b) Interest cover.

Investment measures

EARNINGS PER SHARE (EPS)

EPS is calculated by dividing profit after taxation by the weighted average number of shares in issue. For Hanson PLC for 1992 you might recall that this produced an undiluted earnings per share of 22.6p (see page 86) which was calculated as follows:

$$\frac{\text{Profit after taxation for 1992}}{\text{Weighted average number of shares in issue during 1992}} = \frac{£1,089 \text{ million}}{4,813,529,336}$$

EPS is considered to be an important indicator of corporate performance. However, it is influenced by the accounting principles applied in calculating profit, an issue we look at further in the next two chapters, and also by the capital structure in terms of the balance of funding between share capital or borrowed funds. The more equity that is used to fund a business, the greater the dilutive effect upon the profit attributable to each individual shareholder. While this suggests that debt may be more beneficial, it is not quite so straightforward. As we have indicated, debt creates a charge that has to be met irrespective of business performance so any apparent benefit to EPS from a lower equity base may be more than offset at times by interest affected profits. In fact, debt represents a 'two-edged sword' – at times of boom it may be advantageous, unlike recessionary times when it may be potentially disastrous. EPS is a widely used, conventionally accepted indicator of corporate performance, the importance of which is linked with the price–earnings (PE) ratio.

PE RATIO

The PE ratio is often taken as *one* of the, if not the most, significant indicator of corporate performance and it is widely quoted in the financial press. As shown below, it is calculated by dividing the market price of a share by the earnings per share (or alternatively the total market value by total earnings attributable to shareholders):

$$\text{PE ratio} \quad = \quad \frac{\text{Market price of share}}{\text{Earnings per share}}$$

For Hanson PLC, at the time of writing, this calculation using the 1992 reported EPS of 22.6p and a market price of 250p, yielded a PE ratio of 11.06.

The PE ratio indicates how much investors are willing to pay for a company's actual and perceived earnings. Potential high growth companies tend to have high PE ratios, while those with little or no potential growth have low ratios.

The PE of a company depends not only on the company itself, but also on the industry in which it operates and on the level of the stock market. PE ratios do move over time and in particular with business cycle swings. The level of the PE ratio of *The Financial Times* 500 Index shows this movement very clearly:

500 PE Ratio

– 'Bull' market 1972 19.9
– 'Bear' market 1974 3.7
– 'Bull' market 1987 21.0
– 'Bear' market 1990 5.2
– 'Bull' market 1993 18.3

The Actuaries Share Indices table published in *The Financial Times* every day except Mondays also gives the PE ratio for each industry group and subsection, so any historical PE ratio calculated for a company can be compared with its sector and the market as a whole. The result of comparing it with the market as a whole (usually with the FT 500's PE ratio) is called the PE relative:

$$\text{PE relative} \quad = \quad \frac{\text{PE of the company}}{\text{PE of the market}}$$

This provides a quick indication of whether a company is highly or lowly rated, although differences in the treatment of tax by individual companies do cause some distortions, such that analysts will tend to standardize their calculations.

In general, a high historic PE ratio compared with the industry group suggests either that the company is a leader in its sector or that the share is overvalued, while a low PE ratio suggests a poor company or an undervalued share. It is worthwhile being cautious of companies with ratios much above 20. The company may be a 'glamour stock' due for a tumble or, if it is the PE ratio of a very sound high quality company, the market itself may be in for a fall. One exception is the property sector, where PE ratios may be high because property companies often have a high proportion of borrowed capital and use most of their rental income to service debt, thereby leaving very small earnings per share values. In fact, investors typically buy property company shares more for their prospects of capital appreciation than for their current earnings.

DIVIDEND COVER

Shareholders are also interested in what they get in the form of dividend payments, not just how the company is doing. An important indicator of the ability of a company to pay a dividend is provided by the dividend cover which is calculated as follows:

$$\text{Dividend cover} \quad = \quad \frac{\text{Earnings per share}}{\text{Dividend per share}}$$

For Hanson PLC for 1992 the dividend cover was just over 2, i.e.

$$\frac{22.6 \text{ pence}}{11.0 \text{ pence}} \quad = \quad 2.06 \text{ times}$$

Hanson pays out by way of dividend approximately 50 per cent of its earnings after tax. This is very typical for an industrial company in the

United Kingdom. That which is retained provides an indicator of growth potential and is available for reinvestment in the business – to buy new or replacement fixed assets or to increase (if necessary) working capital. If these funds are not enough, the company may have to borrow or ask its shareholders for more cash by way of a rights issue.

The dividend cover indicates how many times the dividend could have been paid from available earnings. We can use this measure to identify those companies which tend to pay out all or most of their profits as dividends, as well as those which occasionally pay dividends of a greater amount than the profits which they earn. In inflationary conditions this latter type of company will find itself contracting rather than growing, and in recessionary conditions it will often find itself hard pushed to sustain such a policy. However, the pressure not to cut dividend payments is very significant and the policy is not entertained lightly. Despite the apparent discretion available in determining the dividend payment for a year, many companies exercise such discretion very much as a last resort, typically for fear of its impact upon the share price.

DIVIDEND YIELD

The dividend yield indicates the current income yield that the investor receives from the distributed earnings of the company. As for any form of investment, the return or yield to be obtained is a function of both the income to be received and the outlay cost of the investment.

Dividend yield is calculated by dividing the latest annual dividend payable per share (grossed up for tax purposes) by the current purchase price of the share, and by expressing the result as a percentage. Assuming a share price of 250p, Hanson's dividend yield could then be calculated as follows:

$$\frac{14.7p^*}{250p} \times \frac{100}{1} = 5.9 \text{ per cent}$$

The shareholder is equipped, through the use of the dividend yield, to compare the income of one share with another or, indeed, with any other form of investment, for example a bank deposit. However, when other investments are considered which give higher income yields, the fact that shares offer prospective growth in value must also be considered. Actually,

---

*Net dividend of 11p grossed up at Hanson's effective tax rate of approximately 25 per cent. In fact, it is a little more complicated than that, because of Hanson's overseas income.

any investor need make no reference to the annual accounts when requiring the dividend yield of a quoted share – this will have been done already because the yield is quoted, regularly, in the financial press.

Professional investors are likely to be interested in a portfolio of investments, and they will be very concerned with the relative performance of an individual company against other similar companies, and against the stock market as a whole. A common way of measuring relative performance is to look at the history of the market price of the share and to compare it with the industrial sector or all-share index. The purpose here is to find out whether a particular company has 'out-performed' the market. Many professional investors consider that one of their prime aims is to hold shares which out-perform the market.

Operating measures

RETURN ON SHAREHOLDERS' FUNDS

This ratio, like profit on capital employed, relates profitability to the funds used in generating it. However, both the measure of profitability and funds used differ between the two ratios. Return on shareholders' funds focuses specifically on the earnings to shareholders for the year after interest payable and taxation have been deducted. This return is then related to shareholders' funds, for example, by reference to the 'book value' of their stake in the business. As such, this measure ignores the market value of any particular shareholder's investment (that is, the amount actually paid to acquire shares) but it does incorporate the total return attributable to the investors, that is, both the dividends and the profits retained on their behalf. For Hanson PLC, on the basis of 1992 results, the return on shareholders' funds is:

$$\frac{\text{Earnings of the year}}{\text{Shareholders' funds}} \quad \text{x} \quad \frac{100}{1} = \frac{£1089 \text{ million}}{£4224 \text{ million}}$$
$$= 25.8 \text{ per cent}$$

It should be noted that opinions do differ about what measure of shareholders' funds should be used. For example, where a company has preference shares in its capital, return on equity may be calculated by excluding preference shares from the denominator and by deducting preference dividends from the numerator. This 'pure' return on equity is often preferred to the return on shareholders' funds, as it deals with the part of the business's capital that is traded in the market. However, some analysts would contend that such an adjustment is still not really satisfactory. In their eyes the focus of attention should really be upon the yield, that is the return generated from their actual investment in equity rather than its historical value adjusted for retained profits. Given that the decision to invest will typically be based upon a comparison with alternatives forgone, this last view is one with which we concur.

Financial status measures

GEARING

Gearing (sometimes known as 'leverage') expresses the relationship between some measure of interest-bearing capital and some measure of the equity capital or the total capital employed. As suggested by the vagueness of this definition, one potential difficulty with gearing is that there are many alternative measures that can be used, hence the reference to 'some measure' for both interest-bearing capital and equity capital. For example, from one perspective interest-bearing capital would consist of short- and long-term bank and institutional loans, finance leases and preference shares, while to other users quite different measures would be applicable, as the following example serves to illustrate. Consider a company with the following results:

1. Short-term loans £50 million
2. Long-term loans £70 million
3. Preference shares £10 million
4. Ordinary shareholders' funds £200 million
5. Cash at bank £57 million
6. Market value of long-term debt £100 million
7. Market value of shareholders' funds £400 million.

Using these results we can calculate many different gearing ratios and, given a particular perspective, one might be preferred to another, but none is necessarily correct or incorrect. The following calculations illustrate what these different gearing ratios might be:

$$\frac{\text{Long-term loans}}{\text{Total equity } (3+4)} = \frac{\text{£70 million}}{\text{£210 million}} = 30 \text{ per cent}$$

$$\frac{\text{Long-term loans } + \text{ Preference shares}}{\text{Ordinary shareholders' funds}} = \frac{\text{£80 million}}{\text{£200 million}} = 40 \text{ per cent}$$

$$\frac{\text{Long-term loans} + \text{Short-term loans}}{\text{Ordinary shareholders' funds}} = \frac{£120 \text{ million}}{£200 \text{ million}} = 60 \text{ per cent}$$

$$\frac{\text{Long-term loans} + \text{Short-term loans} - \text{Cash at bank}}{\text{Ordinary shareholders' funds}} = \frac{£63 \text{ million}}{£200 \text{ million}} = 31.5 \text{ per cent}$$

$$\frac{\text{Market value of debt}}{\text{Market value of equity}} = \frac{£100 \text{ million}}{£400 \text{ million}} = 25.0 \text{ per cent}$$

What these different calculations serve to illustrate is that in interpreting the results for a particular gearing ratio, it really is important to know how it was defined.

Why is gearing important? A company with a large proportion of debt to equity is said to be highly geared. The importance of gearing is that changes in operating profit in a highly geared company may have disproportionate effects on the return accruing to ordinary shareholders.

In Hanson's case, the gearing ratio would also vary depending upon the measure adopted. One view is that because of the very significant cash balance revealed in the consolidated balance sheet for 1992 (see p. 90), that does not appear to be inaccessible and is therefore potentially available to offset any financial risk, gearing might be calculated using the fourth measure illustrated above. This first of all requires the net debt figure for 1992 to be calculated:

	£ million
Long-term loans (creditors due after one year)	5069
Short-term loans (part of creditors due within one year):	
Debenture loans	2263
Bank loans and overdrafts	1881
	9213
Less Cash at bank	8439
Net debt	774

Using this measure the gearing figure for Hanson for 1992 is:

$$\frac{\text{Net debt}}{\text{Ordinary shareholders' funds}} = \frac{£774 \text{ million}}{£4,224 \text{ million}} = 18.3 \text{ per cent}$$

But, taking a different measure can yield a very different result as the following calculation serves to illustrate:

$$\frac{\text{Long-term loans} + \text{Short-term loans}}{\text{Ordinary shareholders' funds}} = \frac{£9213 \text{ million}}{£4224 \text{ million}} = 218 \text{ per cent}$$

Using net debt in comparison to ordinary shareholders' funds in the measure of gearing indicates no real financial risk. Using total debt shows a very high gearing ratio. Which is appropriate depends upon the view taken of the cash balance shown in the consolidated balance sheet for 1992. For some companies like Polly Peck, which went into administration in 1990, severe misgivings were expressed about the availability of cash balances to the holding company. In a situation like that the use of net debt would hardly be appropriate.

INTEREST COVER

As you can see from the Hanson example, the definition of gearing used does influence the results obtained and also, potentially, the view formed. What must never be lost sight of in calculating any ratio is the purpose of its calculation. In this case, the purpose is to measure financial risk and so far the information we have used for measuring it has focused upon the implications for the company in terms of the capital structure. Equally important is the effect of the capital structure upon the profit generated. To gauge this we can make use of the profit and loss account and examine what coverage there is for interest payments using the interest cover ratio.

Interest cover shows the extent to which earnings are pre-empted by the need to make interest payments. It is directly analogous to 'dividend cover' and it can be used to gauge both the risk-taking attitude of the company's management and the vulnerability of interest (and, thereafter, dividend payments) to fluctuations in operating profit. It is calculated as follows:

$$\text{Interest cover} = \frac{\text{Profit before interest and taxation}}{\text{Interest payable}}$$

For Hanson PLC the interest cover in 1992 was 2.7 times, i.e.

$$\text{Interest cover} = \frac{£1286 + £823 \text{ million}}{£777 \text{ million}}$$

$$= 2.7 \text{ times}$$

Cover ratios do vary with the economic climate. When profits fall and interest payable is high, such as in times of recession, cover ratios will be lower. For example, the cover ratio for all industrial and commercial companies in late 1991 was estimated by the government to be around 2.9 times interest payable. This was comparable with the recession of the early 1980s, but lower than that in the early 1970s. At this time Hanson's ratio was not vastly different from that government estimate, being approximately 2.8 times, thus providing support for the view we expressed earlier of the company not being a particularly high financial risk.

As with all ratios, analysis would be unlikely to rely on the information provided by just one annual report. Typically, use will be made of previous years' annual reports to analyse the ratios over a time span greater than the two years' figures normally found in the annual report. From this analysis, analysts will consider growth or decline in each group of ratios and then, with the aid of other information which they have about the company and the economy, they will attempt to project future trends, for example of sales, profits and gearing, and their potential impact for share prices.

A cautionary note on using published ratios is apposite. Many analysts use data and ratios which have already been calculated for them by someone else. Before doing so, they will naturally check to see how the ratios have been calculated as everyone seems to calculate them slightly differently! The golden rule is: *when you are using someone else's ratios, always make sure that you know how they were calculated.*

9.2 Lenders

The information requirements of lenders are very similar to those of other investors, even though the terms on which they invest may differ. Lenders include:

- Clearing banks
- Merchant banks
- Finance houses, that is, hire-purchase, leasing and factoring companies
- Specialist financial institutions
- Insurance companies and pension funds
- Private individuals, especially for small businesses.

Since their business is to lend money, charge interest on it and then re-lend it, their main uses of accounts are:

- To assess and monitor the repayment capacity of borrowers.
- To identify business development opportunities in companies which are growing.

We can conveniently consider lenders in two categories:

1. Lenders of long-term funds to the business
2. Lenders of short-term funds.

Each group is concerned with the capacity of the business to repay the loan and to pay interest. This involves forecasting the future cash flow position of the company, that is, determining whether it will be able to generate enough cash to make the requisite payments.

A short-term lender, that is, somebody who lends only for a period of, say, up to one year, is primarily concerned with the short-term prospects of the business to generate enough cash to repay the loan with interest.

A long-term lender will certainly be interested in liquidity, but will also be interested in the economic stability and vulnerability of the borrower in the long term. The concern of such an individual, basically, is to judge the risk of default over the term of the loan which may be anything between 2 and 25 years.

The lender will wish to measure interest cover and dividend cover so as to assess how a change in profits would affect the likelihood of interest payments being stopped. Also, the lender would want to have an indication of whether the company had followed a policy of paying dividends solely out of income. As regards the stability of a lender's investment in a company, perhaps the most important ratio is the gearing ratio. Not surprisingly, the view taken of the gearing ratio by the lender and of its counterpart for assessing the financial risk associated with interest payments, interest cover, will often be very conservative. Balance sheet gearing would be looked at very cautiously, including all borrowings and paying particular attention to the existence of any restrictions on the use of cash and liquid balances. Equally, interest cover may well be calculated taking a worst case position, that is by including fixed charges such as lease expenses with interest payable.

From a security point of view, the lender will be looking for a fairly low-geared company with a strong asset base, thus giving security for interest payments and security for the repayment of the loan. One measure of security used is to calculate net assets per share. This ratio measures the underlying net asset value of each share at balance sheet values – that is, it gives a crude indication of the asset backing of each share. It is calculated as follows:

Net assets per share   = $\dfrac{\text{Net assets attributable to shareholders}}{\text{Number of ordinary shares issued}}$

For Hanson PLC for 1992 this ratio is:

$$\text{Net assets per share} \quad = \quad \frac{\text{Net assets attributable to shareholders}}{\text{Number of ordinary shares issued}}$$

$$= \quad \frac{£4224 \text{ million}}{£4820 \text{ million}}$$

$$= \quad 87.6 \text{ pence}$$

One final point worth noting about lenders and financial ratios is that very often a condition of making a loan will relate to the ability of the company to maintain agreed levels for such ratios as interest cover, gearing and the current ratio. Covenants will be imposed by the lender specifying required ratios to be observed as well as consequences associated with defaulting upon them. In this way, lenders, particularly of large sums, exercise some control over the funds of a business.

9.3 Conclusion

In this chapter we have reviewed corporate performance from a shareholder's and a lender's perspective with reference to the 1992 results for Hanson PLC as reported in its Annual Report. Specifically, we have shown how a number of ratios can be calculated to help interpretation of corporate performance. However, this is not the end of the story. As we will illustrate in the next two chapters, considerable care has to be exercised in interpreting results because of dependence upon financial information which may be subject to a number of influences and, therefore, may not necessarily always be appropriate to use.

Other than concerns about the financial information used to calculate ratios, there is a growing view that many conventional measures of performance may not be the most appropriate tools for assessing future performance. This is of particular concern to the general manager who very often will have to devote an increasing amount of time to strategic issues as his or her career progresses. In such circumstances we believe an alternative view that looks at value is more appropriate and this we consider later in the book.

In summary, the main points which need to be remembered from this chapter include the following:

- An understanding of the shareholders' perspective is important to the general manager because of the existence of the market for corporate control.

- There are advantages and disadvantages to borrowing funds, and a real risk associated with high levels of borrowed capital.
- In addition to ratios which calculate past trends of profitability, profit on capital employed, etc., there are other important ratios which fall into the following three categories:

  Investment measures
  Operating measures
  Financial status measures.
- When using someone else's ratios always make sure that you know how they have been calculated.
- Lenders may be categorized into lenders of long-term funds and lenders of short-term funds. Each category is concerned with the capacity of the business to repay the loan and to pay interest, however, the long-term lender will also be interested in the economic stability and vulnerability of the borrower.
- As regards the stability of a lender's investment in a company, possibly the most important ratio is the gearing ratio.
- From a security point of view, the lender will usually look for a fairly low-geared company with a strong asset base. One method used to measure this is to calculate net assets per share.

10
The art of accounting

If you give 20 different accountants the same set of figures you will get 20 different results.

ANON

One common source of frustration about accounting and finance that we have referred to on many occasions, is that it involves a good deal of human judgement. We should not, of course, be too surprised, because experienced managers are aware of the potential to influence the picture provided by internally generated data. For example, it is rare to find the manager who has not been exposed to the budgeting game, where the end result is very often heavily reliant upon the actions of individuals who have exercised a good deal of judgement.

While we know judgement to be the case from the perspective of internal accounting practice, many managers are extremely surprised when they discover just how much scope for creativity there can be in producing financial data for shareholders and other interested parties via media such as the annual report and the accounts.

In this chapter we will look at the art of accounting and we will also draw upon a term 'creative accounting' that was really brought to the fore by Ian Griffith (1986) who observed that:

> Every company in the country is fiddling its profits. Every set of published accounts is based upon books which have been gently cooked or completely roasted. The figures which are fed twice a year to the investing public have all been changed to protect the gentry. It is the biggest con trick since the Trojan Horse!

More recently, this view has been endorsed by Terry Smith (1992) who caused somewhat of an uproar in his book entitled *Accounting for Growth: Stripping the Camouflage from Company Accounts*. Smith demonstrated a number of approaches, which we will review here, whereby companies could use considerable judgement to produce results which put them in the best possible light, while staying within the letter of the law. He drew upon the

Major Companies Accounting Health Check, which was produced in the original research publication by UBS Phillips and Drew and which became affectionately known as the 'blob' guide. This guide uses a blob to illustrate accounting/financial engineering techniques used by a company from a maximum of eleven techniques (and therefore eleven blobs). He identified companies that achieved five or more blobs, that is those using five or more of the eleven accounting/financial/engineering techniques surveyed in *Accounting for Growth*. In the case of all but two which performed well in 1991, Dixons and Next, the share price performance ranged from indifferent to disastrous as indicated in Table 10.1.

Table 10.1   Share price performance of the highest scorers in *Accounting for Growth* checklist

	No of 'blobs'	Relative share price performance in 1991(%)	
LEP	5	−90	
Maxwell	7	−100	(suspended)
ASDA	5	−66	
British Aerospace	7	−44	
Burton	7	−43	
Ultramar*	5	−16	
Blue Circle	5	−10	
Cable & Wireless	6	−5	
Granada	5	−4	
Sears	5	−4	
Laporte	5	+6	
Dixons	6	+40	
Next	5	+234	

* After bid from Lasmo

The implications of this 'blob' guide are that the use of accounting financial engineering techniques may convey no benefit as regards perception by the market expressed in share price performance. In what follows we will develop our discussion of the art of accounting around two measures of business performance that are reckoned to be particularly important to analysts and stockbrokers and therefore to company directors - earnings per share and gearing. Both of these we encountered in the last chapter.

1. *Earnings per share* In response to the requirements of their share-holders, many companies endeavour to ensure steady growth in their earnings per share. Unfortunately, as we will discuss in more depth later, it is possible to show an improvement in earnings per share by influencing the numerator and/or the denominator involved in its calculation. Some ways in which this can be achieved are all too obvious; others may be difficult to detect, even for professional analysts.
2. *Gearing* Similarly to earnings per share, gearing can be influenced by massaging the numerator or the denominator in its calculation. Increasing the equity and/or decreasing the amount of debt can have a significant impact upon a company's gearing. Quite how this, and earnings per share manipulation, may be achieved we will now demonstrate.

10.1 How to shape accounting information

There are many ways in which the information provided by a company can be shaped so as to provide a more favourable picture. We will review two areas that are both important and relatively straightforward to understand.

Brand accounting

Brand accounting became newsworthy in the corporate takeover frenzy of the 1980s, particularly among companies possessing strong, frequently international, brand names. The debate really came to the fore in 1988 when Swiss foods conglomerate Nestlé bid for control of confectioners Rowntree, offering more than twice Rowntree's pre-bid capitalization. The debate about brand accounting raged on later that year when Grand Metropolitan decided to capitalize brands acquired since 1985 but particularly when Ranks Hovis McDougall (now part of Tomkins PLC) moved to capitalize not only acquired, but also internally developed brands. Subsequently, brand accounting became popular and important companies that feature brand name assets in their balance sheets include:

– Cadbury Schweppes
– Grand Metropolitan
– Guinness
– Ladbroke
– Reckitt & Colman
– United Biscuits
– Pearson
– Reed International

- SmithKline Beecham
- Thorn EMI
- United Newspapers.

To be fair, some of these companies had carried intangible assets in their balance sheets prior to the trend for brand accounting. For example, United Newspapers had valued titles and Reckitt & Coleman trademarks.

For internally developed brands, the approach generally adopted has been for directors to assess the value of the brands acquired since a particular date, sometimes with the help of specialist advice, and these are then included as intangible assets in the balance sheet. For example, Ranks Hovis McDougall (referred to earlier) did just this in 1988 when, as a consequence of a valuation of home-grown brands by the consultancy Interbrand, £678 million or approximately one and a half times the value of its tangible net assets were put on the company's balance sheet.

The approach taken by Ranks Hovis McDougall and Interbrand in capitalizing the company's brands was to measure 'brand profitability' and to apply a multiple in the form of 'brand strength'. In a press release by Ranks Hovis McDougall on 16 January 1989 the company identified that the brand profit used was that which resulted from the brand's identity. This brand profit, after tax, was a weighted average over a three-year period. In the case of brand strength it was determined as a result of a detailed review of each brand in terms of its positioning, the market in which it operated, competition, past performance, future plans, risks to the brand, etc. These characteristics were captured in a composite of the following seven weighted factors:

- Leadership
- Stability
- Market vulnerability or volatility
- Internationality
- Trend over a long time period
- Support from investment
- Protection by trademarks or law.

To understand the impact of a brand valuation like this, consider a company 50 per cent geared in terms of its ratio of shareholders' funds. It has a balance sheet with totals as follows:

Balance sheet extract

	£ million
Net assets*	100
Shareholders' funds	100

*Debt of £50 million deducted as 'creditors: amounts falling due'

Now let us assume that brands are valued at £150 million – not an extraordinary situation when one considers the examples of actual practice like Ranks Hovis McDougall! Including the brand names has the following result:

Balance sheet extract

	£ million
Net assets (prior to brand valuation)	100
Intangible assets – brands	+150
Net assets	250
Shareholders' funds (prior to brand valuation)	100
Capital reserves	+150
Shareholders' funds	250

Such brand values need not be amortized via a charge in the profit and loss account if the brand is assumed to have an infinite life, thereby ensuring profits and earnings per share are not affected. In this case, any change in brand values would be reflected by an annual review and an appropriate balance sheet adjustment. For example if, as a result of an annual review, the brand value was considered to have fallen by £50 million, then the balance sheet would be adjusted as follows:

Balance sheet extract

	£ million
Net assets	250
Intangible assets – brands	−50
Revised net assets	200
Shareholders' funds	250
Capital reserves	−50
Revised shareholders' funds	200

The real benefit of brand name accounting is the boost it gives shareholders' funds by increasing the book value of the company's assets on the other side of the balance sheet. It has no effect upon cash flow at all, but it can be shown to improve the gearing ratio. This can readily be seen from our example where before the inclusion of brand values, the debt to shareholders' funds ratio was 50 per cent, i.e.

$$\frac{\text{Debt}}{\text{Equity}} = \frac{£50 \text{ million}}{£100 \text{ million}} = 50 \text{ per cent}$$

After the inclusion of brand values the ratio becomes

$$\frac{\text{Debt}}{\text{Equity}} = \frac{£50 \text{ million}}{£250 \text{ million}} = 20 \text{ per cent}$$

Why did brand accounting become so popular? There are many reasons but one which cannot be ignored concerns accounting rules relating to the goodwill arising from an acquisition where the goodwill is the sum over and above the price paid for the separable net assets acquired. Upon acquisition, companies have a choice of one of two courses of action. First, they can write off the goodwill immediately against reserves, thereby often depleting them severely. Second, they can capitalise it and write off against future earnings. Both of these have shortcomings from the company's perspective – the first weakens the balance sheet and increases gearing because of the depletion of shareholders' funds, and the second reduces future earnings per share. (This issue is dealt with more fully in the next chapter.)

Brand accounting has become particularly contentious and, in common with many areas of financial reporting, there has been a call to tighten up relevant accounting procedures.

Capitalization of costs

The brand accounting controversy discussed above is useful as a basis for understanding the practice of capitalizing costs, which is a fairly prevalent form of creativity. As we illustrated, to minimize damage to earnings, ways have been found to keep items of cost in the form of goodwill and brand amortization charges away from the profit and loss account. Similarly, it is possible to keep other costs away from the profit and loss account by capitalizing them. This is achieved by combining them with fixed assets legitimately and including them in the balance sheet. This is possible because accounting makes a distinction between costs which expire during an accounting period and are written off through the profit and loss account, and assets which do not expire during a single accounting period, and are 'held over'. If a case can be made for such items to be treated as assets, typically that part which expires during an accounting period will be matched as a cost, the remainder being held in the balance sheet as an asset.

Items often found to be capitalised include:

- Interest
- Research and development
- Start-up costs.

To understand how the capitalization of costs works, consider a company which after charging interest payable through the profit and loss account makes a loss of £20 million. If this company did not include this interest payable in its profit and loss account, the £20 million loss would be £20 million profit, the £40 million interest payable being included with the fixed assets. This adjustment from a £20 million loss to a £20 million profit can be demonstrated quite simply by adding back interest payable as follows:

Profit and loss account

	£million
Loss	20
Interest payable	40
Profit	20

However, this alternative treatment of interest payable does not mean that the balance sheet will not balance. While the net assets section increases by £40 million so also does the shareholders' funds side because the loss of £20 million is now a profit of the same amount – an increase of £40 million. This you will recall is reflected in the retained profit in the profit and loss account which is transferred to the revenue reserves (often referred to as the profit and loss account) in the balance sheet.

When and why do companies capitalize interest costs? The practice may often be used, and not unreasonably, for a large project when the interest is considered to be an indistinguishable part of the cost of an asset.

The effect of capitalization is often very beneficial to the current year's profit but this may not be quite as much as illustrated earlier for either the current year or later years. Why? Because often the interest payable will be depreciated together with the asset. For example, we will assume that our company with interest payable of £40 million incurs this in relation to a project with a planned timescale of four years. Depreciating this sum over four years means a reduction in profits for each year of £10 million, assuming a straight-line write-off. The effect is therefore to defer the cost, unless the item never makes an appearance in the profit and loss account – a practice that has been associated with the treatment of investment properties by companies in the property sector.

The level of capitalized interest is important to monitor simply because it is possible for a company to run out of cash while apparently making healthy pre-tax profits. In fact, the level of capitalized interest can be significantly high. For example, for a selection of major companies for the year ended December 1989 capitalized interest costs ranged from 14 to 138 per cent, averaging 42 per cent!

The decision to capitalize research and development expenditure can also have a significant effect upon a company's reported results as the Price Waterhouse review of the accounts of Cray Electronics PLC for 1989 revealed. In this independent review, prompted as a consequence of events arising from the publication of the company's results, Price Waterhouse acknowledged that although Cray's capitalization of development expenditure was quite permissible according to accounting standards requirements, it did not correspond with general practice in the sector. When brought in line with practice elsewhere, the net effect on the pre-tax profit, which was originally £17.03 million, was a reduction of £4.196 million.

There are many other approaches that can be, and have been, used to create a favourable picture of company results. These relate to the following:

– Write-downs on acquisitions
– The inclusion of non-trading profits
– Taking a pension holiday
– Lengthening the time period for depreciating fixed assets
– The decision to treat costs as extraordinary rather than exceptional
– The use of off-balance-sheet finance.

All of these approaches have been used quite legitimately by many UK companies and if you are interested in how they have been applied then you could do no better than to refer to Terry Smith's (1992) book.

Sometimes the adoption of such techniques has almost been dismissed by market reaction, but not always. As you will see in the next section, there have been occasions causing strong market reaction largely because of the recognized consequences of the practices adopted on reported results.

10.2 Consequences of different accounting practices

There have been some staggering examples of creativity in accounting practices, many of which have come to light after a significant event has drawn attention to a business. Polly Peck and Maxwell Corporation referred to earlier are good examples of such circumstances. However, there are many others where major concerns about a company have been expressed, perhaps more directly traceable to the financial picture painted in an annual report. When such concern is expressed it can have a marked effect upon a company's share performance. This was well demonstrated if we refer again to Cray Electronics PLC, which reported an increase in pre-tax profits from £13.1 million in 1988 to £17.03 million in 1989. The stock market responded by marking the shares down 18p to 140p on the day the numbers were released. This reaction suggested that the market realized that the reported pre-tax profit was somewhat unrepresentative of economic reality. This response was probably heavily influenced by analysts' reactions to the accounts. In fact, one review showed that by digging into the notes accompanying the preliminary results, and stripping out property profits of £2.99 million and profits of £1.9 million arising from businesses bought during the year, Cray's trading performance was flat at best. Furthermore, a change in the way in which the company had accounted for £3.7 million of development expenditure, which had been capitalized, raised comment that there had in fact been a drop in trading profits over the period.

Cray left virtually no accounting stone unturned. Such was the reaction to Cray's results that, as indicated earlier, the company brought in an independent accountancy firm, Price Waterhouse, to review its accounting policies. Price Waterhouse recommended changes in virtually every key area: the treatment of development expenditure; the classification of leases; recognition of income, particularly on long-term contracts; and merger accounting. Taking development expenditure first, Price Waterhouse recommended writing it off immediately unless it could be recovered on contracts with third parties. The result, an immediate £4.2 million write-off against reported profits. This, together with the other changes recommended by Price Waterhouse resulted in the following adjustments to profits for 1988/89:

	1988 £000	1989 £000
Pre-tax profit as previously published	17,030	13,120
Accounting policy changes		
– Write-off of development expenditure	(4,196)	(2,298)
– Re-classify sale and leasebacks of properties as finance leases	(2,472)	–
– Other items	(2,232)	–
Post-balance-sheet events review	(2,690)	–
	5,439	10,822

Cray produced and distributed a revised set of published accounts which incorporated the earlier profit restatements. However, its profit restatement was, not surprisingly, greeted with a wave of criticism of the company, its directors and its accountants. What financial commentators viewed as the most depressing part was, that in the absence of accounting rules detailing the exact treatment for every set of circumstances, different interpretations will continue to arise. However, as we have already indicated, there has been a significant move to tighten up the UK regulatory framework since 1990 to help prevent such situations in the future.

10.3 Conclusion

The potential for influencing apparent corporate performance must never be ignored. The most sophisticated analytical techniques available will be of no real value if applied to data of dubious quality. Just imagine applying ratio analysis and attempting to draw meaningful conclusions about Cray PLC from its original 1989 Annual Report!

How do you determine whether creative accounting practices have been applied? For some items like capitalized interest, it will often be evident in the accounting policies in the annual report but for others it is far more difficult to identify them. However, do not ignore the financial press, like *The Financial Times*, and analysts' reports. In our experience, much of the information about creative accounting practices is readily available, albeit with some effort.

In this chapter we have discussed the use and implications of various techniques that may be applied to portray the value of a business in different ways. Key points to remember include the following:

– There are many ways in which the information provided by a company can be shaped so as to influence the financial picture given about its performance.
– Two measures of business performance are particularly widely used by analysts and stockbrokers. These are earnings per share and gearing, both of which can be influenced by creative accounting practices.
– There are many ways of accounting creatively, but the general principles involved can be readily understood with reference to the treatment of goodwill and brands and the capitalization of costs.

11

Variations in financial reporting: the international dimension

A people divided by one common language
AN ANONYMOUS OBSERVATION ON THE DIFFERENCE
BETWEEN THE UNITED KINGDOM AND THE UNITED STATES

One major frustration is that having learnt the layout and principles which underpin United Kingdom profit and loss accounts and balance sheets, a casual glance at similar statements in other countries, even those using the same language like the United States, reveals them as being very different. Differences in layout are relatively simple to deal with, but the principles are quite another story. To understand the impact of accounting principles we only need to refer once again to the annual report of Hanson PLC for the year ended 30 September 1992.

The company discloses a profit available for appropriation according to United Kingdom accounting principles of £1,089 million. When adjusted for US GAAP, the profit is reduced to £903 million. More significant, however, are the differences in the balance sheet, as the company demonstrates and we illustrate below for 1992 with reference to the effect upon shareholders' equity.

	1992 £ million
Ordinary shareholders' equity as reported in the (UK) consolidated balance sheet	4,224
Estimated adjustments (for US):	
Goodwill and other intangibles	+3340
Proposed final dividend	−

	1992 £ million
Revaluation of land and buildings	−166
Pensions	+189
Timberlands depletion and reforestation	−60
Taxation	−102
Estimated ordinary shareholders' equity as adjusted to accord with US GAAP	<u>7425</u>

According to UK GAAP, shareholders' equity is reported as being £4,224 million, in stark contrast to the US GAAP figure of £7,425 million. As you can see, a major source of difference concerns the treatment of goodwill for which the accumulated deduction of £3,340 million would be quite inappropriate in the United States. In fact, this adjustment is a particularly important source of difference between reported profits in different countries, a subject we discuss later in this chapter.

Financial reporting in the United Kingdom differs considerably from practices elsewhere in terms of how the main financial statements are presented. For example, the items grouped together in the different sections within a balance sheet vary, as may the order in which they are presented and, even where a common language is spoken, very different terms may be used to describe the same thing. All of these we will examine in this chapter to help you understand how to deal with variations in financial reporting practices.

First, we will review important variations in national accounting practices in continental Europe and within the European Community, where a harmonization programme has been under way. Second, we will review financial reporting practices within the United States of America where, as we have already indicated, significant differences exist, in spite of being united by a common language. Last, but by no means least, we will look at financial reporting practices more globally by considering action by international bodies to encourage standardization and also those practices adopted by individual corporations within a transnational context.

11.1 The European Community (EC)

The variations in financial reporting practices that exist within the European Community can best be understood by considering the following headings:

1. The legal system
2. Stakeholder orientation
3. The influence of taxation
4. Different accounting practices and conventions.

By comparison with the United Kingdom, much of continental Europe, including the European Community, operates within the principles of Roman law. This approach relies upon a detailed scheme of laws and penalties such that there should always be a law on any matter. For example, some EC countries, notably France and Germany, rely on precise and detailed legislation to control accounting practices. By contrast, common law in the United Kingdom is less prescriptive, and is based upon concepts of reasonableness and equity. In fact, United Kingdom financial reporting practice is reliant upon judgement as to what constitutes a 'true and fair view' of the situation in each individual company, given the broad frameworks established by law, custom and practice.

The development of different legal systems within the European Community has had other implications for accounting. Government rules rather than professional standards predominate so that the form of what is provided is as important as its substance, and tax domination is a key feature. By contrast, in the United Kingdom and for that matter other economies that follow Anglo-Saxon practices, tax and accounting rules are separate, such that the substance of what is produced is given more emphasis than its form, and professional standards rather than government rules are very important. However, you will doubtless recall from the last chapter, the United Kingdom approach has not exactly been trouble free!

Second, as regards stakeholder orientation, the providers of finance and the users of accounting information differ markedly between EC members. In Germany the banking fraternity predominates while in France and Italy it is a combination of bankers, family businesses and the government. This means typically that such groups have good access to company financial data, and secrecy towards others is not uncommon. By contrast, in the United Kingdom, private and institutional shareholders are the most significant providers of finance. As a consequence far more importance tends to be attached to disclosure, rather than secrecy in published data like the annual report.

Third, as already indicated, tax is a more important influence upon financial reporting in some EC member states than others. In the United Kingdom, by the time tax on business income first became important, there was a fully operational system of accounting and auditing already in place, such that taxable profit was based on accounting profit with adjustments. By contrast, in much of continental Europe many of the rules of accounting were determined by Tax Acts, because a coherent system of financial reporting was lacking. For example, in France and Germany, depreciation charges are made with reference to tax tables. Such charges would probably not be viewed as true and fair according to United Kingdom practice, but would be legal and correct in Germany.

Last, but by no means least, the rules and principles applied in financial reporting differ and these are manifested in specific accounting features being peculiar to the United Kingdom which are not characteristic of continental European countries, both inside and outside of the European Community. Important distinguishing features can be summarized in Table 11.1.

Table 11.1   Comparison of UK and continental financial reporting

UK Anglo-Saxon	Continental
Depreciation over useful lives	Depreciation by tax rules
No legal reserves created out of profit	Legal reserves
Finance leases capitalized in the balance sheet	No lease capitalization
Cash flow statement produced	No cash flow statement produced
Earnings per share disclosed	No earnings per share disclosures
No secret reserves	Secret reserves
No tax-induced provisions	Tax-induced provisions
Preliminary expenses expensed against profit	Preliminary expenses capitalized in balance sheet
Goodwill written off immediately through the balance sheet	Goodwill amortized and written off against profits of future years

A significant consequence of the different accounting practices shown in Table 11.1 is that reported profits between EC member countries may well differ, even if the same input data are used! As we will illustrate shortly, if the accounts of one company were to be prepared by a French or German accountant and also by a British accountant using exactly the same data, it is likely that the profit reported by the British accountant would be significantly higher than that reported by the other two. In fact, the nature and impact of such differences was brought out by Touche Ross, where members of the partnership in seven EC states were asked to prepare accounts (in ECU) for the same hypothetical group of companies, thus providing statements which should be directly comparable as between jurisdictions. For the profit and loss account, participants were asked to use the maximum flexibility of local rules, to provide three alternative figures:

1. That which a real company would be most likely to arrive at.
2. The highest profit possible.
3. The lowest profit possible.

The results of the study (Table 11.2) are interesting to say the least!

Table 11.2 Alternative figures for profit and loss accounts of EC countries

	Most likely net profit (ECU millions)	*Maximum net profit* (ECU millions)	*Minimum net profit* (ECU millions)
Belgium	135	193	90
Germany	133	**140**	27
Spain	131	192	121
France	149	160	121
Italy	174	193	167
The Netherlands	140	156	76
United Kingdom	192	194	**171**

The results in Table 11.2 illustrate that not only could the likely profit measurement vary between different member states, but also that the range over which the profit could be measured was different. To take extreme cases, the British profit could have been at worst 171 million ECU, while the German profit could have been at best 140 million ECU.

The main influences on the difference between the net profit figures relate to the treatment of goodwill, taxation and stocks. For example, goodwill can be written off immediately against reserves, or amortized over a number of future years' profits. Within the European Community it is only in the United Kingdom that the immediate write-off of goodwill against reserves in the balance sheet is the most popular practice. In other member states goodwill is normally written off against future profits, with the number of years against which it is amortized varying from country to country, as can be seen in Table 11.3.

The impact of the differences (Table 11.3) can be demonstrated with reference to an example. The results shown in Table 11.4 would be reported in Belgium, France, The Netherlands and the United Kingdom as a consequence of treating goodwill of £150 million purchased in the period according to the respective prevailing practices.

Table 11.3   Amortization of goodwill in EC member states

	Amortization period
Belgium	5 years
Germany	15 years
France	20 years
Italy	10 years
The Netherlands	10 years

Table 11.4 Treatment of £150 goodwill in various EC countries

	Belgium £ million	France £ million	The Netherlands £ million	UK £ million
Profit attributable to ordinary shareholders	70	70	70	70
Amortization of goodwill	30	7.5	15	–
Adjusted profit	40	62.5	55	70
Earnings per share*	40p	62.5p	55p	70p

*Assuming 100 million ordinary shares

As you can see, simply by comparing the first and last columns of Table 11.4 for Belgium and the United Kingdom, the different treatment of goodwill has a significant impact upon adjusted profit and earnings per share.

Harmonization within the European Community

There have been moves to harmonize accounting practices within the European Community. The harmonization of company accounting requirements is achieved through directives addressed to the governments of 12 member states. These directives are legally binding and normally have to be implemented and enforced through national legislation as equivalent measures in each member state. However, in order to achieve political consensus in difficult areas, the directives contain many options and many omissions. For example, we have already seen that goodwill can be treated differently and some issues, as we illustrate below, like currency translation, have not been dealt with at all. There are in fact dozens of provisions in the directives that begin with such expressions as 'Member States may require or permit companies to ⋯ '. So, the exact effects of any directive on a particular country will depend upon the laws passed by national legislatures.

The two most influential directives upon accounting and financial reporting practices are the Fourth and Seventh. The Fourth Directive is based on the German Public Companies Act (Aktiengesetz) of 1965 and introduced standard formats for the balance sheet and profit and loss account (with some options). It contains a number of important accounting principles and valuation rules and also introduced minimum rules regarding the disclosure, publication and audit requirements of medium sized and large companies. However, it also leaves a good deal unharmonized, such as:

– The treatment of leasing contracts.
– Foreign currency translation.
– Pensions.
– Financial instruments and off-balance-sheet financing.
– The requirement to provide a cash or funds flow statement.

Furthermore, on a number of important issues, the Fourth Directive allows member states to choose between alternative options, for example:

– Historic or current market valuation of assets.
– The capitalization of research and development.
– Alternative layouts for the balance sheet and profit and loss account.

It is perhaps not surprising that lacunae and options exist. The aim of the directive was to reconcile very different approaches to accounting in 12 member states where both the level of expertise and the philosophy of the accounting profession varied widely. In particular there were, and still are, significant differences between the Anglo-Saxon approach, heavily influenced by the requirements of sophisticated capital markets, and the tax-driven approach of continental Europe.

The Seventh Directive builds upon the Fourth by laying down consolidation requirements for the accounts of groups of companies. It adopts a precise legalistic approach which describes in detail the conditions under which consolidated accounts have to be drawn up. Many EC countries, such as Portugal, had no group accounting at all or, as in the case of Germany, had it only for public companies. The implementation of the directive makes group accounting obligatory for all public companies and for other groups with over 500 employees, which is a dramatic advance in the publication of group accounts. It has also resulted in many of the specific accounting features of continental European companies, identified earlier, being replaced by United Kingdom Anglo-Saxon methods in the preparation of group accounts.

To summarize then, harmonization provides for considerable latitude in accounting practices. It is also worth noting that their implementation has varied from country to country, as can be seen from Table 11.5.

Table 11.5   Implementation of EC directives

	Implementation dates	
	4th Directive	*7th Directive*
Drafts published	1971/74	1976/78
Adopted by EC	1978	1983
Denmark	1981	1990
United Kingdom	1981	1989
France	1983	1985
Netherlands	1983	1988
Luxembourg	1984	1988
Belgium	1985	1990
Germany	1985	1985
Ireland	1986	1992
Greece	1986	1987
Spain	1989	1989
Portugal	1989	1991
Italy	1991	1991

The directives have been criticized for being slow to be implemented and for ossifying practices, simply because it is virtually impossible to amend a directive. As a consequence, in 1990 the EC Commission announced that there would be no more directives on accounting and a 'forum' has been established to discuss differences.

11.2 United States of America

Despite commonality of language in the United Kingdom and United States, there are important differences in jargon, measurement and presentation. At first glance, one might have expected that the similar legal systems, wide private ownership of shares, similar tax systems which do not heavily interfere in accounting, and strong professions which have controlled the standards of accounting and auditing, would provide the basis for very similar accounting practices. However, there have been different degrees of government intervention between the two nations, considerable differences in terms of the involvement of the accounting professions regulating the practices of their membership, and there are some significant language differences which have had an impact upon the development of accounting terminology used. The net result is that whilst US and UK accounting may appear to belong to the same family, especially when compared to the French or German systems, there are many opportunities for confusion and error when making any sort of comparison between the two.

First, different terminology is used to describe the same items. Consider, for example:

UK	USA
Stock	Inventory
Debtors	Accounts receivable
Creditors	Accounts payable
Shares	Stocks

In our experience, these four are a common source of confusion, particularly stock, which is used by both but with a totally different meaning in each case.

Second, US financial statements, particularly the balance sheet, look very different from those produced in the United Kingdom. In fact, many are similar to those produced in continental European countries in the following respects:

– They are horizontal rather than vertical, with total assets on the left-hand side and total liabilities/equities on the right-hand side.
– They order items differently, e.g. the assets commence with the most liquid (cash) and finish with the least liquid (fixed assets) – quite the opposite of UK practice.
– They display three years' comparative figures rather than two in the case of the profit and loss account.

In fact, US annual reports for publicly quoted companies are far more comprehensive than for UK counterparts because of a much more demanding financial reporting regime. However, it is important to realize that this regime only applies to publicly quoted US companies, which are a very small proportion of the total number of US companies. This is quite unlike the United Kingdom, where the reporting requirements apply to all limited liability companies, although somewhat less detailed reports can be filed for small/medium sized companies.

Last, but certainly by no means least, the rules applied differ substantially in regard to such matters as the treatment of goodwill, which is written off over a period of up to 40 years, the revaluation of assets, the treatment of deferred taxation, and so on. The effect of such differences as we saw at the start of the chapter is well illustrated with reference to the accounts of Hanson PLC.

11.3 Global efforts to reduce national variations

Global efforts to reduce variations in financial reporting practices have been of a voluntary nature and have come mainly from the preparers and auditors of the financial statements of multinationals. For example, in many countries of the world there is uniformity of certain areas of accounting practice via international accounting standards set by the International Accounting Standards Committee (IASC).

The IASC was set up in 1973 to formulate and publish in the public interest basic standards to be observed in the presentation of audited accounts and financial statements, and to promote their world-wide acceptance and observance. Over 80 accountancy bodies from more than 60 countries are members of the IASC. Each member has agreed to support the standards published by IASC and to use its best endeavours to ensure that published accounts comply with the standards, or disclosure is made of the extent to which they do not.

International standards have no direct application in the United Kingdom. However, the provisions of international standards are, as far as possible, incorporated into United Kingdom standards, so that only one document needs to be consulted – the United Kingdom standard. The Stock Exchange requires United Kingdom companies to comply with UK SSAPs/ FRSs and foreign companies with a listing in the United Kingdom to comply with the IASC standards.

A major obstacle to the global harmonization of financial reporting practices has been the lack of strong professional accountancy bodies in certain countries. This means that a body such as the IASC, which seeks to operate through national accountancy bodies, will not be effective everywhere. The alternative to this is a world-wide enforcement agency, which as yet does not exist, although the EC Commission discussed earlier, may well prove to be such an agency for a part of the world. A second problem is nationalism, which may show itself in an unwillingness to accept compromises that involve changing accounting practices to match those of other countries. This unwillingness may arise on the part of accountants and companies, or member states that do not wish to lose their sovereignty.

One major source of global harmonization that should not be overlooked is that emanating from multinational companies themselves. For example, an update of a survey published in 1989 of 206 European companies with multiple stock exchange listings, reviewed the 1990 annual reports in various languages of a number of major European companies whose international financial reporting practices had been found to be particularly innovative in one or more respects (Archer and McLeay, 1992). The main features of the transnational reports are described below.

Adaptation of communication

Adapting communication to meet different audiences and, perhaps, as many as the number of countries in which they operate. By way of an example they cite Volkswagen's 1990 Annual Report which, in addition to there being an English version, is published in German, Chinese, French, Italian, Japanese, Portuguese, Slovakian, Spanish and Czech. The condensed version of the 1990 Annual Report is also available in Polish, Russian and Hungarian.

Convenience currency translation

The term convenience currency translation refers to the restatement of financial statement items from the main reporting currency into one or more other currencies thought to be more convenient either for particular groups of readers or for particular reporting purposes, with a view to enhancing the cross-sectional comparability of the information. These convenience currency translations are of a voluntary nature and need to be distinguished from the currency translations which are a necessary part of the process of preparing consolidated financial statements of multinational groups.

The main reporting currency is normally the domestic currency of the country in which the parent company of the group is incorporated. The convenience currency translation may involve restatement of financial statement items from this currency into:

- one other currency, such as the US dollar
- a composite currency, such as the ECU
- several other currencies.

The majority of companies were found to use the US dollar in convenience currency translations, although some make use of a wider range of reporting currencies. For example, Unilever is a case in point where the key figures are expressed in as many as eight different currencies plus the ECU.

Accounting restatements

The existence of differing sets of accounting ventures in different countries is a major obstacle for foreign readers not familiar with accounting practices in the reporting companies' country and, in some annual reports, the accounts are restated for foreign readers by:

– reformatting the financial statements
– reconciling between different sets of accounting principles and practices
– restating financial statements as a whole.

These restatements can be very helpful, so let us consider what is meant by each.

REFORMATTING THE FINANCIAL STATEMENTS

In this case the original set of accounts is re-presented using a terminology and format customary in a foreign country but without changing the accounting conventions and amounts reported. Thus, the financial statements in the original version of the annual report differ in form to those in the English language version. Often this applies to the consolidated financial statements with the parent company accounts tending to be a literal translation.

RECONCILING BETWEEN DIFFERENT SETS OF ACCOUNTING PRINCIPLES AND PRACTICES

This involves the restatement of financial accounts using domestic and foreign accounting principles and a reconciliation between the two which itself may be more or less detailed. These are normally restricted to key items such as net income or equity and usually appear in both the foreign language versions of the annual report and the original version. We have already demonstrated such reconciliation with reference to Hanson PLC. Another good example is Telefonica, the Spanish communications company, which includes a reconciliation from Spanish to both international accounting standards and US GAAP.

RESTATING FINANCIAL STATEMENTS

In this case the financial statements as a whole are restated using the accounting conventions prevalent in the reader's country. Restatement of the full set of financial statements appears to be less common than the restatement of the balance sheet and income statement in accordance with alternative accounting conventions. A good example of full restatement is provided by many Finnish companies.

Secondary financial statements

Most companies publish a straightforward linguistic translation of the original annual report without major changes. An alternative is to publish a condensed foreign language version or an extract from the official report. Many very large companies publish in a secondary language, but reduce the full foreign language version or, alternatively, an abridged version may be produced.

From a large company perspective, and especially those with multiple stock exchange listings, international harmonization of accounting and financial reporting is making steady progress. In part this may be due to the effects of the European Community directives which, although leaving a number of gaps and having some shortcomings, do have an impact beyond the ambit of the existing Community of Twelve. This is quite simply because a number of other countries are now planning to join the European Community and are thus anticipating the need to comply with the directives.

It cannot also be ignored that many large multinationals wish to project an image that their financial reporting meets the highest of international standards, and annual reports including financial reporting practices form part of the strategy of financial public relations. This may be coupled with the fact that they frequently have to produce financial statements which meet the requirements of stock exchanges in more than one country (e.g. the United States and United Kingdom) and/or countries that have aligned their financial reporting requirements on the standards of the International Accounting Standards Committee (IASC).

11.4 Conclusion

This review of variations in financial reporting has illustrated the existence of considerable sources of difference in the formats and principles applied in producing financial statements, even in parts of the world like the European Community, where there has been a conscious harmonization programme. Such variations are also to be found between countries, like the United Kingdom and United States, despite a common language and comparable legal systems. Financial reporting practices between countries is a veritable minefield and in recognition of this there have been collective initiatives, like the establishment of the International Accounting Standards Committee (IASC). However, in addition we cannot ignore the significance of the company- specific initiatives we have reviewed.

Main points to remember from this chapter include the following:

- Despite sometimes similar presentation, financial reporting practices differ between countries.

- Variations in financial reporting practices within the European Community exist because of differences in the legal system, stakeholder orientation, the influence of taxation, and national accounting practices and conventions.
- The consequence of variations in financial reporting practices is that the profit measurements and the range over which the profit could be measured may differ between countries.
- The main influences on the difference between the net profit figures relate to the treatment of goodwill, taxation and stocks.
- Within the European Community there have been moves to harmonize accounting practices. The two most influential directives in this respect are the Fourth Directive and the Seventh Directive, although these still allow significant differences to exist.
- There are important differences in jargon, measurement and presentation between financial reporting practices in the United Kingdom and the United States.
- Global efforts to reduce variations in financial reporting practices have been of a voluntary nature and have been made mainly by the preparers and auditors of the financial statements of multinational companies.

PART THREE
FINANCIAL MANAGEMENT: THE GENERAL MANAGER AS A FINANCIAL MANAGER

In this section we look specifically at key areas of financial management that the general manager needs to understand because, quite simply, in many cases he or she will be responsible for the performance of his or her part of the business. It is often incorrectly assumed that financial management is the sole responsibility of financial specialists. It is true that to understand the detail of many areas of financial management falls within the domain of financial specialists, however, the general manager who assumes responsibility for running a part of the business must have a sound grasp of such matters.

We will consider issues of financial management relating to the following topics:

- Cash
- Working capital
- Cost control
- Capital expenditure.

Do not let this put you off. In our experience by working through these issues in this way you should develop the ability to 'helicopter' over the minutiae of financial management as dealt with by the financial specialists and be able to ask important questions about the progress of the business and, very importantly, be able to understand the answers you are given!

12
Managing cash

A fool and his money are soon parted. What I want to know is how they got together in the first place

C. FLETCHER

The management of cash is so fundamental to the success of a business that it warrants very particular attention. This is especially so in times of recession when interest rates rise and businesses find cash management particularly difficult. The real problem of cash management is being able to anticipate future requirements and to strike the correct balance between holding too little and holding too much.

In this chapter we will review the key issues to consider in terms of cash management. The definition of 'cash' we will use corresponds with the liquid assets of the business. These include currency on hand plus bank deposits at commercial banks and marketable securities, which are investments that might be held temporarily by the business, but which can be quickly converted into cash. We will also introduce one principle vital for you to understand, discounted cash flow analysis (DCF). This technique provides a means for analysing future decisions in a world characterized by uncertainty. Its potential application is enormous as you will see in the chapters which follow and a good understanding of it is vital to anyone aspiring to general management.

12.1 The advantages and disadvantages of liquidity

The main returns that can typically be expected from holding liquid assets are as follows:

- The interest income earned by investing in marketable securities. Effective marketable security management can easily pay for itself and make an important contribution to the business's overall profitability.
- By having cash on hand the business can take advantage of cash discounts offered by suppliers and therefore lower the cost of items purchased.

– The business credit rating can be influenced by the amount of liquid assets held within the business. Essentially, holding too low a liquid asset level may affect the business's creditworthiness adversely, and the credit rating will be lower, resulting in higher future costs for securing both short- and long-term funds.

The fundamental risk involved in holding too little cash relates to an inability to run the business in the normal way. If cash inflow is a problem, paying bills may have to be deferred, capital expenditures curtailed, short-term financing obtained and assets sold. Any good potential opportunities that present themselves will have to be bypassed. In an extreme situation the business may be forced into liquidation.

There is, therefore, a risk–return trade-off for liquid assets relating to:

– Having enough cash and liquid reserves (in the form of marketable securities or lines of credit) to meet all business obligations.
– Not holding excess liquid reserves, because investments in long-term assets generally provide higher returns than short-term investments.
– Maintaining a minimum cash balance while actively managing the business portfolio of marketable securities to ensure as high a return as possible commensurate with the risk involved.

12.2 Cash management

The flow of cash into and out of a business is continual and while the level at any point in time can be related to many factors, certain cash management principles are fundamental to any business, whatever its size, or industry, or the state of the economy. Two obvious and fundamental principles of cash management involve:

1. Speeding the inflows through a *cash collection system*.
2. The control of the outflows via a *cash disbursement system*.

Cash collection system

The complexity of a business cash collection system depends upon the size of the business and the scope of its operations. Small businesses tend to operate very simple systems, while large businesses typically have very extensive systems.

In any cash collection system the concept of the 'float' is vital, this being the length of time between when a cheque is written and when the recipient receives the funds and can draw upon them. The average collection float is found by multiplying the number of days of float and the average money value amount that is in the collection system. There are in fact three sources of cash gathering float which are:

1. *Mail float* This is the time that elapses between when a customer places a cheque in the mail and when the selling business receives it and begins to process it.
2. *Processing float* This is the time it takes the selling business to deposit a cheque in its bank after receiving it.
3. *Transit float* This is the time required for a cheque to clear through the banking system until the recipient can draw upon it.

The shorter the float period, the quicker cash is received and, therefore, the main objective should be to minimize the float, for which many different approaches may be adopted. Irrespective of the approach, a basic model can be used to assess the cost effectiveness. This model compares the incremental after-tax benefit of the method to be adopted against the incremental after-tax costs. If these incremental benefits of an alternative cash collection method are greater than the incremental costs, then it is worth while changing and not if vice versa. The incremental benefits can be calculated as follows:

$$IB = T \times S \times I \times (1-t)$$

where IB = incremental benefits
   T = the time in days that the float is changed
   S = the size of the transaction
   I = the interest rate
   t = the marginal tax rate.

To understand how this model operates, consider, for example, a business that currently moves funds by paying cheques into its bank which costs nothing directly. This business is contemplating using an automatic transfer system at a cost of £4 per transaction. The marginal tax rate is 40 per cent, the yearly interest rate is 10 per cent, and it is estimated that there would be a reduction in the float time of two days as a result of the change. Our concern is to find out for what size of transaction such a change would be worth while. First, we need to calculate the incremental cost which is:

$$(£4-£0) \times (1 - 0.40) = £2.40$$

This we compare with the incremental benefits, calculated as follows:

$$£2.40 = (2) \times S \times (0.10/365) \times (1 - 0.40)$$

$$S = \frac{£2.40}{(2) \times (0.10/365) \times (0.60)}$$

$$= £7300$$

If the average size of the cheque paid in is at least £7300, then it pays to use automatic transfer. If the reduction in the float time were only one day, the size of the average transfer would have to be £14,600.

Cash disbursement

In designing a cash disbursement system for a business the emphasis is on controlling and slowing down the outflow of cash as long as possible without incurring the ill will of the business's suppliers. The starting point is payment procedures which should be designed so that the business pays just before the due date. Paying earlier simply reduces the time that cash is available to the business.

There are many approaches that can be adopted for controlling cash disbursements, the sophistication of which will depend upon the complexity of the business structure. Two approaches are paying creditors centrally and controlling the time of the week when cheques are issued.

Paying creditors centrally is the type of approach that may be adopted by businesses with many divisions. In such circumstances invoices may be received and verified at the divisional level, but they are actually paid and, therefore, controlled at the business headquarters.

By issuing cheques at certain times during the week the float may be increased. By issuing cheques on Wednesday or Thursday a business may gain an extra two days float over the weekend. Likewise paying the payroll on Friday means that not all cheques can clear the banking system before Monday or Tuesday of the following week.

The benefits and costs of alternative cash disbursement systems have to be evaluated for which the same framework as described earlier can be used. In the disbursing situation, the benefit arises from the additional length of time the business will have the funds available. This has to be weighed against the costs associated with a better control of the disbursement of cash.

12.3 Determining the daily cash balance

Now that we have reviewed the issues associated with cash collection and disbursements, we need to consider how much should be held by way of the daily cash balance. In principle, this should be the minimum amount possible because of the interest-generating benefits that result from holding marketable securities.

We have discussed in principle how to determine this daily cash balance in Chapter 3 with reference to cash flow forecasting. There, we illustrated how using a columnar format we could determine a monthly cash balance from data relating to any balance carried forward from the last month and the difference between the expected cash receipts and payments for the month. This monthly process can be readily adapted for use at more frequent intervals like a week or a day. In practice, this is typically very difficult because of the many assumptions that have to be made. This process really does lend itself to computer spreadsheet modelling so that changes can be made quite straightforwardly. You will also recall that cash flow, profitability and financial position are linked via the three main financial statements. Therefore, changes in the cash flow should be reviewed in line with the effect upon profitability and financial position. Given that the effect of many changes might need to be analysed in a complex business environment with the consequent potential for arithmetical errors, real value can be derived from building a tried and tested computer spreadsheet model.

Large businesses with substantial fluctuating cash flows may well undertake their cash flow analysis daily. In terms of determining a sensible daily balance between cash and marketable securities, historical trends can also be used effectively by building them into the computer model. This balance will, of course, be influenced by the relative costs and benefits which can be established using exactly the same approach as described earlier. But do recognize that it may not be profitable to switch funds to and from the marketable securities portfolio every day. For example, if it costs £50 to move funds in or out of the marketable securities portfolio, the incremental interest from having funds in marketable securities is 4 per cent, and the marginal tax rate is 40 per cent, the relative balance between cash and marketable securities can be determined as follows:

$$\text{Incremental costs} = £50 \times (1 - 0.40) = £30$$

These are matched against the incremental benefits:

$$£30 = (1) \times S \times (0.04/365) \times (1 - 0.40)$$

Solving for S, the size of the transaction, the result is:

$$S = £30 \ / \ [(0.04/365) \times (0.60)] = £456{,}253$$

This means that it is only profitable to transfer sums of £456,253 daily from cash. Any sum less than this will result in incremental benefits of less than the incremental costs incurred.

12.4 Discounted cash flow

We have illustrated how decisions between alternative courses of action can be analysed within an approach that focuses upon the relative incremental costs and benefits. In fact, you will find this cash-flow-oriented approach to be a useful managerial tool, but to make it really powerful so that a longer time frame can be considered we need to introduce an important principle known as 'discounted cash flow analysis'. This involves discounting, or scaling down, future cash flows to ensure comparability with present-day values. It is easiest to understand discounted cash flow analysis by comparing discounting with the more familiar but related technique of compounding.

Compounding is used to calculate what a present sum of money will be worth at some time in the future given a known interest rate. If you were given £1000 today which could be invested for 12 months to give a 10 per cent return, it would be worth £1100 12 months from today. Because of the benefit derived from interest (which is typically compounded), you would not be indifferent between £1000 today and the same sum in 12 months' time. At an annual rate of interest of 10 per cent £1000 now would be comparable with £1100 in 12 months' time and £1210 in 24 months' time (£1100 × 1.10), and so on. Discounting is the opposite. Given a sum of money relating to a future period and a known rate of interest a present value can be determined.

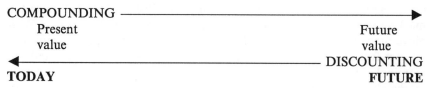

The relationship between compounding and discounting can be seen in Table 12.1 where compounding and discounting at an interest rate of 10 per cent are illustrated.

Table 12.1 Compounding and discounting compared

		Compound interest factors (10%)		*Discount factors (DCF) (10%)*
Year 0		1.000		1.000
Year 1	1×1.10	1.100	$1 / 1.10$	0.909
Year	$1 \times (1.10)^2$	1.210	$1 / (1.10)^2$	0.826
Year 3	$1 \times (1.10)^3$	1.331	$1 / (1.10)^3$	0.751
Year 4	$1 \times (1.10)^4$	1.464	$1 / (1.10)^4$	0.683

The discount factors are calculated quite simply by expressing the value of £1 now as a proportion of its compounded value at some future time. For example, the discount factor for 10 per cent in one year's time is 0.909, that is £1 today divided by the value of £1 in one year's time at 10 per cent (1.10). In our example (Table 12.1) the same value would arise by expressing £1000 in terms of its value in 12 months' time at a rate of 10 per cent (£1000/£1100). However, discount factors are typically expressed in terms of £1 and, fortunately, they do not have to be calculated because tables are readily available in which the present value of £1 has been calculated for a wide range of interest rates.

The principle of discounting operates by scaling down the absolute monetary value of future cash flows to their present value. Thus, information about the value of future cash flows can be compared with the present value of money spent now. How much future cash flows are scaled down is dependent upon the discount rate. The higher the rate of interest, the more severely the cash flows will be reduced.

12.5 Net present value analysis

These discounted cash flow principles can be applied in analysing business problems by using an approach known as net present value analysis (NPV), where for a given rate of interest, future net cash flows can be discounted and compared with present-day cash outflows. If the sum total of these discounted future net cash flows is greater than cash to be spent today, a positive NPV exists, making the proposed course of action acceptable on economic grounds. Conversely, if a negative NPV results it is not acceptable on economic grounds.

We will illustrate this NPV principle with reference to Table 12.2 (p. 150) in which £9 million is to be spent now on a project expected to produce net annual cash inflows of £3 million per annum for six years. The relevant discount factor has been estimated as being 10 per cent. The cash flows (receipts *less* payments) shown in column 2 of Table 12.2 are multiplied by the 10 per cent discount factors in column 1 to produce the annual present value of the cash flows in column 3. These annual present values are then added together to give the total present value of the cash inflows of £13,062,000. The net present value is then calculated by deducting the capital outlay from the total present values of the cash inflows (i.e. £13,062,000 − £9,000,000) giving £4,062,000.

Table 12.2   Illustration of the NPV principle

Year	Column 1 Discount factor (10%)	Column 2 Cash flows (£'000)	Column 3 (Column 1 × Column 2) Present value (£'000)
0	1.000	−9,000	−9,000 (A)
1	0.909	3,000	2,727
2	0.826	3,000	2,478
3	0.751	3,000	2,253
4	0.683	3,000	2,049
5	0.621	3,000	1,863
6	0.564	3,000	1,692
Present value of cash inflows			13,062 (B)
Net present value (B + A)			4,062

The NPV of the proposal is positive, and on economic grounds this proposed project purchase should proceed for the following reasons:

– It exceeds the required rate of return of 10 per cent.
– It produces a sum in excess of the capital outlay.

There is often a fundamental misunderstanding about what we are seeking to do in discounted cash flow analysis, particularly with inflation. Even in a world with no inflation discounted cash flow analysis would be relevant in that the providers of finance would still demand a return, albeit at a lower rate.

At this point we should distinguish between two types of return – real and nominal. The real rate is that which providers of finance would demand in an inflation-free world to compensate for the opportunity cost of using the funds for another purpose. How much this real rate – opportunity cost – is depends upon the relative risk of the purpose for which the funds will be used. When the effects of inflation are combined with the real rate, the nominal or monetary rate is determined. For example, given a real rate of interest of 8 per cent and an inflation rate of 4 per cent, the nominal (money) rate would be 12.3 per cent, i.e.

Nominal rate =
[((1 + real rate) × (1 + inflation rate)) − 1] × 100 =
[((1 + 0.08) × (1 + 0.04)) − 1] × 100

If you work in, or have dealings with, the UK public sector, a real rate is quoted and used, for example in the evaluation of capital projects. The implications of this for discounted cash flow and net present value analyses are that projected cash flows can be left in a real form, that is they do not have to be adjusted for inflation. Quite the opposite is true when the discount rate is of the nominal type, like the rates quoted by the banks and other lenders. If you are using rates like this, then the future cash flows must be adjusted, the principle being that in undertaking discounted cash flow or net present value analysis like should be treated with like – real cash flows should be discounted at a real rate or nominal cash flows should be discounted at a nominal rate. Where cash flows and discount rates do not match one another an adjustment has to be made to one or the other. Typically, it is the cash flows that are adjusted, the mechanics of which we will illustrate later in Chapter 16, when we consider the issues associated with analysing long-term decisions.

12.6 Conclusion

We have discussed managing cash in this chapter within the context of the day-to-day operations of a business and we have introduced discounted cash flow analysis as a tool for considering longer-term issues. To our minds, understanding how to manage cash is vital and, while general management typically demands the ability to manage profitability, to do so without paying close attention to cash will produce limited results. Businesses cannot survive without cash but equally, to hold too much is not good practice, as we have illustrated. In recognition of this, many businesses manage cash as part of their working capital requirement. In fact, working capital management is the subject of the next chapter – there we will broaden our review of managing liquid assets to include stock, debtors and creditors.

In addition to managing cash from this short-term perspective, general management demands the ability to take a long-term view for which a cash flow analysis is ideally suited. How to apply such analysis we will consider together with relevant practical issues in Chapters 15 and 16 where we will draw upon the principles of discounting reviewed here. Key points to remember from this chapter include the following:

- Cash management is fundamental to the success of a business.
- The real problem with cash management is being able to anticipate future requirements and to strike the correct balance between holding too little and holding too much.
- Discounted cash flow analysis involves discounting future cash flows to ensure comparability with present-day values.
- The float is a vital part of managing the cash collection system; efficient manipulation of this should help to maximize cash inflows.

- The concept of cash disbursement is aimed at controlling and slowing down the outflow of cash without incurring the ill-will of the business's suppliers.
- The daily balance should be kept to the minimum amount possible because of the interest-generating benefits that result from holding marketable securities.
- A vital principle to understand in managing all business assets is discounted cash flow analysis.
- Discounted cash flow principles can be applied in analysing business problems, for example net present value analysis (NPV), and will be reviewed and also applied extensively to different business problems in later chapters.

13
Managing working capital

It's been four years and we still don't know what we have in inventory and we still don't know what we're selling

SIR R. GREENBURY,
CHAIRMAN OF MARKS AND SPENCER,
(ON INFORMATION SYSTEMS AT BROOKS BROTHERS,
ITS US CHAIN STORE)

Most organizations give and take credit, and those trading in or manufacturing products rather than providing a service, will have to hold some stock, be it of raw materials, partly finished goods, or completely finished goods. These are all part of the working capital of the business that was discussed in Chapter 6 within the context of business ratios.

There are some important issues for consideration in managing working capital which must be judged within the context of what the business as a whole is seeking to achieve. Financial goals in terms of potential profitability need to be coordinated with marketing and production requirements. This can be seen when determining appropriate levels of receivables and stocks. The marketing department may see a strong case for lenient credit terms and collection policies in order to achieve sales targets. The marketing effort also benefits from high stock levels because immediate delivery can be promised in the knowledge that there will be no loss of sales because of a 'stockout' (no stocks being available). Higher stock levels help the production department as well, enabling it to purchase in larger quantities, use longer production runs, and suffer less downtime or unanticipated adjustments in the production schedule. However, high stock levels conflict with the financial objectives of the business. Other things being equal, a better profit on capital employed will result from minimizing the debtor (accounts receivable) and stock levels. Lower levels have two important financial benefits:

1. Less financing has to be secured because the business has less investment in debtors and stock.

2. Profits should be higher relative to sales or assets, because long-term investments are expected to generate higher returns than investments in short-term assets.

The result must be a trade-off between risk and required return. On the one hand there is the risk of not granting enough credit or having insufficient stock, thereby suffering sales losses. On the other hand, too high a level of debtors and stock has a cost that may offset any sales or production benefits. A coordinated effort, involving marketing, production and finance is required to balance the risks against the required returns. In what follows we will review the important issues to be considered in managing the individual components of working capital. Specifically we will look at:

- Debtors
- Stock
- Short-term financing.

13.1 Managing debtors

The debtors (accounts) receivable required by a business will be influenced by the following three factors:

1. The industry type
2. Total sales
3. Credit and collection policy.

First, such issues as competition in the industry, the characteristics of the product and the production process will influence the amount and return of credit extended to customers. Compare, for example, the hotel industry with the market for consumer durables. Hotels are not renowned for operating on credit terms, which is quite the opposite for retailers of consumer durables. Second, such factors as the state of the economy and the aggressiveness of the business's marketing efforts influence total sales. As total sales increase, the level of credit sales and the debtors necessary to support business activity will increase. Quite the opposite happens in a recession as recent UK experience illustrates all too well. Third, the credit and collection policies of the business also influence the size of the debtors required by the business and also the length of time between the granting of credit and the receipt of cash. As the length of time before collection increases, the required investment in debtors will need to increase. Shortening the average collection period reduces the required investment in debtors.

As a general manager you will need to control the investment in debtors.

Key within this will be the control you can exercise via credit and collection management. A major contribution to such management can be achieved via sound credit analysis, whereby the creditworthiness and paying potential of a customer need to be assessed.

There are many sources available for securing information about customer creditworthiness of which the following are the most important:

1. *Financial statements*   We have illustrated in earlier chapters how a framework of business ratios can be used to form a view about a business.
2. *Credit ratings and reports*   These are provided by credit agencies, like Dunn and Bradstreet. Such agencies provide ratings on domestic and foreign companies, and the following information would be typical for a credit report:
   (a) Summary of recent financial statements.
   (b) Key ratios and trends over time.
   (c) Information from suppliers to the business about its payment pattern.
   (d) Description of the physical condition of the business and any unusual circumstances related to the business or its owners.
   (e) A credit rating indicating the agency's assessment of the creditworthiness of the potential customer.
3. *Banks*   Many banks maintain credit departments and may provide credit information on behalf of their customers.
4. *Trade associations*   Many trade associations provide reliable means of obtaining credit information.
5. *Own company experience*   Large companies may well produce formal guidelines to use as an initial screening of creditworthiness.

Once information has been collected about a potential customer the decision whether or not to grant credit has to be made. One way of tackling this is by classifying potential customers into a number of risk classes (Table 13.1).

Table 13.1   Customer creditworthiness

Risk class	Estimated percentage of uncollectable sales	Percentage of customers in this risk class
1	0–0.5	35
2	> 0.5– < 1	30
3	> 1– < 2	20
4	> 2–3	10
5	More than 3	5

Businesses falling into risk class 1 might be extended credit automatically and have their status reviewed only once a year. Those in other classes might be extended credit within defined limits, with their status being checked far more frequently. Clearly some method has to be established for determining the appropriate risk class. One approach that can be used to make risk class judgements is 'credit scoring'. Credit scoring can involve the use of subjectively determined ratios which are weighted. From this a total credit score is found. For example, one model we have encountered looked at three particular variables:

- Cover for fixed charges provided by operating profit, e.g. with an operating profit of £100 million and fixed charges of £25 million, the cover would be 4 times (£100 million/£25 million).
- Quick ratio.
- Years in business (maximum of 10).

These three, upon the basis of judgement and/or experience, were assigned weightings such that the credit score was calculated as follows:

Credit score = 5(cover for fixed charges) + 10(quick ratio) + 2(years in business)

When a new customer applied for business these three factors would be established, multiplied by the appropriate weightings and then added to determine the credit score. The credit score determined would be used to assign the customer to a risk class and hence determine the level of credit to be allowed.

In addition, considering the terms and conditions of credit sales and credit policy, a business must consider the credit decision. This involves comparing the costs of granting credit against the benefits to be derived from granting credit, taking into account risk and the timing of the cash flows. Quite simply, we can apply the net present value principles outlined in the last chapter to compare the investment made in holding receivables against the future cash flows associated with them. Whether such an approach is warranted depends upon the level and significance of receivables in the business. In our experience this approach seems to have a theoretical rather than a practical appeal, with the decision about such matters more often being based upon far broader business issues like the need to be competitive. Nevertheless, the logic is unassailable and the principle of monitoring receivables to ensure that there are benefits from such an investment should not be overlooked. Certainly, we have found a number of organizations with very sizeable receivables, using a variant of this approach by comparing the benefits from receivables with the relative benefit to be obtained from investing short term.

The final step in managing debtors is following up, or chasing customers, to ensure that sums outstanding are collected. The rate that debtors are converted into cash measures the efficiency of a collection policy.

What techniques are available for monitoring debtors? In fact, we have encountered one of these already in the form of the debtors' collection period in Chapter 6. You may recall that for HMC Ltd the following equation was used:

$$\text{Debtors' collection period} \quad \frac{£23.4 \text{ million}}{£130 \text{ million}} \times 360 = 65 \text{ days}$$

Such calculations are easy but not very effective for internal use in monitoring a business's collections. This is because it is an aggregate measure which tends to hide differences between customer payment profiles.

A more specific measure that can be used is known as the 'debtors' pattern'. The debtors' pattern is that percentage of credit sales remaining unpaid in the month of sale, and in subsequent months. The key to understanding debtors' patterns is to remember that *each* month's credit sales are kept separate, as well as the collections received on these credit sales. Consider a business that has credit sales of £100,000 in January. Collections on the £100,000 are as shown in Table 13.2.

Table 13.2 Debtors' pattern

Month	Receivables from January sales	Payment pattern	Collections outstanding at end of month	January debtors' pattern
January	£10,000	10%	£90,000	90%
February	£30,000	30%	£60,000	60%
March	£30,000	30%	£30,000	30%
April	£30,000	30%	0	0

Ignoring, for simplicity, bad debts, 10 per cent of the credit sales are paid in January, followed by 30 per cent in each of February, March and April. The debtors' pattern, which is just 100 per cent minus the cumulative percentage payments, declines from 90 per cent in January to zero in April.

Since the debtors' pattern approach relates uncollected debtors to the months in which they arose, it has two significant advantages from a management standpoint. First, it disaggregates the debtors into their collection pattern relative to the month in which they occurred. Second, because debtors are related to sales in the month of origin, they are not sales dependent. No matter what the sales pattern, any changes in payment behaviour can be recognized immediately.

Using the debtors' pattern approach, control can be achieved by comparing actual results with expected, or budgeted, figures.

Table 13.3   Budgeted versus actual debtors' patterns

	January	February	March
Budgeted			
% of same month sales	**91%**	91%	90%
% of 1 month before	61%	**61%**	62%
% of 2 months before	22%	20%	**20%**
Actual			
% of same month sales	**90%**	88%	89%
% of 1 month before	66%	**65%**	65%
% of 2 months before	30%	28%	**30%**

In Table 13.3, which shows both budgeted and actual debtor patterns over a three-month period, the budgeted pattern for January credit sales was 91, 61 and 20 per cent for January sales, whereas the actual debtors are 90, 65 and 30 per cent. In both the first and second months after the credit sales, the collections came in slower than expected.

13.2 Managing stock

Like debtors, stock typically represents a sizeable investment that must be managed effectively. It is important to appreciate that there may be more than one type of stock, of which the most important categories are raw materials, partly finished goods (work-in-progress), and finished goods.

The purpose of holding stock is to uncouple the acquisition of goods, the stages of production, and selling activities. Without stock in a manufacturing environment, particularly work-in-progress, each stage of production would be dependent upon the preceding one finishing its operation. Stock of all types uncouples purchasing and selling functions from production.

While manufacturing firms hold all three types of stock, wholesale and retail businesses typically hold only finished goods. Service businesses may have no stock except for a few supplies related to their activities.

In addition to uncoupling business operations, there are a number of other potential benefits associated with the investment made in stock.

– *Taking advantage of quantity discounts* Often suppliers will offer customers quantity discounts if they purchase a certain number of items at the same time. To take advantage of such discounts, businesses need to hold stock.
– *Avoiding stock outages* If a business runs out of stock it may disrupt the production cycle and even cause it to stop. If finished goods are not on hand, sales may be lost and the business's reliability as a supplier comes into question.
– *Marketing benefits* Often there are distinct marketing benefits in terms of increased sales associated with having a full and complete line of merchandise. Also, developing the reputation for always being able to supply needed items may be a key part of the marketing strategy of a business.
– *Stock speculation* When prices are rising such as in times of inflation, businesses can benefit by increasing stockholdings. Other things being equal, this will increase the profitability of the business.

The costs of a business's investment in stocks consist of three main elements – carrying costs, ordering costs, and costs of running short.

1. *Carrying costs* Carrying costs include the direct investment the business has in its stocks, including storage, insurance, property tax, and spoilage and deterioration. In addition, there is an opportunity cost associated with having funds tied up in non-productive or excess stock. Thus, if it keeps £3 million in stock when only £1 million is needed, the business has £2 million tied up that could be used elsewhere.
2. *Ordering costs* The primary costs associated with ordering stock include the clerical costs of placing the order, and transportation and shipping costs.
3. *Costs of running short* The main costs associated with running short (stock outages) include lost sales, loss of customer goodwill and disruption of the business's production process.

Because of these costs, the control of stock levels may be very important. How can this be achieved? One approach is what is known as the '123' method which is applied as shown in Table 13.4. Consider a business with thousands of stock items, ranging from very expensive to very inexpensive.

Table 13.4   123 method of stock control

	% *Stock volume*	% *Stock value*
Category 1	10	50
Category 2	30	35
Category 3	60	15
	100	100

The Category 1 items (Table 13.4) require a high investment and in this case represent 10 per cent of the volume but account for 50 per cent of the value of stock investment. Category 2 items constitute say 30 per cent of the items and 35 per cent of the money value, while the Category 3 items account for 60 per cent by volume, but only 15 per cent of the value. By separating stock into different groups, a business can concentrate on items where effective control is most important. A formal system involving extensive and frequent monitoring is likely for Category 1 items. Items in Category 2 will be reviewed and adjusted less frequently – perhaps quarterly – and Category 3 items may be reviewed only annually.

The 123 method has two advantages. First, it focuses attention where it will do the most good and, second, it makes the financial management of inventory paramount. That is, attention is paid to the key requirements of the business in terms of marketing, production, purchasing, etc., but their implications need to be gauged as regards stockholding by the business.

An alternative approach uses just-in-time (JIT) principles, whereby businesses contract with suppliers to receive goods only as and when they are required. The notion with this approach is that a business ideally wants to maintain almost a zero stockholding so as to minimize its costs. This means that suppliers need to be located nearby in order to make a delivery on a daily, or even an hourly, basis. From the business's standpoint, the method requires a totally different approach to the production and management process. In fact, it may often take a new or completely redesigned plant and labour contract to achieve the anticipated benefits from lower investment in stock. Effective management of a business's stock involves a balancing of the costs and benefits associated with the investment in it. Various statistical models have been developed for determining the size of a stock order to place, but investment in stock is really no different from any other decision to invest where future cash benefits have to be judged against cash costs. This means that the net present value framework outlined in the last chapter can, in principle, be employed to assist in deciding whether to increase or decrease investment in stock.

13.3 Short-term financing

In addition to managing debtors and stock, a business must also pay attention to short-term finance, which often represents a significant proportion of working capital.

There are many alternative sources of short-term finance. Certain of them, like taking trade credit, are often spontaneous in so far as they tend to expand or contract automatically as the debtors and inventory of the business expand or contract. Others are negotiated between a borrower and a lender.

To determine what sources of short-term finance to employ, four specific issues need to be considered:

— Risk matching
— Cost
— Availability
— Flexibility.

By risk matching we mean that the business must decide how much risk it is willing to incur in financing temporary assets with temporary liabilities. An aggressive stance will lead a business to employ more sources and amounts of short-term financing than a conservative one.

The second issue that influences the selection of short-term financing is its cost, which often cannot be separated from the availability of credit. If a business cannot borrow through an unsecured loan, then some type of secured means will have to be employed.

Third, over the course of the business cycle, certain sources of funds may be more or less available. Thus, availability refers to both the amount and the conditions attached to the short-term financing. Only by examining both features will managers be in a position to consider the business's short-term financing sources over time.

Finally, there is the issue of flexibility. Flexibility refers to the ability of the business to pay off a loan and still retain the ability to renew or increase it. It also refers to the ease with which a business can secure or increase financing at short notice. Some forms of short-term financing, like trade credit, may be increased relatively quickly and easily, but others, like a negotiated short-term loan, may take longer to secure.

All four issues need to be considered when a business looks at its sources of short-term financing. Although the direct cost is a key element, it does not always provide the final answer. This is because there may be opportunity costs relating to risk matching, availability and flexibility that have to be considered. For example, seeking one source of short-term finance because it is relatively more available may well reduce future flexibility. However, it is difficult to quantify opportunity costs. A practical approach to the problem is to rank sources according to their direct costs, and then consider these other factors. If the opportunity costs are significant, the ranking of the desirability of one source of short-term financing compared with another will probably change.

Finally, since business financing needs change over time, multiple sources of short-term financing should be considered even if some of them are not employed presently. However, great care needs to be taken to ensure that a business does not overstretch itself in terms of the short-term financing it raises. Many businesses in the United Kingdom have suffered from the consequences of borrowing too much both in the short term and longer term and have found it difficult; and in some cases impossible, to support the costs of borrowing from dwindling profits.

13.4 Conclusion

Working capital is vital for business survival. Manage it incorrectly by having too little or too much stock, too many debtors and too much by way of short-term finance, and the risks of survival will increase dramatically. Working capital enables the necessary flow of cash through the business so that a profit can be made. This is why it is crucial to manage it effectively.

What is often not appreciated about working capital is that it really does deserve conscious management. Unlike major discrete business decisions, it is often not characterized by requiring a significant single outlay of funds and yet its financial impact and consequences may be as great, if not greater.

Furthermore, and of particular importance, the responsibility for effective working capital management rests with general management. Decisions as to the level of stock to hold and the amount of investment in debtors are business-led and not simply the responsibility of the financial officers in a business.

Main points to remember from this chapter include the following:

- Managing the working capital of a business involves controlling current assets like cash marketable securities, trade debtors and stock as well as current liabilities like trade creditors, short-term loans and overdrafts.
- A coordinated effort involving marketing, production and finance must be employed in managing the individual components of working capital.
- Managers face a trade-off between risk and required returns when determining appropriate levels of debtors and stocks.
- One way of evaluating the credit allowance of a customer is by classifying potential customers into a number of risk classes determined by 'credit scoring'.

- The principle of managing debtors will be influenced by the industry type, total sales, and the credit and collection policy.
- A specific technique for monitoring debtors is the 'debtors' pattern'.
- The costs of business investment in stocks consist of three main elements: carrying costs, ordinary costs and costs of running short.
- In addition to managing debtors and stock, managers do need to pay attention to short-term finance. To determine what sources of short-term finance to employ, four specific issues need to be considered: risk matching, cost, availability and flexibility.

14

Managing costs to support business decisions

A decision is the action an executive must take when he has information so incomplete that the answer does not suggest itself

A. W. RADFORD

Managing costs is a key challenge for all organizations. As was demonstrated in Chapter 5 with reference to business profitability ratios, the successful management of costs can have a significant impact upon profitability. You will probably recall from that chapter that anything that improves the profit on sales percentage will feed through to improve profit on capital employed percentage. This is because profit on capital employed percentage is the product of profit on sales percentage and sales as a multiple of capital employed.

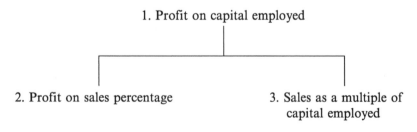

1. Profit on capital employed

2. Profit on sales percentage

3. Sales as a multiple of capital employed

Improvements made in managing costs are a key source for improving profit on sales percentage. However, they may be difficult to achieve because the one fact about costs that most of us can relate to is that they increase far more readily than they fall. Very often the only way they can be readily affected is by the use of appropriate monitoring and control mechanisms.

164

Such mechanisms involve the comparison of actual against expected performance and the identification of exceptional differences, or variances. These variances are then reported to the individuals responsible for them who are then required to take appropriate courses of action. Of course, as is often the case in business, there is much more to achieving sound monitoring and control than simply the mechanical process. The human element in particular can never be ignored!

In addition to managing the day-to-day or routine performance of the business in which cost control is a vital feature, most general managers have to make decisions of a non-routine nature for which there are some important issues relating to the cost data to be used. These issues and how to manage costs to support non-routine, or *ad hoc,* business decisions are covered later in the chapter.

Last, but by no means least, it may be necessary at times to question the fundamental assumptions that underpin the cost base. In addition to dealing with routine day-to-day cost control issues, how to organize and select data to support non-routine decisions, there may be substantial benefits to be gained from questioning the rationale for the costs incurred by parts of the business. As indicated earlier, one feature of costs is that they all too readily go up but only come down with a concerted effort. Techniques do exist to assist in questioning the cost base. What they are and their implications we will discuss in the last section of the chapter.

14.1 Monitoring and controlling routine performance

Most organizations use some form of variance analysis for monitoring performance. Quite what form it will take tends to depend upon how responsibility is assigned. In an organization where individuals are held responsible for achieving profit targets, then variances will be sought and analysed in terms of both costs and revenues. By contrast, if individual responsibility relates only to costs, then cost variances will predominate. However, for most general managers this distinction will be arbitrary. Such individuals are typically responsible for controlling all aspects of performance.

Within the total system for monitoring and controlling routine performance, cost control will usually feature as being particularly important. In many businesses the achievement of better returns may be all too dependent upon managing costs successfully – there being limited latitude for improvements in any other way because of the competitive nature of the market. The same limitations upon improved performance also apply in times of recession, as recent UK experience has served to show.

Severely affected sales, combined with a desire to meet shareholder return expectations, have caused many companies to engage in severe cost cutting programmes.

What form does cost variance analysis take? There is no standard format. Organizations apply variance analysis to suit their own individual circumstances.

Manufacturing businesses typically analyse variances in accordance with the different types of production cost they incur, like labour, materials and production overheads. Such variance accounting may be highly developed into an approach known as standard costing, where technical specifications will be used in determining the standard set. Service businesses, on the other hand, will often analyse their cost variances with reference to a budgeting procedure rather than technical specifications. In effect, this means that estimates of expenditure will be made by type of cost to be incurred, for example advertising and promotion, against which actual costs incurred will be monitored. Such estimates will often be made for one year ahead in detail, being broken down by week and/or month.

Estimates of expenditure for longer time periods are made by many organizations as part of their medium-term planning process, the detail of such estimates being limited. It is also important to note that some businesses use rolling forecasts whereby short-term estimates are revised as a consequence of actual performance achieved.

How might cost variances be reported? Let us consider this with reference to a simple example concerning advertising and promotion expenditure (Table 14.1). The total variance for advertising and promotion for the year to date is £400,000 and represents an overspend situation. Such situations of overspend are usually referred to as 'unfavourable' or 'adverse' variances, by comparison with 'favourable' variances for underspend situations. The reason for this is that any overspend will have an unfavourable effect upon net profit, while underspend will be reflected by increased profits.

We have seen that it is normal practice in accounting to show unfavourable or negative numbers in brackets, and this also applies to the

Table 14.1 April 1992 year to date actual v. budget advertising and promotion expenditure

	Actual (£'000)	Budget (£'000)	Variance (£'000)	Volume (£'000)	Timing (£'000)
Spend to April	1400	1000	(400)	(150)	(250)

reporting of variances. In our example the variance in the third column and the numbers in the columns headed 'Volume' and 'Timing' are all bracketed. In fact, these columns illustrate that there is a £400,000 unfavourable advertising and promotion variance which has arisen because:

– £150,000 more advertising and promotion was incurred than was allowed for – a volume variance.
– £250,000 of advertising and promotion expenditure was incurred in a different time period than allowed for – a timing variance.

Volume variances can be as dependent upon the ability to forecast and formulate an accurate budget as the actual sequence of events which occurs. While a successful system of variance analysis is critically dependent upon regularly reported actual information, there is an equally important need for accurate forecasting. In short, the managers responsible must ensure that each category of cost is realistic and as accurate as possible. This applies particularly to what is commonly known as 'reforecasting' which we alluded to earlier with reference to rolling budgets.

In many organizations, usually after some six months of a current budget period has elapsed, managers are asked to provide a reforecast for the remaining six months and to produce a forecast for the 12 months thereafter. In producing a realistic reforecast there is a real need for managers to avoid being over- or under-optimistic about both volume and timing. Quite simply, as much realism as possible is required.

There are some additional practical points to consider in monitoring costs using variance analysis. These can best be appreciated by extending our earlier example (Table 14.1) as shown in Table 14.2 (p. 168). The budget has been adjusted to correct it for an error in its preparation. It was prepared incorrectly on a cash rather than an accounting basis. In effect the original budget for £1 million made allowance for the month in which costs were to be paid rather than when they were to be incurred. As you will know from earlier chapters, the distinction between cash flow and profit is important. Because the concern in analysing cost variances is upon profit, accounting principles should be used in preparing estimates.

Having adjusted the budget to £1,240,000 what is the cause of the variance with actual expenditure? The unavailability of suitable advertising signage space reduced promotion costs and therefore has a beneficial effect upon profit. Against this favourable variance, there is an unfavourable variance of £205,000 caused by media costs being incurred earlier than anticipated.

Clearly in such circumstances the reason for such variances would have to be investigated and accounted for by the individual responsible. This is an important point: a good system of cost control requires that those involved

Table 14.2   April 1992 year to date actual v. budget advertising and promotion expenditure

	Actual (£'000)	Budget (£'000)	Variance (£'000)	Volume (£'000)	Timing (£'000)
Spend to April	1400	1000	(400)	(150)	(250)
Adjusted budget for error in preparing on a cash basis	1400	1240	(160)		
Advertising budgeted but not taken				45	
Media costs incurred earlier than budgeted					(205)
	1400	1240	(160)	45	(205)

in preparing the estimates and responsible for the costs involved are held accountable.

One approach for ensuring that appropriate comparisons are made between actual and expected performance is to 'flex' the estimates, the logic being that it is meaningless to compare actual results for promoting, say, 120,000 units with a budget based on 100,000 units. Rather what should be calculated is a variance showing a comparison of what actually resulted at 120,000 units with what should have resulted had 120,000 units been the anticipated volume. In this case there would be a flexing upwards of costs by 20,000 units, the process being facilitated by a knowledge of those items which were volume related and those which were not. Quite how this might be achieved in principle we will consider shortly.

There is little doubt that such a system of flexing has much to commend it but it may prove difficult to apply simply because the necessary information may not be available and/or it may be too complex to implement. As a consequence, in practice, variances may often be calculated by comparing original estimates with actual performance.

14.2 Managing costs associated with non-routine decisions

In addition to the need to control costs relating to the day-to-day running of the business, general managers have to deal with one other important issue concerning how costs can be managed to support important business decisions that fall outside of day-to-day needs. For the general manager responsible for running a part of the total business, the types of decision warranting such consideration may include such issues as:

– Is it more profitable to produce X good or provide Y service?
– Is the business costing more to run than it should?
– Should a short-term business opportunity be accepted at a lower than normal price?

A major problem to be faced in dealing with decisions of this kind concerns the data that should be used. Very often data contained in the accounting records may not be relevant to the decision being considered, and/or may have been derived using inappropriate methods for the purpose in hand. Often, available cost data will relate to past periods of time and will be categorized by business function whereas what is required is a future-oriented view broken down, for example, according to how costs change with levels of business activity.

In fact, the key to managing costs to support business decisions lies in recognizing that there is no single view of costs. Costs that may be accurate for one kind of decision may be totally misleading for another.

Whereas the data produced by an organization in the normal course of events may be appropriate for the day-to-day management of the business, non-routine, or *ad hoc*, decisions may well require specific adjustments to be made to normal cost data. With this in mind let us consider types of cost information and how it may be used.

Full costs

Many organizations, particularly those involved in manufacturing, produce full cost information in order to value stocks. It is also not unusual to encounter such information being used for diagnosing profitability and as a guide in setting selling prices.

A full cost actually means that a share of all manufacturing costs has been assigned to a product. It usually excludes selling, distribution and administrative costs outside of the plant.

Variable and fixed costs

One popular way of viewing costs for supporting business decisions is with reference to their behaviour over time. As we will illustrate by making a distinction between what are known as variable and fixed costs, some fairly simple but powerful analysis can be undertaken. In order to perform such analysis three basic terms need to be identified. These are:

- *Variable costs* Costs that change proportionately to a change in the level of activity.
- *Fixed costs* Costs that remain (relatively) unchanged in total for a given time period despite wide fluctuations in the level of activity.
- *Contribution margin* The difference between sales revenue and variable costs.

Their significance can be appreciated by making reference to the following simple definition of profit

$$\text{Sales revenue} - \text{Expenditure} = \text{Profit}$$

We can now separate the various items of expenditure into the two groups of cost defined above, variable and fixed costs, to give an interim indicator of profitability, known as the contribution margin:

$$\text{Sales revenue} - \text{Variable costs} = \text{Contribution} - \text{Fixed costs} = \text{Profit}$$

As we will demonstrate, this separation of costs can be used quite powerfully to interrogate the viability of a business proposition. If the fixed costs to be covered can be measured, then the number of units required to achieve the point at which the proposition will break-even can be readily calculated as follows:

$$\text{Break-even point} = \frac{\text{Fixed costs}}{\text{Contribution per unit}}$$

For example, given the following information and ignoring stock:

	Per unit £	Total £
Sales revenue	10	
Variable costs	6	
Contribution margin	4	
Fixed costs		60,000

If each unit contributes £4 towards fixed costs, we can readily see that 15,000 (£60,000 /£4) is the required number to break-even, i.e.

		Total £
Sales revenue	(15,000 × £10)	150,000
Variable costs	(15,000 × £6)	90,000
Contribution	(15,000 × £4)	60,000
Fixed costs		60,000
Profit		0

Sales over 15,000 will contribute towards profit because all fixed costs have been covered. At 15,001 units £4 profit will result and, if we want to determine the volume to achieve a given profit, then we simply add this sum into the numerator of the calculation. For example, if a profit of £40,000 is required, the volume is found as follows:

$$\frac{\text{Fixed costs} + \text{Required profit}}{\text{Unit contribution}}$$

$$= \frac{£60,000 + £40,000}{£4} = 25,000 \text{ units}$$

Using this approach, known as 'cost–volume–profit' (CVP) analysis, back of the envelope type calculations can be used quite powerfully to get a feel for business opportunities. Of course, the calculation of variable and fixed costs may be difficult with real precision but, perhaps, this is not necessary. Less precision and an interrogation of the numbers using an approach known as 'sensitivity analysis' may be all that is required. The mechanics of this approach can be best understood with reference to the following illustration, in which the effect upon the break-even point of a 10 per cent shortfall in each of the key input variables in our earlier example is considered.

1. *Sales volume 13,500 units*

	Total £
Sales revenue (13,500 × £10)	135,000
Variable costs (13,500 × £6)	81,000
Contribution (13,500 × £4)	54,000
Fixed costs	60,000
Loss	6,000

Given that the only change we are measuring is a 10 per cent volume shortfall, the break-even point remains 15,000 units, i.e.

$$\frac{\text{Fixed costs}}{\text{Unit contribution}}$$

$$= \frac{£60,000}{£4} = 15,000 \text{ units}$$

2. *Unit sales revenue £9*

	Total £
Sales revenue (15,000 × £9)	135,000
Variable costs (15,000 × £6)	90,000
Contribution (15,000 × £3)	45,000
Fixed costs	60,000
Loss	15,000

The effect of this change is to increase the break-even point to 20,000 units simply because the result of a lower unit sales revenue, other things being equal, is a reduction in the unit contribution. Thus, the new break-even point is:

$$\frac{\text{Fixed costs}}{\text{Unit contribution}}$$

$$\frac{£60,000}{£3} = 20,000 \text{ units}$$

3. *Unit variable cost £6.60*

	Total £
Sales revenue (15,000 × £10)	150,000
Variable costs (15,000 × £6.60)	99,000
Contribution (15,000 × £3.40)	51,000
Fixed costs	60,000
Loss	9,000

The result of a 10 per cent increase in unit variable costs is to increase the unit break-even point to 17,647 units, i.e.

$$\frac{\text{Fixed costs}}{\text{Unit contribution}}$$

$$= \frac{£60,000}{£3.40} = 17,647 \text{ units}$$

The CVP approach can also be used to help to explain why some business propositions may be far more risky than others, simply because of the fixed costs that will be incurred. Such a situation corresponds with what is referred to as a higher level of 'operating leverage', or 'operating gearing'. This may arise when a business substitutes fixed costs in order to decrease variable costs. Thus, a business with a high operating gearing would have a large amount of fixed asset costs (depreciation) and relatively small variable costs. An increase in automation is often a good example of an increase in operating leverage.

The implication of higher operating leverage can most readily be seen when we extend our earlier example to consider the impact of introducing more automation – the business thereby increasing fixed costs but at the same time decreasing variable labour costs. (While many employment costs may be considered to be relatively fixed, those associated with manual skills are normally considered to be variable for purposes of CVP.)

	Current manufacturing process £	New manufacturing process £
Sales revenue/unit	10	10
Variable costs/unit	6	5
Contribution margin	4	5
Fixed costs	£60,000	£75,000
Break-even units	15,000 units	15,000 units
Profit on marginal unit (incremental profit)	£4	£5

Current manufacturing process £	At 15,000 unit volume	New manufacturing process £
150,000	Sales revenue	150,000
90,000	Variable costs	75,000
60,000	Contribution margin	75,000
60,000	Fixed costs	75,000
0	Profit	0

As a consequence of such a change in the manufacturing process, some very real benefits can be seen:

– Lower variable costs
– Higher incremental profit.

However, the 'two-edged' nature of the operational gearing sword can also be seen when the potential downside risks are considered:

– Higher fixed costs to be met
– Greater potential loss below break-even levels.

This simple example illustrates the importance of understanding CVP relationships. To invest in a new manufacturing process, or any new business venture that will incur substantial fixed costs, is commercial suicide without having a good understanding of the potential of the market to provide the volumes required. It only takes a downturn in business optimism to change success into failure. The same observation also applies to 'financial gearing' or 'financial leverage' which, you will recall, we have discussed within the context of ratio analysis. Taking on high levels of debt may be very beneficial when interest rates are low and business confidence is good. However, replace business confidence with pessimism as we have seen in the recent UK recession and an interest payment burden remains that has to be met from dwindling profits.

It is important to appreciate that the forgoing discussion of CVP type analysis is recommended only as an initial method of trying to understand the riskiness associated with business propositions. Think of the approaches discussed as representing screening devices. Much deeper analysis may well be warranted when the distinction of costs by behaviour, that is fixed and variable, does not correspond readily with what will actually happen to them in the event of a decision being made.

For purposes of considering decisions it is often helpful to use the term 'differential' costs. Quite simply, these are those costs that will change as the result of a specific decision. Variable costs may approximate for differential costs of a decision only when the circumstances assumed in calculating the variable costs are consistent with those involved in the decision. In fact, variable costs will approximate differential cost only for those short-term decisions that affect a limited volume of production where adequate capacity exists. The message is quite simple – do question what will happen to all costs as a consequence of the decision and do not get locked arbitrarily into the distinction simply between fixed and variable costs. For example, if a decision requires more goods to be produced or services to be provided than is possible given existing capacity then recognize that costs over and above the variable costs will have to be incurred. You should also bear in mind two other issues associated with costs.

First, in the case of most decisions there will be 'opportunity' costs whereby a benefit will be forgone as a consequence of taking an alternative course of action. For example, assume that a manufacturer can sell a semi-finished product that has a full cost of £80 to an outside buyer for £100 each. However, he chooses to finish them and sell them for £150. The opportunity cost of the semi-finished product is £100 because this is the amount of economic resources that the manufacturer gave up. Note that no cash has changed hands in determining the opportunity cost of £100 and this is a unique feature of an opportunity cost. No exchange of economic resources is necessary because opportunity costs result from forgoing an alternative which involves no transaction. This means that opportunity costs are usually not reflected in the regular cost accounting records.

Opportunity costs often cause some problems in real-life situations and are often incorrectly ignored, quite unlike the second problem area, 'sunk' costs which are often included when they should not be. Sunk costs represent economic resources that have already been committed, which cannot be recovered and are not relevant in evaluating a future course of action – for example, the amount of money spent to date on a research project that has not yet yielded results. Another example of a sunk cost is the purchase price of a fixed asset which is irrelevant in considering its potential replacement. What is relevant is the net amount that could be realized from its sale. The key point to recognize is that sunk costs have no relevance in calculating the financial impact of future decisions other than providing an historical reference point, and should be ignored.

14.3 Questioning the cost base

We have made reference to one key problem concerning costs – they tend to increase effortlessly but rarely decrease in the same way. This has been recognized by many organizations, particularly as a consequence of recessionary times, where the only scope for maintaining performance or even survival may hinge upon the more effective control of business costs.

Those costs that may provide the greatest scope for improvement are often fixed costs typically referred to as overheads. In their case a number of approaches have been developed which focus upon questioning the necessity for incurring them. One of the longest standing of these approaches was developed in the United States and had its origins in public expenditure programmes. Known as zero base budgeting (ZBB), it requires the relevance of all costs to be questioned and may be readily contrasted with conventional budgeting procedures which tend to operate on an incremental basis, that is last year's performance represents the starting or reference point for this year's budget. The real problem with incremental budgeting is that it perpetuates any past inefficiencies and there is only really a challenge to justify proposed cost increases and not the cost base upon which any increases are based. In recognition of this, various approaches have been developed with the most extreme requirement being that the projected expenditure for *existing* programmes should start from base zero, with each year's budgets being compiled as if the programme were being launched for the first time. In effect, those responsible for preparing budgets are challenged with presenting their requests for appropriations in such a fashion that all funds could be allocated on the basis of cost/benefit, the approach being an attempt to ensure 'value for money'. In effect, the long-standing assumptions about particular functions are challenged and systematically examined. The types of question typically asked are:

- Should the function be performed at all?
- What level of service should be provided? Are we doing too much?
- How much should it cost?

ZBB can yield some substantial benefits but it is very time consuming and, therefore, costly. As with all financial techniques it really is important to be able to evaluate the potential benefits against likely costs. Rather than starting from a zero base for all activities, an alternative is to examine costs by prioritizing them in some way. In fact, this approach has been developed into what is known as priority base budgeting (PBB) and has a distinct advantage in not requiring a complete 'bottom up' analysis of costs. Nevertheless it still requires a major time commitment and the involvement of key staff. Many of those organizations that have employed this approach have recognized and acted upon the need to educate and train staff who typically would have been involved in an incremental approach. The transition from making adjustments to historical data for, say, inflation and other expectations to a detailed analysis of resource needs to support business requirements is by no means insignificant.

The last, but by no means least, approach we will review briefly is known as activity based costing (ABC) which has become very popular in recent times. ABC emphasizes the need to obtain a better understanding of indirect cost behaviour than is provided by many traditional cost accounting methods which have long been associated with rather arbitrary approaches to allocating overheads. It attempts to focus attention towards what causes costs to be incurred and that products (or other selected cost objects) such as customers consume activities in varying amounts. A link is made, therefore, between activities and products by assigning the cost of activities based on an individual product's demand for each activity.

ABC had its origins in manufacturing but has been adapted by many different types of organization in both the for-profit and not-for-profit sectors. Its design as a system involves the following steps, irrespective of organization types:

- Identification of the key activities that take place.
- Creation of a cost pool/cost centre for each major activity.
- Assignment of costs to activity cost pools.
- Determination of the cost driver for each activity cost pool.
- Determination of the unit cost for each activity.
- Assignment of costs of activities to selected cost objects (e.g. products) according to the cost objects' demand for each activity.

To understand better how this might operate let us relate it to an organization we can all relate to, a bank.

The first stage requires that an activity analysis is undertaken in order to identify the major activities performed in the organization. Such activities are simply the tasks that people or machines perform in order to provide a product or service. In the case of a bank activities would be processing a deposit, issuing a credit card, processing a cheque, getting a loan, opening an account or processing monthly statements.

The next stage requires that a cost pool (or cost centre) is created for each activity. Costs are then analysed and assigned to the appropriate activity cost pool so that, for example, the total cost of processing a deposit might constitute one activity for all deposit processing related costs. But separate cost pools should be created for each type of deposit account if different types of deposits consume resources differently.

The third stage is to identify the factors that influence the cost of a particular activity. The term 'cost driver' is used to describe the events or forces that are the significant determinants of the cost of the activities. For example, if the cost of processing deposits is generated by the number of deposits processed, then the number of deposits processed would represent the cost driver for deposit processing activities.

The cost driver selected for each cost pool should be the one that, as closely as possible, mirrors the consumption of the activities represented by the cost pool. Examples of cost drivers that might be appropriate in a clearing bank include:

- Number of applications processed for setting up a loan
- Number of mortgage payments past due date for processing activities relating to mortgage arrears.

The next stage divides the cost traced to each activity cost pool by the total number of driver units in order to calculate a cost per unit of activity.

Finally, the cost of activities is traced to products (or other cost objects) according to a product's demand for the activities by multiplying unit activity costs by the quantity of each activity that a product consumes. A product or service in ABC is viewed as a bundle of the individual costs of the activities that are required to deliver it. Its intended purpose is to measure as accurately as possible the resources consumed by products or services rather than relying upon the traditional arbitrary cost allocation systems that may have distortive effects. For example, a traditional costing system might allocate deposit transaction processing costs to customers, or different types of deposit accounts, on the basis of the number of customer accounts. The approach will lead to distorted product costs if deposit processing costs are driven by the number of transactions processed. Allocating costs according to the number of customers will lead to low value deposit accounts that may involve numerous transactions being undercosted, whereas high value infrequently used accounts may be overcosted. In contrast, the ABC approach would establish a separate cost centre for deposit processing activities, ascertain what causes the costs (i.e. determine the appropriate cost driver, such as the number of transactions processed) and assign costs to products on the basis of a product's demand for the activity.

14.4 Conclusion

Managing costs to support business decisions is an important issue to come to terms with. For routine control of costs a sound understanding of variance accounting and the analysis of variances is invaluable but, as we have identified, there are some pitfalls to be aware of.

As regards decisions of a non-routine nature, there is a very real need to come to terms with the issue of the relevance of the cost information for any decision being examined. And while, as we have demonstrated, there are techniques like cost–volume–profit analysis that can be used to assist decision making, they will only be as good as the quality of information associated with their use.

Last, but by no means least, the need to question the cost base must be acknowledged. Overheads can grow out of all proportion and some means has to be used for examining their need. Techniques like zero and priority base budgeting can be used to ask fundamental questions about the necessity of particular costs, as can activity based costing by linking costs incurred to the activities that caused them.

In summary, the main points in this chapter include the following:

- The successful management of costs can have a significant impact upon profitability.
- Improvements made in managing costs are a key source for improving profit on sales but can be more difficult to achieve as they tend to increase far more readily than they fall.
- Most organizations use some form of variance analysis for monitoring business performance.
- A succesful system of variance analysis is critically dependent upon regularly reported actual information.
- The key to managing costs to support business decisions lies in recognizing that there is no single view of costs.
- One popular way of viewing costs for supporting business decisions is with reference to their behaviour over time.
- A separation of costs into variable costs, fixed costs and contribution margin enables a powerful but relatively simple approach known as cost–volume–profit analysis (CVP) to be applied.
- The CVP approach can also be used to help to explain why some business propositions are more risky than others.
- Sensitivity analysis can also be applied to data to get a feel for the potential sources of risk relating to a business proposition.
- It may be necessary at times to question the fundamental assumptions that underpin the cost base. Methods to facilitate this include: zero base budgeting (ZBB), priority base budgeting (PBB), and activity based costing (ABC).

15
Managing capital expenditure: the principles

Nothing is more difficult, and therefore more precious, than to be able to decide

NAPOLEON BONAPARTE

Businesses can only grow via internal expansion or external acquisition. As such, one of the tasks of senior management is to identify and evaluate potential investment opportunities, and to select and implement those that should be successful. A major problem to be faced in this respect is that, as with any decision based upon the future, there will always be some uncertainty as to the outcome.

In managing the capital expenditure in a business there are many financial tools that may be employed to help to evaluate alternative investment opportunities. In this chapter we will review the main financial tools that as a general manager you need to understand. While it may not be your job to prepare evaluations it is highly likely that you will assume responsibility for approving sizeable proposals that are referred to you. This being so, a good understanding of the advantages and disadvantages of each of the financial tools that can be used for evaluating investment opportunities is essential.

The effective management of capital expenditure is not only reliant upon the evaluation process, but also the monitoring and control of expenditure that has been committed. This monitoring and control may include the review of past capital expenditure decisions by way of a post-completion audit. The principles involved in monitoring and controlling capital expenditure via a post-completion audit will, therefore, also be reviewed.

In what follows it is important to recognize that there are different motives for undertaking capital expenditure, not all of which will be directly related to increasing the future profitability of the business. The various evaluatory techniques we will review can, however, be applied to all types of capital expenditure proposal.

15.1 General considerations

When assessing investment opportunities it is all too easy to become lost in detail and not to be able to 'see the wood for the trees'. To help avoid this there are some general considerations which should be borne in mind:

- Only those investment opportunities which meet the objectives of the business should be selected, i.e. those which provide what the business regards as a satisfactory rate of return for the risks involved.
- The expected rate of return from any opportunity must exceed the financing cost that the capital expenditure will necessitate.
- The most financially desirable opportunity must be selected from the range available (assuming, as is normally the case, that resources are limited and that not all opportunities can be undertaken).
- A broad perspective must be taken of each opportunity so that both financial and non-financial considerations are given appropriate weight.

With these points in mind, what are the main financial variables required for evaluating a potential investment opportunity? These can be summarized as follows:

- The initial capital outlay including the cost of fixed assets, working capital and, if appropriate, deliberate start-up losses.
- The expected useful economic life.
- An estimate of the residual value of assets remaining at the end of its useful economic life.
- The amounts and timing of all cost and revenue components associated with the investment opportunity.
- Expected price level changes for each cost and revenue component.
- Taxation assumptions and any regional grants likely to affect the corporate position.
- The relevant cost of capital, in terms of the returns required to satisfy the financiers of the business.
- Likely estimates of variation for each of the above variables.

15.2 Popular financial tools

We will review the financial tools used for evaluating capital expenditure proposals that you are most likely to encounter. Some may be known by more than one name, however, the most widely recognized are:

1. Payback period
2. Rate of return
3. Discounted cash flow

(a)   net present value
(b)   internal rate of return.

Unlike the rate of return, the payback period and discounted cash flow are calculated using cash flows rather than profit. Further, only discounted cash flow tools take into account the time value of money which, as we will demonstrate, means that money received in the future is scaled down in order to make it comparable with current-day money.

A comparison of these financial tools and their respective advantages and disadvantages is best illustrated using financial data. Accordingly, we will use as an example the following data from an imaginary business contemplating three alternative investment proposals:

	Proposal 1 (£'000)	Proposal 2 (£'000)	Proposal 3 (£'000)
Cash outlay now	−9000	−7500	−6000
Net annual cash inflows (after deducting cash outflows):			
Year 1	3000	3500	2500
Year 2	3000	3000	2600
Year 3	3000	2400	2400
Year 4	3000	2600	
Year 5	3000	2500	
Year 6	3000		

Payback period

The payback period measures how long it will take to recover the capital outlay from net annual cash flows. It is calculated using cash flow data and is expressed in terms of a number of years, or years and months. For Proposal 1, which has a capital outlay of £9 million and cash inflows of £3 million for each year of its expected life of six years, the payback is clearly three years (3 years × £3 million = capital outlay of £9 million).

If you try to calculate the payback period for the other two proposals you will find that it does not occur exactly at the end of a year. For example, Proposal 2 generates the following cash inflows:

	Net annual cash flows (£'000)	Accumulated annual cash inflows (£'000)
Year 1	3500	3500
Year 2	3000	6500
Year 3	2400	8900

The cash flows for the first two years amount to £6.5 million. In the third year, only £1 million of the net cash flows are required to make the accumulated net cash flows equal to the £7.5 million capital outlay. By assuming that the net annual cash flows occur evenly throughout the year, we can find the payback period in years and months. The years we have established as being two and the number of months can be found by expressing the net annual cash flows during year 3 required to pay back as a fraction of the total cash inflows during year three, and then converting the result to months, as follows:

$$\frac{\text{Cash flow required to pay back}}{\text{Net annual cash inflow during year 3}} \times 12 \text{ months}$$

$$\frac{£1 \text{ million}}{£2.4 \text{ million}} \times 12 \text{ months} \qquad = 5 \text{ months}$$

The same calculation for Proposal 3 produces a payback period of 2 years 4.5 months and the results for all three proposals may be summarized as:

	Proposal 1	Proposal 2	Proposal 3
Payback period	3 years exactly	2 years 5 months	2 years 4.5 months

A major objective in using any evaluatory technique may often be to find out which proposal should be selected from a number of competing alternatives. A simple ranking, in this case based on the proposal offering the shortest payback period, shows that Proposal 3 is marginally more desirable than Proposal 2. However, to form a more complete view we need to review the proposals using other evaluatory methods.

The payback period has appeal because it is relatively simple to calculate, understand and use. Against this the payback period focuses specifically upon the time taken to recover the capital outlay such that cash flows generated after the payback period may easily be overlooked. One other major shortcoming, the substance and importance of which will become evident shortly in our discussion of the discounting principle, is that unless the cash flows are specifically adjusted, the time value of money is ignored.

Rate of return

The rate of return can be likened to the profit on assets or capital employed ratio, which was be discussed in detail in Chapter 5, in so far as the return generated by a proposal is expressed as a percentage of the investment outlay. Unlike the payback period the data used in its calculation include data relating to its whole life. You must be aware, however, that it is calculated with reference to a proposal's profit rather than cash flow which is a source of criticism because, as we have illustrated in earlier chapters, it can be calculated in a number of different ways. Indeed, as we demonstrated in Chapter 11 with reference to the Touche Ross study, different users could arrive at different rates of return using the same input data, and what is even more confusing is that none of the resulting calculations is necessarily incorrect!

The first step in calculating the rate of return is to accumulate the estimated annual profit flows to establish the total profit of the proposal. If only cash flow information is available then the annual cash flows must be summed, from which the depreciation on the proposal (a proxy for which is the capital outlay) must be deducted to give the total profit. The total profit is required in order to calculate the average annual profit. This is found by dividing the profit by the estimated life of the proposals and is illustrated for our three example proposals in Table 15.1.

Table 15.1 Average annual profits for the three proposals

	Proposal (£'000)	Proposal 2 (£'000)	Proposal 3 (£'000)
Total net annual cash inflow	18,000	14,000	7,500
Outlay	−9,000	−7,500	−6,000
Total profit (a)	9,000	6,500	1,500
Life (years) (b)	6	5	3
Average annual profit (a)/(b)	£1,500	£1,300	£500

The rate of return is then calculated by dividing the average annual profit by the outlay. For Proposal 1 the calculation is:

$$\text{Rate of return (per cent)} = \frac{\text{Average annual profit}}{\text{Outlay}} \times 100$$

$$= \frac{£1.5 \text{ million}}{£9 \text{ million}} \times 100$$

$$= 16.7 \text{ per cent}$$

Similar calculations for Proposals 2 and 3 produce rates of return of 17.3 and 8.3 per cent respectively. A simple ranking, which in this case is based on the highest rate of return, shows that Proposal 2 is slightly better than Proposal 1.

	Proposal 1	Proposal 2	Proposal 3
Rate of return (%)	16.7	17.3	8.3
Ranking	2	1	3

It was indicated earlier that using the same input data, different rates of return can be produced. How can this happen? Some organizations use average rather than total capital outlay, and, as you will appreciate, anything that reduces the outlay in the calculation will increase the rate of return. The potential ambiguity in rate of return results is sometimes presented as being a theoretical shortcoming. Nevertheless, the technique is popular in some organizations and in many the potential for ambiguity is avoided by manuals of capital expenditure procedure which are used to provide a specific definition of the items included in rate of return calculations.

Discounted cash flow

The two remaining techniques for discussion are reliant upon a principle which involves 'discounting', or 'scaling down', future cash flows. Essentially, where a capital expenditure proposal involves an outlay in the anticipation of future cash inflows, discounted cash flow analysis is appropriate. We will illustrate the two most popular forms of such analysis: net present value and the internal rate of return. However, you may recall that we have already introduced the first of them in Chapter 12.

NET PRESENT VALUE

We will now illustrate the application of the net present value (NPV) technique introduced in Chapter 12, where we showed the calculation of the NPV for a project requiring £9 million to be spent now which would produce net annual cash flows of £3 million per year for six years. In fact, the data correspond with data relating to Proposal 1 to be evaluated and produce an NPV of £4.062 million, calculated as shown in Table 15.2.

Table 15.2   Application of NPV technique

Year	Column 1 Discounted cash flow factor 10%	Column 2 Net annual cash flows £'000	Column 3 (Column 1 × Column 2) Present value £'000
0	1.000	−9,000	−9,000 (A)
1	0.909	3,000	2,727
2	0.826	3,000	2,478
3	0.751	3,000	2,253
4	0.683	3,000	2,049
5	0.621	3,000	1,863
6	0.564	3,000	1,692
Present value of net annual cash flows			13,062 (B)
Net present value (B−A)			4,062

You will recall that the net annual cash flows shown in column 2 of Table 15.2 are multiplied by the 10 per cent discount factors in column 1 to produce the annual present value of the cash flows in column 3. These annual present values are then added together to give the cumulative present value of the net annual cash flows of £13,062,000. The NPV is calculated by deducting the capital outlay from the cumulative present value of the net annual cash flows (i.e. £13,062,000 − £9,000,000) giving £4,062,000.

Table 15.3   Net present values for Proposals 2 and 3

	Proposal 1 £'000	Proposal 2 £'000	Proposal 3 £'000
Cumulative present value of net annual cash flows	13,062	10,790	6,223
Outlay	−9,000	−7,500	−6,000
Net present value	4,062	3,290	223

The same calculation for Proposals 2 and 3 produces the values shown in Table 15.3 which are summarized alongside those for Proposal 1.

The results show that for all three proposals, the net present value is positive, and on economic grounds each should be accepted because they all:

- exceed the required rate of return of 10 per cent
- cover the capital outlay
- produce a sum in excess of the capital outlay.

INTERNAL RATE OF RETURN

Whereas the calculation of the net present value is reliant upon the company's cost of capital as data input, the internal rate of return (IRR) is not. Just what then is the IRR? The IRR is a discounted cash flow method which seeks to find the discount rate at which the present value of net annual cash flows exactly equals the capital outlay. In other words at the IRR the net present value is zero.

The IRR is compared with the cost of capital in order to establish the economic acceptability of a proposal. The principle is that if the IRR exceeds the cost of capital, then the proposal is acceptable according to economic criteria, and vice versa if the IRR from the proposal is lower than the cost of capital.

Without the aid of a computer spreadsheet or a programmable calculator a number of trial and error calculations are usually required to find the IRR, i.e. the discount rate corresponding with a zero NPV. For example, the trial

Table 15.4 Trial and error calculations to find the IRR for Proposal 1

Year	Cash flows £'000	DCF factor 20%	Present value £'000	DCF factor 25%	Present value £'000
0	−9000	1.000	−9000(A)	1.000	−9000(A)
1	3000	0.833	2499	0.800	2400
2	3000	0.694	2082	0.640	1920
3	3000	0.579	1737	0.512	1536
4	3000	0.482	1446	0.410	1230
5	3000	0.402	1206	0.328	984
6	3000	0.335	1005	0.262	786
			9975 (B)		8856(B)
NPV		(B−A)	975		−144

and error calculations necessary to find the IRR for Proposal 1 are given in Table 15.4 (p. 187).

When discounted at 20 per cent the cash flows for Proposal 1 produce a NPV of £975,000. To find the IRR where the NPV will be zero, the present value must be lower and the discount factor must be decreased. This corresponds with the selection of a higher interest rate, i.e. the interest rate and the discount factor are inversely related. The result of increasing the rate to 25 per cent shows that the NPV is negative at −£144,000. The IRR must therefore fall between 20 and 25 per cent and simply by looking at the NPVs corresponding with each of these two rates, we can see that it must be closer to 25 than 20 per cent. In fact, it can be approximated by measuring what proportion of the 5 per cent difference in discount factors corresponds with the point at which the net present value is zero. This is calculated as follows for Proposal 1:

$$\text{IRR} = 20\% + (\frac{£975}{£1,119*} \times 5\%)$$
$$= 20\% + 4.4\%$$
$$= 24.4\%$$

* (£975 −(− £114))

Similar calculations for Proposals 2 and 3 produce the following results which are shown alongside that calculated earlier for Proposal 1:

	Proposal 1	Proposal 2	Proposal 3
IRR %	24.4	27.3	12.1

These results achieved by using the manual calculations for the IRR produce satisfactory results provided that the difference between the two discount factors is not too large (e.g. greater than 5). However, you will often find it much more convenient to use a programmable calculator or computer spreadsheet.

The IRR does have to be used somewhat guardedly. Whereas the NPV decision rule assumes that cash flows resulting during the life cycle of a proposal have an opportunity cost equal to the discount rate used, the IRR decision rule assumes that such resulting cash flows have an opportunity cost equal to the IRR which generated them. The NPV approach also provides an absolute measure of the increase in value of the company if a particular proposal is undertaken, but the IRR provides a percentage figure from which the size of the benefits in terms of wealth creation cannot always be gauged. This can be readily seen with reference to Table 15.5.

Table 15.5 Why the IRR has to be used with caution

	Proposal 1 (£'000)	Proposal 2 (£'000)	Proposal 3a (£'000)
Present value of cash inflows	13,062	10,790	62,230
Capital outlay	−9,000	−7,500	−60,000
NPV	4,062	3,290	7,770
IRR %	24.3	27.3	12.1

In this case Proposal 3 has been replaced by Proposal 3a which is exactly ten times its scale. Although its NPV is ten times larger than for Proposal 3 and substantially larger than for Proposals 1 and 2, it still produces a lower IRR.

Our review of the popular financial tools has demonstrated quite different results from applying them to the financial data relating to the three proposals. The difference in results is summarized in Table 15.6 which shows the relative ranking of each.

Table 15.6 Relative rankings of the three proposals

	Proposal 1	Proposal 2	Proposal 3
Payback	3	2	1
Rate of return	1	2	3
NPV	1	2	3
IRR	2	1	3

While in theory the net present value method is to be preferred, it may not be the most used in practice, as we will demonstrate in the next chapter. In some circumstances it can be likened to 'using a sledgehammer to crack a nut', however, it really does come into its own outside the realms of evaluating capital projects and in particular for valuing strategic options like acquisitions. This application we review in a later chapter.

15.3 Monitoring and controlling capital projects

In addition to the responsibility for evaluating potential benefits to be derived from capital expenditure, another key challenge for the general manager concerns the monitoring and control of committed capital expenditure. The responsibility for capital expenditure does not end with its evaluation – it really is necessary to keep track of committed expenditure to ensure that expected benefits are actually being realized.

The monitoring and control of capital projects is as important as their evaluation, but it is surprising how little attention may be devoted to projects under way. Greatest emphasis is often placed upon 'before the event' control by questioning project proposals and within this process of questioning, senior management can play an important part. While it may be rare for capital projects to be turned down by senior management, studies of practice have shown that senior managers do intervene directly in various ways to influence projects as they evolve. Such intervention includes the following:

– Wearing two hats, i.e. senior managers who wear both a group and a divisional hat, for example, by having at least one board director on each divisional board.
– Questioning assumptions either formally or informally.
– Testing for commitment, i.e. by the senior managers on the group board being tough reviewers.
– Setting limits and deadlines, for example the go-ahead being given conditionally on the project not exceeding the estimate in the proposal. Setting such deadlines and limits by an external body in a position of authority in the hierarchy can be useful and effective as a focusing device. The problem, however, is that those who are distant from the problem may not understand the pressures and realities involved and may interpret the inevitable delays as signs of bad faith, lack of commitment or incompetence.
– Imposing additional project criteria, i.e. by introducing supplementary project specific criteria.
– Influencing the direction of divisions through senior management appointments.

After a capital investment proposal has been approved, the financial control system should provide a means of follow-up. We have seen that what is involved in capital investment is the physical investment in assets which will subsequently result in a stream of profits or earnings.

From a project management point of view, it is a relatively simple task to keep an eye on the progress of the initial investment. We have all heard of cost over-runs in large capital projects, but it is the job of the project manager to keep within the cash limits set at the commencement of the decision. Otherwise, all the good work emanating from the resources subsequently will literally be sunk by the sunk cost overspend up front.

It is usually much more difficult to compare actual profits or earnings with the proposal. This may be for a number of reasons:

1. It is often quite difficult to disaggregate all the cost and revenues of a new product from the costs and revenues of the business as a whole. Most accounting systems are not designed to keep track of revenues and costs by capital investment.
2. Where a project is justified on the basis of cost savings, by definition, the costs which are to be saved will no longer exist! For example, if an old piece of equipment is replaced because of its exceptional repair costs, there is no knowing exactly what those repair costs would have been if the equipment is replaced.
3. The conditions, both internal and external to an enterprise may change so radically, that it is impossible to judge the success or otherwise specifically attributable to a project.

While the logic of after the event monitoring seems unassailable, actual practices vary widely. Some organizations undertake post-project monitoring quite actively with the express intention of gauging areas of benefit for future projects, while others do little or nothing. There are many reasons for this, some of which we have already made brief reference to, i.e. the difficulty of comparing the results of an investment with what was envisaged.

15.4 Post-completion auditing

Capital investment decisions taken now may affect an organization for a long time to come and are not easily reversed. On the other hand, for the well-being of the enterprise, it is usually essential to keep up the investment in long-lived assets to maintain competitive advantage and cost efficiency. Capital investment decisions have to be taken with great care and with the best forecasts that are possible in any particular circumstances. Seldom will actual events work out quite as planned, but, as far as is possible, management must try to see that the project achieves what was planned when it comes 'on stream'.

As capital expenditure projects are 'one off' – the same project is unlikely to be repeated exactly in the same way – there is not much point in reviewing the outcome of an investment, as such. None the less, there is great benefit in looking back over the process of the decision making – the aim to be to improve decision making in the future rather than to apportion blame. The purpose of a post-completion audit should ensure that past errors in the investment decision process are not repeated.

The post-completion audit would be expected to look at the following:

– *Strategic impact of the project* – looking at issues such as: have the strategic benefits of the investment been achieved, surpassed or not gained? What lessons can be learnt about future strategy and the 'fit' of projects with the overall strategy.
– *Appraisal of the project* – looking at how such matters as the following were dealt with: data collection and original presentation; sensitivity analysis; consideration of options.
– *Implementation of the project* – looking at aspects in the initial stages of the project such as: control of the capital cost of the project; appropriateness of the technical specifications of the activity; accuracy of the original operating cost estimates.
– *Final post-audit* – looking at what was expected when a project was implemented and what actually happened.

What actually happens in practice? Organizations' practices vary considerably, even among the very largest of corporations. However, to provide an illustration of what form of post-completion auditing may take, let us consider the practice adopted by one specialist UK materials group. Its procedures for post-implementation state that all projects requiring main board approval will, in principle, be subject to post-audit review, typically two to three years after approval. Projects for review are selected and agreed with top management, but those selected are the responsibility of, and are intended to be carried out by, the management (or their successors) who originally put up the proposal, although they may if they wish get help from elsewhere. All reviews are subject to scrutiny by someone from the centre to ensure that the right questions have been asked and that the answers are reasonably objective.

Reviews are kept short and to the point, usually three or four pages, with the emphasis being typically upon establishing broadly whether the assumptions were right and the project has been carried through in the manner anticipated rather than concentrating on detailed nit-picking. Reviews are seen as an exercise in lesson learning and not in blame apportionment. The format is kept fairly open, but is intended to include:

1. A summary of the key cost, sales and profit figures as they were shown in the original proposal, as they actually turned out and (where relevant) how they are expected to develop for the remainder of the life of the project.

2. A short commentary covering the overall success or failure of the project, any significant variances in the key figures, and any significant variances against the key economic, operational or financial assumptions on which the case was based.
3. Comments on any obvious mistakes made or lessons that can be learnt; in particular, whether the project would have been carried out differently (or indeed at all) with the benefit of hindsight.

15.5 Conclusion

We have reviewed the basic principles relating to the evaluation of capital expenditure proposals. Popular financial tools like the payback period, rate of return, net present value and internal rate of return are instrumental in forming a view about the potential economic viability of a proposal but, as you will see in the next chapter, there are some important practical considerations that have to be borne in mind in applying them.

You should now understand the basic principles behind the management of capital expenditure within a business. Important points to remember include the following:

- Many financial tools exist to help evaluate alternative investment opportunities.
- The most popular financial tools include: payback period; rate of return; and discounted cash flow analysis in the form of the net present value or internal rate of return method.
- The payback period measures how long it will take to recover the capital outlay from cash inflows.
- The rate of return is similar to the profit on capital employed ratio. However, it differs from the other two as it is calculated using profit rather than cash flow.
- Discounted cash flow analysis is reliant upon discounting future cash flows, the aim being to calculate the net present value expressed in money value, or the internal rate of return at which rate the present value of the cash inflow and outflow are equal.
- The monitoring and control of capital projects is as important as their evaluation.
- A major objective of post-auditing is to feed information into the company's decision-making system and, therefore, improve future company performance.

16
Managing capital expenditure: the practice

The only limit to our realization of tomorrow will be our doubts of today
F. D. ROOSEVELT

Capital expenditure decisions typically play a major part in shaping the future of a business. In recognition of this considerable attention is paid, particularly in large organizations, to ensure that they are managed appropriately. Such attention is directed to all aspects of managing capital expenditure, including the evaluatory techniques used, administrative procedures, and methods for ensuring satisfactory monitoring and control processes are in place.

Many studies have been undertaken to find out how organizations manage their capital expenditure decisions. In this chapter we will begin by reviewing the results of these studies. Thereafter, we will consider a number of important practical issues surrounding capital expenditure decisions to ensure the best results possible.

With reference to the studies that have been undertaken, most have been orientated towards the practices of large organizations to which the following general observations apply:

1. The most frequently used technique is the payback period. This is often in conjunction with other techniques, however, it may be used on its own for smaller projects.
2. When a discounted cash flow technique is used it is more likely to be the IRR method rather than the NPV method.
3. Qualitative judgement is regarded as very important.
4. The rate of return is used despite the potential ambiguities in definition we identified in the last chapter.
5. The use of techniques is guided by standard procedures usually in the form of a capital budgeting manual of practice.

6. The formal analysis of risk is used in many organizations in testing the sensitivity of key inputs and underlying economic assumptions.
7. Inflation adjustments are made in appraising projects using rates applicable to specific inputs although the use of a single general rate is also practised.

One important question which emerges from the studies of practice is why is the IRR far more popular than the theoretically preferred NPV technique? This has been attributed to a number of reasons, such as managers' preference for a target expressed as a percentage. It should also not be ignored that the IRR does provide a ranking of projects of different timescales and outflows without the need for a predetermined cut-off rate although, as indicated earlier, this ranking may be inferior to that provided by NPV calculations.

Associated with there being no need for a predetermined cut-off rate is the political appeal of the IRR. One recognized feature of the appraisal process is the potential for playing the system by ensuring that projects which have acquired the personal commitment of management will always meet the prescribed hurdle. If the hurdle is not formally communicated then it is arguable that this problem can be removed. Certainly our observations of practice have found confirmation of this view in some organizations. In such cases, the IRR, usually in conjunction with other techniques, is prescribed for use below corporate level. At corporate level, however, the desired hurdle is known and the NPV technique plays a more significant role.

In the absence of technological developments and computer software we might speculate about whether the popularity of the IRR would be as significant. Certainly the development of relatively easy to use computer software in the form of spreadsheets and tailor-made packages has been found to be associated with the use of more sophisticated appraisal methods, like the IRR and the assessment of risk.

With regard to the evaluatory techniques used and the procedures adopted, it is important not to underestimate the significant part often played in practice by the capital budgeting manual. As well as detailing procedures to be followed in relation to evaluating capital expenditure, the manuals provided by some organizations provide broader guidance on issues such as project monitoring and control.

The purpose of all procedures relating to the capital budget is to ensure that the best use is made of scarce financial resources by way of evaluatory screening and also to ensure that top management time is used most effectively. Ultimately, the most senior management is responsible for the long-term future of the business resulting from capital expenditure. Clearly it should not be burdened with dealing with all such projects personally. Some form of delegated responsibility is, therefore, necessary. Often this delegation will be via the size of investment in terms of the sum of money required or the type of investment. In this way the majority of real decisions are effectively taken by management below board level in a way typically prescribed by formal systems.

The formal systems developed in many companies do have to be viewed in context. While the development of formal capital expenditure procedures manuals is a notable recent feature, some studies of practice have shown them often to be hard to locate, and such observations have caused some researchers to describe formal systems as instruments of apparent ritualism. However, it is important not to ignore the benefits associated with such systems in terms of forcing those involved to be more explicit about their key assumptions, both to themselves and in justifying them to others.

Within the overall process there is a key role to be played by the general manager, both at board level and below. The span of business knowledge typically possessed by such managers often plays a significant part in decisions about capital expenditure with major funding and strategic implications. However, the amount of time available to devote to such decisions does typically represent a major constraint, and time spent will typically vary with seniority. One recent study demonstrated that the group deputy chairman reckoned a significant project with noteworthy strategic ramifications took at least a whole day of his time. By comparison, the divisional board member in charge of the proposal estimated that he spent the equivalent of eight months on it prior to approval and his project team members apparently spent a further two years.

One prerequisite for managing capital expenditure decisions effectively and efficiently is that the amount of general management time devoted to a project will decrease with seniority. This and the volume of paperwork generated are key indicators of the operation of the system. Just as with the amount of general management time devoted, the volume of paperwork should also decrease as projects move upwards through the management hierarchy. For example, in one large divisionalized company we studied recently more than 150 documents could be identified with a major project. In all this represented some 1750 pages about the project which were reduced to a 20-page document and 30 pages of appendices for group finance and a three-page summary for main board consideration.

In our experience these two facets of the system provide a good initial indication of its likely success. Those organizations where the amount of general management time devoted to a project does not decrease with seniority and where the volume of paperwork grows as a project moves upwards through the management hierarchy are likely to face some very significant difficulties in managing capital expenditure.

16.1 The importance of good quality data

In any capital expenditure decision great care must be taken to ensure that the quality of input data is as good as possible. There are two important issues concerning such data:

- How are initial estimates to be generated as accurately as possible?
- How can the importance of the various components within the estimates be judged?

With regard to the first of these, forecasting methods can be used which are reliant upon one or more of the following – subjective managerial judgement, sensitivity analysis, consensus of expert opinion, and computer simulations. The evidence available suggests that most large companies use two or more of these and, where larger capital expenditures are involved, more quantitatively orientated methods reliant upon probability theory may well be used.

Further, and related to the second issue, the initial estimates should be broken down as far as possible. For example, in discussing the basic principles we used information only about annual cash flows from a project. This alone would be unsatisfactory for larger and, therefore, riskier projects which would require that such information should be broken down into key factors, the importance of which can then be investigated via the use of computer spreadsheet packages.

Just exactly what are the factors that should be used in cash flow estimation? It is difficult to be entirely prescriptive because some factors will

Table 16.1 Factors in cash flow estimation

Financial factors	Marketing factors	Operating factors
Inflation	Sales forecast	Operating costs
Risk	Product life	Material and
Taxation	Discount policy	supply cost
Residual value	Promotional costs	Start-up costs
Working capital	Selling costs	Shut-down costs
	Market test costs	Maintenance costs
	Competitive	Repair cost
	advantages and	Capacity
	disadvantages	utilization
	Transportation costs	

vary from project to project but a useful way of considering them is within the following three groupings:

− Financial factors
− Marketing factors
− Operating factors.

Within these headings one might expect to find individual factors as shown in Table 16.1 (p. 197). Once these factors have been identified they should be incorporated within the cash flow analysis in as much detail as possible. The following extract from the EuroDisney offer for sale provides a good example of this.

Operating expenses

The principal operating expense assumptions are based on the following estimates:

* labour costs (including related taxes) have been estimated on the basis of experience at Disney parks, adjusted to the conditions of the French labour market. They include a premium on operating labour of approximately 10 per cent over the market average, with the intention of attracting high quality personnel. On this basis, it has been assumed that gross operating labour costs will be FF 424 million for the MAGIC KINGDOM and FF 232 million for the second theme park (measured in 1988 French Francs) in the respective opening years of these parks, and that they will increase at the rate of inflation, taking into account increased employment associated with higher attendance levels; and

* cost of sales have been estimated on the basis of experience at Disney parks, adjusted to reflect factors specific to EURO DISNEYLAND. The assumptions are:

	Cost of sales (per cent. of revenue)
MAGIC KINGDOM	
Merchandise	40–43
Food and beverage	31
Second theme park	
Merchandise	41.5
Food and beverage	31

16.2 Handling inflation

As we have stressed, the evaluation of any investment opportunity requires good financial judgement to be exercised about a future which is uncertain. If prices are expected to change because of inflation, for example, then this must be incorporated within any appraisal. Many managers make the mistake of believing that by adopting discounted cash flow techniques, inflation has automatically been incorporated into the financial appraisal. Nothing could be further from the truth.

As we demonstrated in Chapter 2, discounting is related to the principle of compounding used in compound interest calculations. Even in a world with no inflation some compound interest would be present in so far as the providers of finance would require some compensation for forgoing their wealth for a period of time. This being so the principle of discounting would be equally applicable. The omission of inflation from an evaluation can completely change the economic viability of a proposal as we will illustrate with reference to the net present value calculation for Proposal 1 from the last chapter, reproduced here as Table 16.2.

Table 16.2   NPV of Proposal 1 from Chapter 15

Year	Column 1 Discount factor 10%	Column 2 Net Annual cash flows £'000	Column 3 (Column 1 × Column 2) Present value £'000
0	1.000	−9,000	−9,000 (A)
1	0.909	3,000	2,727
2	0.826	3,000	2,478
3	0.751	3,000	2,253
4	0.683	3,000	2,049
5	0.621	3,000	1,863
6	0.564	3,000	1,692
Present value of net annual cash flows			13,062 (B)
NPV (B−A)			4,062

Using a 10 per cent discount factor and, in the absence of inflation, we showed the NPV to be £4.062 million. Assume now that upon investigation we discover that the cash flow forecast for the six years shows that cash flows are expressed in real terms, but that the 10 per cent discount factor is a nominal (or money) rate in which an allowance for inflation has already been included.

The NPV of £4.062 million really needs to be adjusted for the effect of inflation because like cash flows it has not been compared with a like discount rate. In other words, a rate adjusted for inflation has been incorrectly applied to pure or real cash flows. Theory requires that either inflated cash flows should be discounted at a rate which incorporates an adjustment for inflation, or uninflated cash flows should be discounted at a rate which does not incorporate an adjustment for inflation.

What effect might this have? For example, let us consider that upon examining the £3 million annual net cash flow estimate for Proposal 1 it is found that today this is comprised of £6 million of cash cost outflows and £9 million of cash revenue inflows. However, future inflation will impact upon today's cash flows and, because of a strongly organized labour market, it is estimated that cost inflation will be 12 per cent per annum while that affecting revenues will be 5 per cent. The effect of such inflation and the impact upon the cash flows is given in Table 16.3.

Table 16.3   Inflationary effects on cash flow

Year	Revenues inflated at 5% £'000	Costs inflated at 12% £'000	Annual net cash flows £'000
1	9,450	6,720	2,730
2	9,923	7,526	2,397
3	10,419	8,430	1,989
4	10,940	9,441	1,499
5	11,487	10,574	913
6	12,061	11,843	218

The previously constant £3 million stream of annual cash flows is eroded progressively over the six-year period when the differential effects of revenue and cost inflation are taken into consideration. The true impact of such inflation upon the economic desirability of the project can be seen in the revised NPV calculation (Table 16.4). Proposal 1, which was previously acceptable according to economic criteria, is now unacceptable because it will produce a negative net present value of £1.33 million.

There is one other point about inflation which we should bear in mind and which may be of relevance to our analysis. This is that individual cash flow elements in the appraisal, such as the sales revenue, labour costs, material costs and the like, may not all be subject to the same degree of inflation or price variation. In such circumstances, where there are different rates of inflation applicable to each, then an adjustment should be made to each.

To summarize, inflation has to be dealt with in its own right and must

Table 16.4 The impact of inflation on NPV

Year	Column 1 Annual net cash flows (£'000)	Column 2 Discount factor (10%)	Column 3 Present value (£'000)	Column 4 Cumulative present value (£'000)
0	9,000	1.000	−9,000	−9,000
1	2,730	0.909	2,482	−6,518
2	2,397	0.826	1,980	−4,538
3	1,989	0.751	1,494	−3,044
4	1,499	0.683	1,024	−2,020
5	913	0.621	567	−1,453
6	218	0.564	123	−1,330

never be ignored. The adjustments which have been discussed are appropriate irrespective of the techniques used in the financial evaluation. Depending upon the evaluatory technique, cash flows or profit flows must be adjusted for inflation and, as illustrated, such an adjustment can have a significant impact upon the financial outcome.

16.3 Managing risk

Any investment opportunity with long-term implications must, by definition, be subject to some risk or uncertainty. Somehow this risk must be captured in any economic valuation and it should come as no surprise to find that there is more than one way of achieving this. Here, we will consider the most popular approach we have encountered which is known as sensitivity analysis.

With this approach the assumptions surrounding a project can be fed into a computer to produce a base case, about which changes in assumptions can easily be made to gauge the effect upon the economic viability of a project.

To understand the principles involved in using this approach consider the following data taken from a proposed investment opportunity which is to be evaluated using the IRR method:

1. Capital costs
   (a) Initial expenditure £15 million
   (b) Life 10 years
   (c) Scrap value £1 million.
2. Annual revenues

(a) Sales volume 600,000 units } £18 million
(b) Selling price £300 per unit } per annum
3. Annual costs
   (a) Labour £50 per unit
   (b) Materials £150 per unit } £14.5 million
   (c) Specific fixed £2.5 million } per annum
      per annum

First, the data provided are used to find the base case IRR of 19.7 per cent. This is the percentage that equates the net annual cash flow of £3.5 million (£18 million − £14.5 million) over 10 years and the scrap value of £1 million at the end of 10 years with the initial expenditure of £15 million. Then, without the need to use any more data each of the input variables, the scrap value, the sales volume, price, labour cost, materials cost and the fixed cost can be changed to determine the impact upon the base case IRR. This is illustrated in the following tables where each of the input variables has been varied adversely by 10 per cent and the IRR has been recalculated:

	Original estimate	Varied adversely by 10%
Capital cost	£15 million	£16.5 million
Life	10	9
Scrap value	£1 million	£900,000
Sales volume	600,000	540,000
Selling price	£300	£270
Labour cost	£50	£55
Materials	£150	£165
Fixed cost	£2.5 million	£2.75 million

	IRR
Selling price	3.3%
Materials cost	12.0%
Sales volume	14.6%
Capital cost	17.0%
Labour cost	17.2%
Fixed cost	17.6%
Life	18.6%
Scrap value	19.7%

As a result of doing nothing other than amending the original data, one really sensitive variable – the selling price – has been identified. If the selling price were not £300 but £270, but all other data remained unchanged, then the project would generate an IRR of only 3.3 per cent. In the case of all other input variables, the internal rate of return is over 11 per cent.

If the company's required rate of return is 10 per cent then a £30 fall in selling price could be a disaster. But, with knowledge of this potential problem area, an investigation could be undertaken by the marketing department to establish whether difficulties in achieving a selling price of £300 are really likely. If so, then despite the acceptable base case IRR, the project really may not be acceptable on economic grounds. This, of course, has assumed there is no sales volume/selling price relationship. A reduction in price to £270 might well be associated with a compensatory increase in sales volume. Such analysis permits sensitive variables to be identified without the evaluator having to input any additional data. In practice, the analysis would be extended much further than in the example so as to explore changes in a number of variables and any interrelationships between variables.

How sensitivity analysis is actually used in practice can be seen with reference to the EuroDisney offer for sale we discussed earlier. In the section on 'Returns to Investors and Sensitivity Analysis', the effect upon internal return over period to 2017 assuming an issue price of FF72 per share was shown as:

		per cent
Company's projections		13.3
(i)	Reduced attendance assuming 10 million visits in the first year of operations of the MAGIC KINGDOM	12.7
(ii)	Increased attendance assuming 12 million visits in the first year of operations of the MAGIC KINGDOM	13.8
(iii)	Reduced per capita spending assuming per capita spending at both theme parks is lower by 10 per cent	12.3
(iv)	Increased per capita spending assuming per capita spending at both theme parks is higher by 10 per cent	14.1
(v)	Delay assuming a six-month delay in the opening of the MAGIC KINGDOM	12.8
(vi)	Increased construction costs assuming costs of construction of Phase 1A are higher by 10 per cent	13.2
(vii)	Reduced resort and property development income	

	assuming that income from all resort and property development is lower by 10 per cent	13.0
(viii)	Increased resort and property development income assuming that income from all resort and property development is higher by 10 per cent	13.5
(ix)	Higher inflation assuming 7 per cent inflation after 1992 and unchanged real interest rates	15.3
(x)	Lower inflation assuming 3 per cent inflation after 1992 and unchanged real interest rates	11.2
(xi)	Higher real interest assuming real interest rates 1 percentage point higher after 1992	13.2
(xii)	Lower real interest assuming real interest rates 1 percentage point lower after 1992	13.3
(xiii)	Higher residual value assuming a P/E ratio of 14.5 in 2017	13.4
(xiv)	Lower residual value assuming a P/E ratio of 10.5 in 2017	13.1

16.4 Dealing with taxation

One other area which will impact upon a cash or profit stream to be used in evaluating capital expenditure concerns taxation. The specifics of taxation are complex and well beyond the scope of this book, however, the general principle to follow is similar to that discussed with regard to inflation. Just as in discounting cash flows to calculate a project's net present value, inflated cash flows must be discounted using an interest rate which contains an allowance for inflation, so too, the cash flows must be discounted either before or after tax depending upon whether the required discount rate is a before- or after-tax rate.

The detail of taxation adjustments is not the concern of the general manager, but what is important to understand is the principle of comparing 'like' cash flows with a 'like' discount rate. If these two are not expressed in the same terms such that taxation adjustments have to be made, it is time to involve a taxation specialist!

16.5 The life span of the project and its residual value

One element that should never be overlooked is the residual value of a capital project. Often it may be insignificant, but on occasions it may be an important contributor to the NPV or IRR of a project. Whether this is so can often be established using sensitivity analysis as illustrated earlier.

16.6 What about working capital?

In addition to an immediate capital outlay capital projects may also require substantial working capital. This working capital support will typically be required over the project life, a substantial amount of it being released at the end of a project's life. However, at this time, its value will probably be markedly different because of the impact of the time value of money. For example, a capital project associated with an immediate working capital outlay of £1 million will have a present value of £1 million × 1.000 at the outset, but at the end of a five-year life at a cost of capital of 10 per cent its present value will be £621,000 (£1 million × 0.621).

16.7 What about competitors' reactions?

The significance of competitors' reactions has been demonstrated with the development of specific expert systems. What they show is that in evaluating investment opportunities it is all too easy to consider only the detailed numerical input about sales and cost of sales over an estimated lifetime for internal consistency. Often no attempt may be made at modelling the potential effect upon the cash flows as a result of competitors' reactions.

Why is the analysis of competitors' reactions so important? The successful introduction of a new product will attract competing products. Competition will tend to force prices to levels at which further investment may not be economically worth while. The first entrants with new products have a head start on the competition and may have some longer-term competitive advantage, for example, in terms of product protection via trade marks. Nevertheless, cash flow projections undertaken should recognize market developments and likely competitors' reactions. How, you might be thinking, can such competitor reaction be measured? A useful starting point is by harnessing internal managerial knowledge and experience.

16.8 Conclusion

There are some important practical issues that have to be taken into consideration in evaluating capital expenditure proposals. The quality of available data, inflation, risks, taxation, competitors' reactions and so on, all have to be managed explicitly and a failure to pay them due consideration can have disastrous effects. In this chapter we have tried to highlight these factors and to demonstrate how the importance of the various evaluatory techniques may be assessed, and how these may be applied in practice. Useful points to remember include the following:

— The IRR tends to be more popular than the NPV technique.
— The development of computer software in the form of spreadsheet and tailor-made packages has been found to be associated with the use of more sophisticated appraisal methods like the internal rate of return and assessment of risk.
— The management of capital expenditure may well be guided by manuals of practice.
— The omission of inflation or taxation from an evaluation can completely change the economic viability of a proposal and both should be accounted for.
— The most popular way of accounting for risk in any economic valuation is by sensitivity analysis.
— Important issues such as working capital requirements, residual value and the potential reaction of competitors should never be overlooked.

17
Assessing and managing corporate financial risk

Unless you enter the tiger's den you cannot take the cubs
JAPANESE PROVERB

One major requirement of general management is to be able to guide the organization into an uncertain future as successfully as possible. The uncertainty created by the unknown means that a good general manager will try to assess and manage all facets of the business that might impede corporate progress and, at worst, corporate survival.

We only need to look at UK experiences during the early 1990s to see why good risk management is vital in order to prevent unacceptable changes in income and cash flow. As we have seen, such changes can all too easily jeopardize corporate survival, for example, because of the action of creditors who, perceiving a sinking ship, seek all or part of what they are owed by pressing for corporate liquidation.

Can a business do anything to protect itself from unnecessary risk? In our minds the answer to this question is yes. To this end in this chapter we will consider:

– What are the primary causes of corporate financial risk?
– What techniques can be used to assess whether the business is currently at risk?
– What methods can be used to understand and manage the riskiness of a business?

In addition to being able to assess and manage risk within his or her own business, the general manager will often be responsible for ensuring that any exposure to risk is minimized in dealing with other businesses. As we will illustrate there are some financial tools that can be used to identify risk and, therefore, help to minimise exposure to it.

17.1 Sources of corporate risk

In order to understand the sources of corporate risk it is perhaps simplest to refer back to the basic principles involved in deriving income and cash flow. Income, or profit, we know is calculated from revenues *less* expenditure, and cash flow is calculated from receipts *less* payments. For reasons we have discussed in earlier chapters, revenues and receipts may differ substantially over the same time period as may expenditure and payments, such that at two extremes a business may be unprofitable but be generating sound cash flows, or it may be profitable but consuming more cash than it generates.

Risk, therefore, arises in those circumstances when confidence in the ability of the business to generate a satisfactory return and/or maintain its solvency may be called into question because of sudden and/or unexpected:

- decreases in revenues and/or receipts; and/or
- increases in expenditure and/or payments.

What can cause any of these to happen? There are many ways in which risk can be classified depending upon the perspective being considered. For our purposes here, we will consider the following possible sources of risk:

- Business risk
- Operating risk
- Financial risk
- Catastrophe risk
- Political risk.

It is worth noting that these five are not mutually exclusive. There may often be considerable overlap between them, but identifying them individually permits some important financial issues to be identified.

Business risk

Business risk is a major problem that all general managers have to face. It can stem from many sources, e.g.

- Foreign competition
- Price competition
- Substitute products
- Technological obsolescence
- Fluctuations and changes in the national economy.

We can find numerous examples of all of these sources of risk in real life. In the case of the first two, the car market and the role played by Japanese manufacturers serve as a good illustration. The production of cheaper and more reliable models has had a major impact upon the market share of European and US manufacturers, and hence on their income and cash flow.

In the case of the third source, substitute products, British Plaster Board used to occupy a dominant position as regards the supply of plasterboard in the United Kingdom. However, it was affected significantly by two key events. First, the investment by Redland PLC in 1987 of some £50 million in a plasterboard plant in Southwest England using imported Spanish gypsum. Second, also in 1987, the development of artificial gypsum as a by-product of smokestack cleaners in coal burning power plants produced a substitute for natural sources.

A good example of technological obsolescence can be seen with reference to telecommunications and the replacement of analog by digital technology. Income and cash flow have been adversely affected for the providers of telecommunications services who have had to invest in order to be competitive.

Last, but by no means least, fluctuations and changes in the national economy have a far reaching effect upon income and cash flow, as the UK recession of the early 1990s serves to illustrate only too well. Falling consumer demand combined with rising interest rates squeezed income and cash flow from both sides with catastrophic results for many businesses, both large and small.

Of course, these business risks are those that strategic planners attempt to identify and control but, unfortunately, not everything can be anticipated and, therefore, planned for. For example, how easy was it for strategic planners in British Plaster Board to anticipate the development of artificial gypsum? Very often sudden surprises occur in business and when such events happen action may need to be taken immediately to minimize the damage.

It is our belief that financial tools we will discuss can help in assessing some risky situations, though clearly not unforeseen surprises. It is better if risk can be managed by attempting to anticipate its effects. As we will illustrate, these financial tools, some of which we have reviewed already, can be used to measure, and therefore manage, some aspects of corporate risk.

Operating risk

This arises from the substitution of costs that vary with the level of activity by those that do not. Consider, for example, the introduction of a new manufacturing system to replace manual labour. A heavy fixed cost is incurred that now has to be covered irrespective of the level of activity. In buoyant business conditions this may be financially beneficial, but in times of recession it may have a harmful effect upon cash flow and income.

Financial risk

This is similar to operating risk in so far as it relates to the use of a method of financing activities that is reliant upon an interest charge which must be met in good times and in bad. This you will recall we discussed in Chapter 9 with reference to gearing. Gearing is a 'two-edged sword', in so far as such financing may be beneficial during boom times when, given a fixed charge, all excess revenue is turned to income, but very harmful during recessionary periods when the fixed charge has to be met irrespective of business performance. In fact, as we have seen in the United Kingdom during the 1990s, a major problem of such financial risk is that it often goes hand in hand with business risk, thereby exacerbating the detrimental effects upon cash flow and income.

Catastrophe risk

This can, in principle, be managed relatively straightforwardly. The chances of a catastrophe such as a fire or an earthquake occurring can be managed by insuring against it. Whereas for many potential catastrophes the likely source of a problem can be identified, for some it may be difficult to recognize that a risk exists.

Political risk

This is one source of risk that it is vital to be able to recognize and be able to deal with. Government and political pressures can have a fundamental impact upon business in numerous ways. One obvious influence on future performance can arise from taxation, an issue about which there are very different political perspectives.

17.2 Recognizing a risky business

It is important to be able to identify the potential risk within any business that you will be supplying with substantial amounts of goods and/or services on credit. The value of such identification has been made all too clear in the United Kingdom during the recession of the late 1980s and early 1990s when numerous businesses were placed at risk, some even being forced into liquidation because of the failure of their customers.

To assist you, there are a number of approaches that can be used which include:

– Analysis of key ratios and business cash flow

- *Z* scoring
- Qualitative analysis
- Beta scores
- Credit rating.

Key ratios

Most banks make use of ratio analysis and business cash flow analysis to measure business risk. Which ratios they will emphasize typically depends upon the type of lending required. For example, for seasonal lending to meet peak needs of a short-term duration, cash flow and solvency indicators are more important than earnings. By contrast, in any long-term lending situation earnings as well as cash flow measures are likely to be critical.

In earlier chapters we have discussed many ratios that can be used to form a view about a business, these include the following:

- Current ratio
- Liquid ratio
- Stock days
- Debtor days
- Creditor days
- Interest cover
- Gearing ratio
- Profit (or return) on capital employed
- Profit (or return) on shareholders' funds.

The only way such ratios can be used effectively is by comparing them with other companies within the industry and also by interrogating them. As we have demonstrated in Chapter 10, comparisons with other companies can be potentially difficult because the policies used in preparing published accounts even within the same sector may differ. This problem can be overcome to some extent by using the services of organizations like Dunn and Bradstreet, Datastream and Extel which do provide financial information, including ratios.

In the case of business cash flow analysis there are many different measures that can be used. Certainly in our experience, many lenders use at least depreciation adjusted profits (profit plus depreciation), although we will demonstrate in the next chapter how this may be usefully refined to give a more effective evaluation.

To our minds a very useful way of understanding business risks via ratio and cash flow analysis can be achieved using spreadsheets like Lotus 1-2-3 or SuperCalc to build up a picture from historical data. By building a model based upon profit and loss account and balance sheet data, business cash flow and key ratios can be challenged by questioning assumptions about future performance. Such challenging, referred to earlier as 'sensitivity analysis', is used by many banks as part of their tool kit in assessing the lending risks associated with a potential borrower.

Z scoring

In addition to ratio analysis, or as an alternative, you might contemplate using Z scoring. This is an approach which seeks to find an index of riskiness and, in particular, is concerned with identifying potential business failures.

In a nutshell, depending upon whose model is used, the principle of Z scoring is that a number of ratios are calculated, often with reference to the published accounts. These ratios are then weighted and summed to yield a Z score. A Z score above a certain level is indicative of a business that should not fail, whereas below a certain level there is good likelihood of failure.

The most widely known Z score model is that which was developed by Professor Altman and published in 1968. His model based upon an analysis of US companies determined five ratios that could be used to measure corporate failure together with a weighting for each ratio to show those companies that had failed, as distinct from those that had not.

In terms of the application of Altman's model, the sum of the products of the five ratios and associated weights can be used to produce a Z score, where the Z score is calculated as follows:

$$Z = (1.2 \times X_1) + (1.4 \times X_2) + (3.3 \times X_3) + (0.6 \times X_4) + (1.0 \times X_5)$$

where Z is the sum of the products of the ratios and the weights, and the individual ratios are defined as:

X_1 = working capital/total assets
X_2 = retained earnings/total assets
X_3 = profit before interest and tax/total assets
X_4 = market value of equity/book value of total debt
X_5 = sales/total assets.

A Z score of 2.675 was established by Altman as a cut-off point, such that when the score is less than 2.675 a business is considered to be likely to fail, by virtue of having similar financial characteristics to past business failures. However, a band or range of scores between 1.81 and 2.99 was recognized and termed the 'zone of ignorance'. It represented the area where a misclassification could occur, i.e. a business could in error be classified as a failure, or vice versa.

This approach was developed by many researchers subsequent to Altman's original work, including some in the United Kingdom. It has very simplistic practitioner appeal because it implies that all that is necessary is to calculate a number of ratios, multiply them by the relevant weightings and then add the result to obtain a prediction of corporate failure. However, we are sceptical about Z scoring, primarily because we have found circumstances where it has been used without being properly understood.

Qualitative analysis

In contrast to the statistically determined Z scoring method, a number of methods involving more qualitative analysis have been proposed. A good example of qualitative analysis is the approach developed by John Argenti.

Underpinning Argenti's approach is the observation that, as a general rule, most companies fail for broadly similar reasons, and in a broadly similar manner. The failure sequence appears to take many years, typically five or more, to run its course and falls into three essential stages:

1. The occurrence of specific defects in a company's management and business practices in particular at the very top.
2. Subsequently, possibly years later, top management makes a major mistake because of the specific defects.
3. Ultimately, signs and symptoms of failure begin to appear, in the form of both financial and non-financial matters.

Defects identified by Argenti relate to the following:

1. Management
2. Accountancy systems
3. Failure to respond to change.

Management defects take many forms, but one major defect identified by Argenti is an autocratic chief executive, particularly where he or she is also the chairman. Such an individual is a problem because he or she is 'the company' and will tend to have managerial advisers whose advice he or she has no intention of taking.

What are other management defects? The board may consist of passive, non-contributing directors, arguably a desirable situation for an autocratic leader, but not for the company. Second, the directors may lack all-round business skills. Third, there may be lack of strong financial direction, often indicated by poor working capital management. For example, there may be no proper cash flow forecasting, which will present difficulties in terms of managing future borrowing requirements.

Companies that fail are often found to have poor or non-existent accounting systems, a defect which can be related to poor financial direction. In addition, many companies that fail are those which have either not noticed a change in their business environment or have not responded to it. Examples of defects provided by Argenti are an old-fashioned product, an old-fashioned factory, out-of-date marketing, strikes attributable to outmoded attitudes to employees, an ageing board of directors, and no development of information management within the business like the use of up-to-date technology.

Three types of mistake have been identified by Argenti as being responsible for failure:

1. Too high a level of gearing.
2. Overtrading – expanding faster than the ability to generate funds.
3. The big project that dominates the business and is so large as to put it at risk, e.g. Laker's Sky Train.

What are the symptoms of a company moving towards failure? The first symptoms are financial signs, such as those detectable using ratio analysis which we have already discussed. Second, the prospect of failure has been known to encourage the accounting system to be used very creatively, particularly where financial information is required to be reported externally to outside parties. Third, a company heading for failure may also exhibit numerous non-financial signs of distress as well as financial ones, examples of which are: management salaries are frozen; capital expenditure decisions are delayed; product quality or service deteriorates; market share falls; staff turnover rises; morale deteriorates; rumours abound; the dividend is not cut when there would seem to be sound reason for so doing.

At the very end of the process what are referred to as 'terminal signs' appear, such that when failure is imminent, all of the financial and non-financial signs become so severe that even the most casual observer can see them.

We only have to reflect upon some of the big failures of the 1980s and 1990s and the commentary that has been associated with them to realize that such a framework has more than just a grain of truth!

Beta scores

Our focus so far has been upon recognizing business risk from the perspective of a lender or supplier, but that is not the only aspect of risk that a general manager particularly in a public limited company has to understand. As well as having responsibility for managing the market for goods and services within the business, the most senior general managers have to manage within a market for share ownership which we referred to in Chapter 9 and is known as the 'market for corporate control'. Actions taken in the past concerning the scope of business activity and how it has been financed will typically be reflected in movements in the share price relative to the rest of the market as measured for example by the FT-A All-Share Index.

The riskiness implied by the business activities and the way in which they are financed can in fact be measured. This measure, known as a beta, is used by fund managers as one means of determining the make-up of their portfolios. It can also be used in measuring the cost of capital, the yardstick for determining major investments, as you will see in a later chapter.

Just how is this beta determined? Few business opportunities have the same degree of risk attached to them and it should not come as any surprise that the providers of finance will expect to be compensated for greater risk by demanding a greater return. The real challenge is to get a handle upon such risk. This can be achieved by using the Capital Asset Pricing Model (CAPM), a statistical model developed in the mid-1960s, which is based upon the observation that some shares are more volatile than others. This means that when stock markets rise these shares rise faster and higher than the markets, and when stock markets fall they fall faster and further.

It is generally agreed that markets use information efficiently such that share prices are adjusted quickly and continue to reflect new information about a company's risks and prospects. Thus, the fact that some shares are riskier than the average should reflect something about the riskiness of their underlying business. Armed with this it has been shown that it is possible to measure the sensitivity of a share's price to market movements by calculating their beta. The beta can be measured in a number of ways, but the most common method of estimating it is by using standard regression techniques based upon historical share price movements. The historical estimation period generally accepted is five years, using monthly returns. This is the method used by a major beta provider in the United Kingdom, the London Business School's Risk Measurement Service.

The market as a whole has a beta of one. Any share moving in line with the market would also have a beta of one – a share twice as volatile as the market (that is when the market climbs 10 per cent the share climbs 20 per cent) would have a beta of two; one that is half as volatile would have a beta of one-half.

Risk measured by the beta is that part of the total risk a business faces which is not diversifiable because it originates from macro-economic forces, is market related and affects all businesses in some form. There are in fact two components of such risk: the activity risk associated with business activities and the financial risk associated with the financial structure of the business. Other than that arising from macro-economic forces, there is a second source of risk to a business which can be related to the business specifically and which is, therefore, manageable by company-specific actions. For example, the specific risk associated with a credit card company having only one major computer installation for managing its client base.

The significance of the beta measurement is that it can be used effectively to view a business portfolio from a strategic perspective and can be invaluable in directing the business from a financial perspective. As we saw in the last two chapters, the present value of a future course of action is dependent upon the cash flows it will yield and the opportunity cost associated with it, as expressed in the cost of capital. The higher the cost of capital and hence the discount rate, the lower will be the resulting present value. What causes a higher discount rate? The answer is a higher degree of risk, this being captured to a large extent in the beta.

There is a risk–return relationship which beta analysis helps us to understand. As we will demonstrate in the following chapters, using such analysis the various component businesses that make up the whole can be judged relative to one another – making use of a particular approach that can be thought of as an extension to net present value analysis.

Credit rating

A credit rating is an opinion on the risk of default of a fixed income security and so credit ratings are a measure of the quality of a company's (or sometimes a country's) debt. They are meant to be predictive and there are three main parties that have a specific interest in them:

- Borrowers, i.e. debt issuers who have their debt rated to help providers of funds to judge them.
- Investors who are interested in the ability of debtors to meet their obligations.
- Regulatory authorities.

There are different rating agencies, but two particularly well known are the US firms, Moody's and Standard and Poors. They have different rating systems for different categories of debt, but perhaps they are best known for their long-term investment grades which include:

- AAA (known as 'Triple A') which is the highest degree of safety with overwhelming repayment capacity.

- AA, associated with a very high degree of safety and a very strong capacity for repayment.
- A, a strong degree of safety and capacity for repayment.
- BBB, a satisfactory degree of safety and capacity for repayment.

In between each of these there are intermediate gradings and there are also grades below BBB, these normally being attached to risky debt instruments, like 'junk' bonds (in the USA) which are high yield but high risk bonds used for highly geared deals such as buyouts, so that bondholders often bear as much risk as the shareholders. Such bonds have a significant probability of going into default, hence their low rating.

Credit ratings are based on both qualitative and quantitative factors, some of which are as follows:

- Gearing ratio
- Interest cover
- Current ratio
- Security availability
- Stability of sales and earnings
- Political risk from overseas operations
- Accounting policies
- Environmental exposure.

Credit ratings are important to companies because they are indicators of default risk and will have a direct impact upon the rate of interest at which a company can borrow. Second, most bonds are purchased by institutional investors which may well be restricted by bond gradings. For example, they may be prohibited from holding bonds below BBB, making it very difficult for any firm with such a rating to sell its bonds.

17.3 Exposure to overseas operations

One very real risk that has to be faced and managed is that concerning transactions involving foreign currencies. This is referred to as transaction exposure and is a firm's vulnerability to loss, or its chance of gain, when an outstanding obligation incurred in a foreign currency is paid off. The most common unsettled obligations are foreign exchange to be paid for imports or to be received for exports. Other unsettled obligations arise from the purchase of services on credit and because of borrowing or lending denominated in foreign currencies. A firm may also have a transaction gain or loss because of obligations incurred under outstanding forward foreign exchange contracts.

How does transaction exposure arise? Consider the following example of a UK aircraft manufacturer which sells an aircraft to a French airline. The sales price for the aircraft is £40 million; and, since the current exchange rate is FF7/£, the aircraft is sold for FF280 million. Payment is to be made in FF six months after the date of sale.

If, on payment date, the exchange rate is FF8/£, the French airline will remit FF280, which the UK company will exchange for £35 million. Because the UK company had booked an account receivable of £40 million and only received £35 million, it experiences a transaction loss of £5 million. This loss is a realized loss for both accounting and tax purposes, meaning that the UK company is out of pocket by £5 million, which it had already booked as profit at the time of sale and expected to receive. The £5 million loss will reduce the UK company's profit for the year but will also reduce its tax.

Proceeds from the sale might well have ended up being some other amount. Had the exchange rate been FF6.8/£ on the payment date, the UK company would have received £41,176,470, which is more than the £40 million booked as an account receivable. If the exchange rate had been FF9/£, the UK company would have received only £31,111,111. In other words, the actual sterling proceeds are at risk and could be the same as, greater than, or less than the expected sterling amount.

Avoiding exposure

The exchange risk could have been avoided by insisting that payment for the aircraft be in pounds sterling. This does not eliminate the risk but simply transfers the risk from the seller to the buyer. If the French airline was obligated to pay £40 million, the cost in francs would be FF320 million if the exchange rate in six months was FF8/£ but only FF272 million if the exchange rate was FF6.8/£. Which currency is used as the currency of denomination for a credit sale is a matter of negotiation between the two parties. However, whoever assumes the foreign exchange risk should include the cost of the offset in calculating the true price of the aircraft.

There are other ways of dealing with such a transaction exposure, one of which involves currency operations in what is known as the 'forward market'. For example, assume that on the day the aircraft is sold for FF280 million the six-month forward rate for the French franc is FF7.2/£. The UK company could sell FF280 million forward six months at FF7.2/£ and, in six months, receive £38,888,888. The advantage of such a forward contract is that the £ proceeds of the sale are certain: the proceeds will be £38,888,888 – neither more nor less. The company has no further foreign exchange risk, but the disadvantage is that it receives fewer pounds sterling – in this instance, £38,888,888 instead of £40 million. The difference, £1,111,112, can be regarded as the amount forgone in order to have a certain sum (£38,888,888) instead of an uncertain sum (£40 million).

Of course, the company should have considered the £1,111,112 cost of the hedge in setting the price of the aircraft and perhaps raised its price to FF288 million. If this amount was sold forward at FF7.2/£, it could have yielded exactly £40 million, the amount the company wanted in pounds sterling. However, at the higher price of FF288 million the French airline might not have purchased the aircraft! Clearly, the cost of foreign exchange protection is a component of the total bargaining process.

Another alternative would be for the UK company to borrow French francs against the account receivable. Assuming an interest rate of 10 per cent per annum, or 5 per cent for six months, the amount to be borrowed would be:

$$\frac{FF280,000,000}{1.05} = FF266,666,666$$

The company would borrow FF266,666,666 on the day of sale and would immediately invest it. Six months from the date of sale, the company would receive FF280 million from the French airline and would use that sum to repay the loan and interest payable on it.

There are other approaches that can be used to manage, or 'hedge', transaction exposure that you may have heard about. One approach involves the use of foreign currency options. A currency option is the right (but not the obligation) to buy or sell a specified amount of foreign currency for base currency at a particular exchange rate within or at the end of a given period.

The particular exchange rate at which the option holder can buy or sell the currency is known as the strike or exercise price. Furthermore, if the option can be exercised at any time during its life it is known as an 'American style' option since this was the type of contract originally traded on the Philadelphia exchange. If the option can only be exercised on its expiry date then it is known as 'European style' option, being the style of option originally traded on the Amsterdam exchange.

An advantage of a currency option over other methods of currency hedging is that only one side of an exchange rate movement is protected. This enables the company to benefit if the exchange rate moves in the company's favour.

What form does such an option take? If a six-month French franc receivable is sold forward, a rate of say 7.8 will be obtained. The company could alternatively purchase an option to sell (known as a 'put') French francs at a rate of 7.8. If the pound rises resulting in a loss on the receivable this will be cancelled out by a gain on the option. If the rate moves to 8.75 the option would allow the company to sell French francs at 7.8 and buy at 8.75.

If the rate moved in the other direction and the pound fell to say to 6.5, a profit would be made on the receivable which can now be converted into sterling at this rate. The option would expire worthless because a loss would be made in exercising it.

Needless to say, an initial price has to be paid for the option. This is known as the premium. In our example if the pound falls the company will not be concerned because of the profit that can be made on converting into sterling and it is covered by the option should the pound rise. One can regard the price of the option as a mixture of gambling and insurance – the gamble that the pound will fall together with insurance if it does not.

The last alternative would be for the UK company to remain unhedged. As was shown in the beginning of the example, this is not really satisfactory because it could result in more, less, or the same ending pounds sterling proceeds, depending on the exchange rate in six months. The key point about forward and money market hedges is that they give a certain end result, while under the best of conditions the unhedged alternative allows a great deal of variation about a most likely result that is the same. For this reason, many firms will hedge in the forward market or the money market in order to reduce their transaction risk – that is, the variability of expected results.

You may be thinking that dealing with risks from overseas operations is complex. It often is and what makes for even greater complexity are the alternative instruments potentially available. When it comes to dealing with complex specific issues it is definitely worth drawing upon those with expertise in such matters!

17.4 Conclusion

In this chapter we have examined some of the major sources of financial risk likely to be faced by a business and some of the ways of identifying and, where possible, dealing with it.

Risk is important to understand and manage. It is one of the most difficult issues the general manager has to face because of its potential impact upon the business. Understanding the likely sources of risk to your business is a very good starting point. Only when you know where it might come from can you attempt to manage it.

In addition to dealing with risk in a short-term context, there is a need to be able to manage its long-term implications. This is particularly relevant in dealing with issues involving the financial direction of the business which we explore in the following chapters.

The important points considered in this chapter are as follows:

- There are five sources of risk: business risk, operating risk, financial risk, catastrophe risk and political risk.
- To recognize a risky business there a number of approaches which can be used. These include:

    analysis of key ratios and business cash flow

    Z scoring

    qualitative analysis.
- The riskiness implied by a business activity can be measured by a beta score.
- A credit rating is a measure of the quality of a company's debt.
- Transaction exposure is a measure of a firm's vulnerability to loss, or its chance of gain when an outstanding obligation incurred in a foreign currency is paid off. It can be managed by hedging through the use of the forward market, the money market and options.

PART FOUR
FINANCIAL DIRECTION

Corporate direction is the ultimate responsibility of those at the very top of an organization, typically the board of directors in a publicly quoted company. For them the challenge is not only to ensure that the goods produced and/or the services provided satisfy the requirements of the market, but also the other stakeholders in the business.

As we have indicated earlier, for publicly quoted companies the 'market for corporate control' means that the share price has to be a key consideration and directors have to ensure value is provided. A failure to provide value to the shareholders may well result in a loss of control by the board and a drastic change in the business as it stands.

'Maximizing shareholder value' is an objective espoused by many publicly quoted companies. However, as we will demonstrate in this part of the book it can be defined in a number of ways. To some it means achieving results expressed in conventional accounting terms and can even be equated with a number of key ratios that we have discussed in earlier chapters, like return on equity. To us and others it means something quite different. For reasons we discuss in Chapter 18, there are good reasons to doubt the ability of conventional accounting-oriented approaches for assisting in understanding issues of corporate direction in financial terms. We believe that for very sound reasons there is a preferable alternative that can be used far more effectively, but which requires us to extend and develop issues like appraising capital investments and the cost of capital which we discussed in earlier chapters.

In what follows, we will review this alternative approach, discuss the cost of capital to which we have made extensive reference throughout the book, and discuss how a value-based framework can be used in understanding matters of corporate direction in financial terms. However, while the focus of attention is initially upon large quoted and, therefore, publicly owned companies, do not believe for one minute that the approach is not relevant to other types of organization. The very principles upon which it is built at their simplest require the measurement of future cash flows and the return required from the organization, both of which can be related to any organizational setting.

18

Strategic financial analysis and measuring the value of a business

Crank – a man with a new idea until it succeeds

MARK TWAIN

Do you find that many traditional accounting methods restrict your ability to look towards the long-term future of your company? A fundamental problem with the accounting techniques we have discussed in earlier chapters is that they can be used in a very short-termist fashion. This point was raised in the Preface with reference to a study by Paul Marsh, Professor of Management and Finance at the London Business School, called *Short-termism on Trial*. He reviewed the notion that Britain and America's competitive edge has been dulled by the two countries' failure to emphasize long-term investment, and that this, in turn, is the fault of their financial markets. He found no support for this, but rather the fault lies with UK managers and he concluded his study by stating the way ahead as being for UK managers to get on with managing as if tomorrow mattered.

If managers are to be able to behave any differently they need an approach that is not reliant upon conventional accounting techniques, and in this chapter we will consider an alternative to it. This alternative to the accounting approach takes a long-term and more strategic business perspective and draws heavily upon the principle of present value analysis discussed in earlier chapters.

We believe this to be important because management will be poorly equipped for managing in the 1990s without being able to use an approach suited to taking a more forward-looking perspective. This is simply because of the considerable attention since the early 1960s that has been given to the 'market for corporate control', which refers to the market for buying and selling companies, as distinct from the market for products and services. This market for control over companies, their assets, and the opportunity to generate value from them was particularly important during the 1980s and will continue to be so during the 1990s. A consequence of this market for corporate control is that management, particularly in quoted companies, must pay careful attention to maximize the value generated by the part(s) of the business for which it is responsible. However, business value can only be managed effectively if it can be measured effectively and it is to this issue we will now turn. We believe such measurement requires the use of the principles of discounted cash flow for reasons we will demonstrate and discuss after a brief review of traditional accounting-oriented approaches.

18.1 Traditional measures of business value

There are many valuation methods some of which have been touched upon in earlier chapters and which have traditionally been used for measuring business value. Many of these are simple to apply, however, they may not provide the full picture. What are these methods? The following list represents the more popular traditional measures:

– Book value
– Liquidation value
– Market capitalization
– Market-to-book (MB) ratio
– Price-to-earnings (PE) ratio.

We have already encountered the first two of these. Book value is concerned with the values of assets and liabilities as shown in the business's balance sheet. It is measured in terms of the net asset value of the business, that is total assets after the deduction of creditors falling due within one year, after one year and provisions and liabilities. In other words, book value corresponds with shareholders' funds. It can in fact be linked with liquidation value, which represents what would be obtained from the sale of these business assets after meeting all debts corresponding with shareholders' funds. In other words, the book value may not be truly representative of the historic values shown in the balance sheet. For example, there may be assets, like land and buildings, the value of which are understated in the balance sheet.

Market capitalization is very straightforward to calculate, but only applies to publicly quoted companies. Value via this approach is simply the product of the number of issued ordinary shares and the market price of the share. With 3 million issued ordinary shares and a market price of £4.50 then the market capitalization value would be £13.5 million.

The market-to-book ratio expresses the relationship between the book value and the market value of shareholders' funds (market capitalization). In terms of business valuation, it can be used for valuing an unquoted company by drawing upon financial information about a comparable publicly quoted company, or companies. From the comparable company or companies, one or a number of market-to-book ratios can be calculated by dividing the market capitalization by shareholders' funds reported in the balance sheet. By multiplying the book value of the business to be valued by relevant market-to-book ratios an estimate of its market value can be found. For example, with a market-to-book ratio of 5 for a comparable business and a book value of the business to be valued of £2.5 million, its estimated market value would be 5 × £2.5 million = £12.5 million.

However, the most popular method, particularly for valuing a business as a going concern is the price-to-earnings (PE) ratio, which we discussed in Chapter 9. It is used in valuing a business in a manner similar to that described above for the market-to-book ratio. By taking the price-to-earnings ratio of a comparable business and multiplying it by the post-tax earnings of the business to be valued, an estimated value can be obtained. For example, if a comparable business has a price-to-earnings ratio of 10 and the business to be valued has post-tax earnings of £1 million, then the estimated business value will simply be 10 × £1 million = £10 million.

All of these valuation measures suffer from distinct shortcomings, many of which we have discussed in earlier chapters. For example, both earnings and book value (shareholders' funds) are influenced by accounting policies and different national practices. Such matters as the treatment of goodwill and taxation may well have a significant effect upon each and would have to be taken into consideration.

Second, and particularly relevant to the popular PE-based approach, investments in working capital and fixed capital are needed to sustain and make a business grow but are excluded from the measures dependent upon earnings and profit calculations. It is, therefore, possible for a business to achieve high profits and earnings even though the associated cash flow figure is much lower. Consider the following example of a business which reports a net profit of £1 million but only generates £50,000 cash:

	£'000
Net profit	1000
+ Depreciation	100
Operating cash flow	1100
− Capital expenditure	900
	200
− Working capital	150
Free cash flow	50

As illustrated, the difference between the two figures is a result of capital expenditure of £900,000 and working capital expenditure of £150,000. In the long term to achieve good performance a relatively good immediate net profit need not be associated with such an increase in economic value from the cash flow generated, which might at first sight be expected.

Third, accounting-based indicators of performance have been shown to fare relatively poorly as measures of shareholder returns, as measured in terms of dividends plus capital appreciation. As we outlined in the Preface, the UK study by Barron and Lawless (1988) found overall only a modest relationship between shareholder return and earnings per share growth and virtually no relationship at all with return on equity, which was confirmed more recently by Dennis Henry and Geoff Smith of P-E International (1991). From accounts available to them by 12 June 1991 for a sample of 250 of the largest UK industrial and commercial companies, they found that over a five-year period there was no correlation at all between earnings per share and shareholder return. By contrast, a substantial body of empirical research in the United Kingdom and United States has shown a strong relationship between cash flow measures of performance, particularly that known as 'free cash flow' which takes account of working and fixed capital requirements associated with generating an earnings stream, and shareholder returns. In other words, it seems that it is not that earnings per share growth is of no importance in determining returns expected by shareholders, rather it is incomplete without further important information.

To complement this empirical research, a recent study by MORI on behalf of Coopers and Lybrand Deloitte (1991) found that the City judges business less by reference to accounting profits than to sustainable cash flows, and concluded that businesses and investors should adopt measures of performance that concentrate on the present value of cash flows. In other words, a successful business is one that creates value for its owners and, as we will show, the creation or destruction of value can be gauged more effectively using an alternative to conventional measures of value.

18.2 Discounted cash flow analysis and business valuation

In the last section we discussed some of the shortcomings of using the conventional indicators of performance for strategic financial analysis. In this section we will review an alternative approach which is more appropriate for strategic financial analysis and makes an understanding of the issues involved clearer, because numerous diverse aspects can be drawn together and expressed meaningfully in financial terms.

The fundamental assumption in this approach (known as shareholder value analysis or SVA for short (Rappaport, 1986)) is that in broad terms the value of a business can be determined by discounting its future cash flows using an appropriate cost of capital, and it provides a framework for understanding and measuring the ramifications of all types of strategic decisions. You might be thinking that this sounds very much like the net present value approach we reviewed in Chapters 15 and 16 with reference to the evaluation of capital projects. Indeed it has many similarities in so far as it draws upon the principles of discounted cash flow analysis, but it has some additional features that make it distinctive.

The framework allows trade-offs like the immediate cash flows associated with significant capital investment to be weighed against longer-term cash flows. These are captured via a number of what are known as 'value drivers'. There are seven of these which represent the basic value drivers. They can be expanded and analysed in far more detail. This is often so in real-life situations, but the concern here is to demonstrate the integrative and holistic nature of this alternative approach. These seven value drivers are:

1. Sales growth rate
2. Operating profit margin
3. Cash tax rate
4. Fixed capital requirements
5. Working capital requirements
6. Planning period
7. Cost of capital.

Cash flows within the model are determined by focusing upon the first five value drivers which can be divided into two groups corresponding with decisions about managing operations and investment within a business. The first group of value drivers consisting of sales growth rate, operating profit margin and cash tax rate is instrumental in determining cash inflows. The second, consisting of fixed and working capital investment, is instrumental in determining cash outflows. The difference between these two represents what is known as 'free cash flow' which we have indicated recognizes the cash outflows that may be necessary in the form of fixed and working capital requirements, to generate future cash inflows. As a consequence, it need not and may often not be positive. For example, in a start-up situation, or when introducing a new product, significant fixed and working capital investment may well be required. Such investments in fixed and working capital may often represent a significant drain on immediate cash flow, but the intention in incurring such expenditure will be to benefit from a larger cash flow from operations in the future than would otherwise be the case. In other words, long-term value is intended to be driven from a decision with immediate cash flow implications. Similarly, a decision not to invest in such a situation will yield higher immediate cash flows, but is likely to generate less future value.

It is important to be quite clear about how the free cash flows are calculated, so let us consider this calculation using the following assumed values for the five value drivers:

1. Sales growth rate   15%
2. Operating profit margin   10%
3. Cash tax rate   30%
4. Fixed capital requirement   15%
5. Working capital requirement   10%

Each of the value drivers is expressed as a percentage, so let us see what these mean. First, the sales growth rate of 15 per cent in sales revenue simply means that sales revenue next year is expected to be 1.15 times that for this year. Once this has been calculated in money terms to establish total cash receipts to the business, then the operating profit margin percentage, and cash tax rate percentage can be applied, thereby permitting the cash inflows after paying costs and taxes relating to receipts to be calculated. Of course, as you will recall from the early chapters of the book, depreciation must also be added back to convert profits to cash flows.

The incremental fixed and working capital requirements in this case are expressed as percentages and have also been related to sales revenue, so that to convert all of these value drivers into annual free cash flows we only need one other piece of information, sales revenue, which we will assume to be £1000 million. In effect, as sales increase it is assumed that additional fixed and working capital will be required, this requirement being expressed in a simple percentage assuming some sort of linear relationship. Other than the incremental fixed capital expenditure, there will be a requirement to maintain the quality of existing capital assets, hence the inclusion of replacement for which a value equivalent to the depreciation charge has been assumed to be appropriate.

To understand how the free cash flows are derived from the value drivers given above let us consider year 1. The first step is to apply the sales growth rate to the sales revenue figure. Thereafter, the percentages are applied as follows:

		£ million
£1000 million × 1.15	=	£1150
		×
Operating profit margin		10%
		=
		£115
		×
Cash tax rate		(100 − 30%)
		=
		£80.5
Plus depreciation		£10.0
Operating cash flow		£90.5
Less		
Replacement fixed capital		£10.0
Incremental fixed capital investment		
((£1,150 million − £1,000 million) × 15%)		£22.5
Incremental working capital investment		
((£1,150 million − £1,000 million) × 10%)		£15.0
FREE CASH FLOW		£43.0

Similar calculations could be undertaken for the second year and as far into the future as desired, but in order to add such cash flows together meaningfully to arrive at a value it has to be recognized that money has a time value. As we demonstrated in Chapter 15, £1 received in the future does not have the same value as a £1 received today. To incorporate this time value we need to discount the cash flows for which the cost of capital value driver is required. As you can now appreciate, over a given time frame and armed with knowledge of seven value drivers, free cash flows can be calculated which then have to be adjusted for the time value of money to arrive at a value.

Applying the discounted cash flow analysis approach in practice

While being readily understandable by virtue of its relative simplicity, the discounted cash flow analysis approach could not be used to provide particularly accurate forecasts in real-life situations. Not only would the likely values of each value driver change over time, but also the composition and breakdown of each. For example, over the course of time the range of products or services produced or provided by a business will typically change, and it is desirable to disaggregate the sales growth rate to reflect this. Similarly, over the course of time the cost of capital may well change to reflect the different expectations of the providers of funds.

How is this dealt with? The answer is that available data can be modelled and shaped but within a framework that uses exactly the same principles as those illustrated earlier. Quite simply, when concerned with valuing a company from available published information, the contents of its annual report and accounts can be used to obtain an historical picture of past value drivers. This historical picture is then used as an important base from which to make future projections. This approach was adopted for obtaining a valuation of Glaxo Holdings plc, where modifications were made to historical trends by making projections based upon comments found in the 1992 Annual Report and Accounts for the company.

By applying this alternative approach to the financial information available for a publicly quoted company, like Glaxo Holdings plc, its share price in the market can be compared with perceptions of its value. This will be demonstrated by valuing a business in its entirety, but the approach can be and is applied to measuring the value of component parts of a business.

In recognition of the long-term nature of the drugs and pharmaceuticals business the projections for Glaxo were undertaken for a period of 10 years and were analysed for each of the company's following therapeutic groupings.

- Anti-ulcerants
- Respiratory
- Systemic antibiotics
- Anti-emesis
- Dermatologicals
- Cardiovascular
- Anti-migraine
- Other.

The sales growth potential in each of these areas was reviewed upon the basis of the information provided to build up as realistic a pattern of future sales revenue as possible. Other assumptions also had to be built in to determine the cash flows and these included no change in either the cost of sales percentage or the commitment of resources to research and development. The result was the following free cash flows which were calculated by applying the principles discussed earlier:

	(£ million)
1993	510.14
1994	697.53
1995	948.46
1996	1,209.98
1997	1,521.97
1998	1,896.31
1999	2,347.76
2000	2,890.68
2001	3,556.23
2002	4,339.55

In this case 10 years' figures have been used as representing an appropriate planning period. How might such a planning period be determined for any given business? This is not an exact science and may present some real difficulties in practice. But, literature on business strategy provides several strategic frameworks. For example, Michael Porter (1986), in *Competitive Strategy*, provides one such framework that can be used to good effect. He has identified the five forces which drive industry. These are:

1. Rivalry among existing firms.
2. Threat of new entrants.
3. Threat of substitute products or services.
4. Bargaining power of suppliers.
5. Bargaining power of buyers.

The combined interaction of these five forces can be used, albeit with some difficulty, to determine a point in time where competitive advantage will disappear.

We can use knowledge of such a time period to our advantage because it enables the value to the business from such a decision to be calculated relatively straightforwardly. Rather than having to undertake an infinite number of cash flow calculations to determine value, the process can be greatly simplified by viewing the value of the business as consisting of two parts – that from the planning period and that which will be generated beyond. That from the planning period is found in the manner illustrated earlier and that from beyond it is found by treating the very last cash flow in the planning period as though it will be received forever. In other words, it is assumed that providing replacement capital expenditure is undertaken, a constant cash flow that diminishes with time in terms of its present value will be received in perpetuity. The rationale for wanting to value this time period beyond the planning horizon can be understood if we consider the components of value for a company's shares, where a relatively small part of its present value is accounted for by near-term cash returns to shareholders. The problem, of course, is how to value longer-term returns which the perpetuity assumption overcomes relatively straightforwardly, but as with all assumptions it can be changed if it is considered to be inappropriate.

The valuation of a perpetuity is very simple. Given knowledge of the cash flow to be received in perpetuity, all that is needed is the return associated with it. Thus, given a perpetuity of £100 and a return of 10 per cent, its value would be £1000 (£100/10 per cent). In fact, the same value would result from discounting the £100 by 10 per cent every year into the future and summing the resulting present values. Using the perpetuity approach simplifies the calculations required and avoids the need to undertake cash flow forecasting way into the future. Imagine, for example, being required to arrive at a realistic cash flow for your organization 200 years from now! This approach was applied in the case of Glaxo Holdings plc with the results you will see shortly, once we have completed the valuation of the planning period.

The sum of the annual free cash flows from the assumed planning period for Glaxo of 10 years is £19,918.61 million but, as we know, these free cash flows must be discounted to determine the value derived from the planning period in present-day value terms. In order to discount them the relevant discount rate, or cost of capital, is required and using an approach we will review in the next chapter we found this rate to be approximately 12 per cent (11.665 per cent in fact).

The result of discounting the cash flows for the 10 years at this rate is a sum of £9367.96 million. Now this is only the value to be derived from the 10-year planning period to which the value that will arise beyond must be added. As indicated earlier, the perpetuity approach was used to produce a value which, when discounted by the cost of capital to express it in present-day terms, produced a value beyond the planning period of £15,191.90 million.

Year	Cash flow	Present value cash flow	Cum PV of cash flow	Present value of residual value	Cum PV of cash flow + PV of res. value
	£ million	£ million	£ million	£ million	£ million
1993	510.14	456.85	456.85	8,187.48	8,644.32
1994	697.53	559.41	1,016.25	8,803.87	9,820.12
1995	948.46	681.19	1,697.45	9,276.84	10,974.28
1996	1,209.98	778.23	2,475.68	9,832.58	12,308.26
1997	1,521.97	876.64	3,352.32	10,474.43	13,826.75
1998	1,896.31	978.15	4,330.47	11,207.11	15,537.58

Year	Cash flow	Present value cash flow	Cum PV of cash flow	Present value of residual value	Cum PV of cash flow + PV of res. value
	£ million	£ million	£ million	£ million	£ million
1999	2,347.76	1,084.51	5,414.98	12,036.77	17,451.75
2000	2,890.68	1,195.81	6,610.79	12,971.05	19,581.84
2001	3,556.23	1,317.46	7,928.25	14,019.15	21,947.40
2002	4,339.55	1,439.71	9,367.96	15,191.90	24,559.86

The combined value from the planning period and beyond is £24,559.86 million. This is not yet a measure of the value to shareholders because it excludes any business assets from which other non-trading profits may be generated in the form of investments outside of normal business activities, and it includes a proportion of business value attributable to the lenders of funds. To calculate value to the shareholders, two more steps are necessary, these being to add short-term investments and to subtract the market value of debt as follows:

	£ million
Business value (from above)	24,559.86
Short-term investments	1,725.00
Corporate value	26,284.86
Less: Market value of debt	543.00
Shareholder value	25,741.86
Shareholder value/share	£8.55
Share price	£7.79
Premium	+9.78%

By adding short-term investments from which profits are derived and by deducting the market value of external debt and obligations we arrive at the value to shareholders, or shareholder value. In this case it is approximately £25,741.86 million and by dividing it by the number of issued ordinary shares we can establish what this means per share. For a quoted company this means that a comparison can be made with the published share price. For Glaxo Holdings plc the result is a value per share of £8.55 by comparison with its market price at the time of writing of £7.79.

Making changes to the base case

As a result of basing assumptions upon the 1992 Annual Report and Accounts for Glaxo Holdings plc we have arrived at a value per share of

£8.55, a premium over the share price at the time of writing of 9.78 per cent. Of course, analysis should not and would not normally stop here – this is just the start. Many questions would probably need to be asked about the realism of the assumptions and whether any improvements could be made.

Changes to the assumptions about the value drivers may have a significant effect upon shareholder value. Indeed one of the advantages of the approach which may be so easily overlooked is in helping to understand the consequence(s) of pursuing an alternative course of action. For example, by changing the assumptions about the commitment of fixed and working capital investment it would not be unreasonable to expect a lower future sales growth to result. That is, without adequate investment it may be very difficult to justify the forecast sales growth rate.

As shown in the Glaxo valuation, continuing value may and often will be the largest component of business value. Given the significance of its size, it is not uncommon to find additional approaches to the base case perpetuity approach being used by way of a cross-check.

Three potential approaches which use the traditional valuation techniques reviewed earlier are the calculation of a realizable value at the end of the planning period, and/or the estimation of the market value at this point in time using price-to-earnings (PE) or market-to-book (MB) ratios.

18.3 Benefits of strategic financial analysis

For a quoted company like Glaxo Holdings plc, this exercise is potentially very useful because it may, as in this case, reveal a 'value gap' which is a difference between one's view of the economic potential of a company and how the stock market views it. Now, of course, whether this value gap is real is very much dependent upon the assumptions made and in any serious valuation more analysis and evaluations of different scenarios would be warranted. Nevertheless, an awareness of potential value gaps is very important, and Hanson PLC which we discussed earlier is a good example of one company that has been able to identify their existence. For example, after buying Imperial Tobacco for £2.5 billion and selling off the group's Courage and Golden Wonder businesses and other relatively small businesses for £2.3 billion, Hanson retained businesses worth about £1.4 billion.

We are not suggesting that Hanson PLC specifically uses the valuation approach we have described, but it must take a forward looking view covering the issues we have identified. Certainly the framework serves as a good example of how information about the underlying business dynamics of an enterprise can be used to gain an understanding in financial terms of future potential courses of action. What is more, the approach does not have to be confined to large quoted companies, although admittedly it is more straightforward. Free cash flow is relevant to all types of organization whether of the for-profit or not-for-profit type and whether publicly or privately owned. What represents a real challenge is determining the cost of capital to be applied in each case. As you will see in the next chapter, the world of finance has dealt with this issue extensively for quoted public companies, but not so well for others.

18.4 Conclusion

The discounted cash flow approach to business valuation has some distinct advantages over conventional accounting-oriented approaches. Free cash flow is a relatively unambiguous concept by comparison with measures like earnings and can be readily understood in all types of organization. However, perhaps the most significant of these benefits of the discounted cash flow approach we have described is the opportunity for being able to understand the financial implications of managerial actions. These financial implications are also considered within a framework that is able to capture risk and uncertainty over the long rather than the short term and which is supported by empirical studies.

We have identified how the approach can be used to understand the underpinnings of a share price using publicly available financial information. As we are sure you can appreciate, this application and others we will discuss subsequently are critically dependent upon the assumptions used, but we believe that the approach can be instrumental in helping directors to avoid unnecessary changes in corporate control because of an unspotted value gap, and also for helping to identify potential business restructuring opportunities. However, before we delve into any more applications we really do need to consider one fundamental issue which is extremely influential in determining the resulting value from the discounted cash flow approach – the cost of capital. This we examine in the next chapter.

Key points to remember from this chapter are:

- General managers cannot afford to ignore the measurement and management of business value, because of the importance of the market for control over companies, their assets, and the opportunity to generate value from them.
- There are many traditional accounting techniques which may be used for measuring business value. These are book value, liquidation value, market capitalization, market-to-book ratio, and price-to-earnings ratio. However, these suffer from distinct shortcomings, not least of which is that

they often err in favour of taking a 'short termist' approach; the application of DCF allows the manager to take a more long-term view.
- Use of the discounted cash flow approach for analysing and valuing businesses does overcome many of the shortcomings of traditional accounting-oriented approaches and it does have a well-established pedigree in the United States.
- The power and relevance of SVA derives from the association between management decisions and value in a clear objective framework.
- The fundamental assumption in the discounted cash flow approach is that a business is worth the net present value of its future cash flows, discounted at the appropriate cost of capital.
- Using SVA, business value and management decisions are linked via seven key value drivers:
  The planning horizon
  Sales growth
  Profit margin
  Tax rate
  Working capital needs
  Fixed capital needs
  Cost of capital.
- SVA facilitates the spotting of possible value gaps, but as with any financial tool it does have limitations and is no insurance against mistakes. However, it can be used to help prevent important decisions being taken without understanding their full implications.

19
The cost of capital

I often tell people I sleep like a baby. I wake up every ten minutes screaming

T. RYAN

We sincerely hope that you won't find this chapter has this effect upon your sleep, but the cost of capital is an area which is relatively complex and, therefore, sometimes difficult to grasp. What is the cost of capital? All organizations require funding to exist and as we have seen in earlier chapters, the funding for a quoted public limited company will take the form of shareholders' funds and loans. To attract such funds a company will have to give a return to investors and this return is known as the cost of capital. What is a return to the providers of funding is a cost to the recipient.

An understanding of the cost of capital is important, and it has reared its head in earlier chapters. First we made many references to it in discussing how to evaluate capital expenditure, where we assumed values for the cost of capital (or discount rate) while only making brief references to the issues involved in its calculation. Second, in discussing the management of business risk we discussed beta values which we indicated can be an important component within a cost of capital calculation. Last, but by no means least, it was shown in the last chapter to be a major determinant of business value.

The real problem with the cost of capital lies in its estimation. Various approaches have been developed to assist in its calculation, particularly for quoted companies, and in what follows we will provide a review of these methods. Please do bear in mind that the contents of this chapter are very much the domain of the financial specialist. We would, therefore, not be surprised if you find it more difficult than earlier chapters. But do bear in mind that an appreciation of the key components of, and issues associated with, the cost of capital is important.

19.1 Cost of capital

The information required to estimate the cost of capital is best understood with reference to Fig. 19.1.

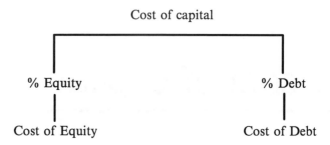

Figure 19.1   Cost of capital

Determining the cost of capital is a difficult task. In what follows we will discuss its calculation using the following three steps which can be related to Fig. 19.1.

1. Calculate the cost of equity.
2. Calculate the cost of debt.
3. Determine the cost of capital by weighting the cost of equity and the cost of debt by the projected proportion of debt and equity in the capital structure.

Cost of equity

The cost of equity can be calculated in a number of ways, the two most common methods being:

– Dividend valuation model
– Capital Asset Pricing Model (CAPM).

DIVIDEND VALUATION MODEL

The dividend valuation model considers that the return shareholders will require, and hence the cost of equity to a business, can be determined with reference to the future dividend stream they require. At its simplest, this return can be calculated using the dividend yield ratio which, you will recall, is defined as the ratio of current dividends to the current price per ordinary share, i.e.

Dividend yield per cent $= \dfrac{\text{Dividend}}{\text{Price}} \times 100$

However, this simple approach will not represent the cost of equity unless a very special set of circumstances apply, namely, that the current dividend per share must be paid out at the end of each year forever and that the amount of dividend must never change (i.e. never grow). This is an extremely unrealistic set of assumptions. Also, if the dividend yield is to be employed as a measure of the cost of equity, the company must pay a dividend and the approach is useless if current dividend payout is zero. Last, but by no means least, a low dividend yield implies a cost of equity capital that is less than the cost of debt – an unimaginable situation.

Of course, as an alternative you might encounter the earnings/price ratio, which you will recall is the earnings yield. This is the ratio of the current annual accounting earnings per share to the current share price, i.e.

$$\text{Earnings yield per cent} = \frac{\text{EPS}}{\text{Price}} \times 100$$

It has the advantage of being 'usable' even though a company may have no dividend payout. However, it leads to a number of difficulties. Not least among them is that it implies a negative cost of equity capital when earnings are negative. Also, it may lead one to conclude that for high price–earnings ratio companies, which are often those with high rates of growth, the cost of equity is lower than the cost of debt – hardly a likely situation. Equity in a geared company, being a residual claimant, is always more risky than debt. Finally, it relies upon accounting information, which may not reflect the underlying economic value of the business. Different costs of equity could be determined for the same company depending upon, for example, the method of depreciation adopted.

The most likely dividend valuation model you will encounter for valuing the cost of equity is known as the Gordon Growth Model. This model considers that the cost of equity can be derived by assuming that a company's dividend per share grows at a constant rate forever and that the company's risk will remain unchanged. If we call *Ke* the cost of equity, the model is:

$$Ke \text{ per cent} = \left(\frac{\text{Expected dividend}}{\text{Price}} + \frac{\text{Change in price}}{\text{Price}} \right) \times 100$$

Since change in price divided by price is just a growth rate Gordon's Growth Model is typically expressed as:

$$Ke \text{ per cent} = \left(\frac{d\,(1+g) + g}{P} \right) \times 100$$

where,

Ke = Cost of equity
d = Current dividend
P = Market price
g = Expected dividend or price growth rate provided that investors expect dividends to grow at a constant rate in perpetuity

Thus, if a company had a current dividend per share of 10p, a market price of £1, and an expected growth rate of 10 per cent, its cost of equity would be:

$$Ke \text{ per cent} = \left(\frac{10p\ (1+10\%)}{£1} + 0.10 \right) \times 100$$
$$= 21 \text{ per cent}$$

This definition of the cost of equity is fairly popular, particularly for valuing preference shares where g reduces to zero. In this case, the calculation of a cost of equity is quite straightforward if it is irredeemable, that is the dividend is paid in perpetuity. For a 10 per cent irredeemable preference share with a nominal value of £1 and a market value of £2 the cost of the preference share using this approach would be:

$$K \text{ pref.} = \frac{\text{Annual dividend}}{\text{Market price}} \times 100 = \frac{10p}{£2} \times 100 = 5 \text{ per cent}$$

If the preference share is redeemable then an internal rate of return calculation is required to find the percentage (cost of preference shares) which equates all future cash flows from dividend payments and redemption with the current market value of the share. This is known as the 'yield to redemption' or 'yield to maturity'.

However, for calculating the cost of equity relating to ordinary share capital the dividend valuation approach has to be used with care. First, the growth rate g is a long-run growth rate over an infinite horizon, and as such is a difficult parameter to conceptualize. It relies upon accurate estimates of growth rates that can be reliably projected into the future – a daunting task given that few businesses have a history of constant growth. Second, the long-run growth rate must, by definition, be strictly less than the cost of equity, Ke. This can be demonstrated by rearranging terms to solve for the present value of equity

$$P = \frac{d(1 + g)}{Ke - g}$$

If the long-run growth rate is equal to the cost of equity, the implied value of the company is infinite. If g is greater than Ke, the implied value is negative. Both results are impossible. Third, the parameters of the Gordon Growth Model are interdependent. It would seem that a higher growth rate implies a higher cost of equity. However, this is not true because the higher rate of growth will imply a higher current share value. The net effect will reduce the cost of equity. But if one estimates a higher growth rate, how much greater should P become? The answer is unclear. Finally, the model provides no obvious answer to the question – what cost of equity should be applied when the company is considering projects of different risk than its current operations?

CAPITAL ASSET PRICING MODEL (CAPM)

Modern financial theory suggests that a better way to estimate the cost of equity is from the demand side. Rather than looking at what the company pays out, it can be estimated from analysing the return investors require for buying a share. And, in a nutshell, the more risk an investor is required to take on, the higher the rate of return he or she is likely to expect.

We have already introduced an important part of the CAPM via the risk measure it requires in the form of the beta. However, to arrive at the CAPM cost of capital two other components must be determined:

– Risk-free rate
– Market risk premium.

The *risk-free rate* represents the most secure return that could be achieved. Anyone wishing to sleep soundly at night could invest all available funds in government bonds which are largely insensitive to what happens in the stock market and, therefore, have a beta of nearly zero.

The *market risk premium* represents the excess return above the risk-free rate that investors demand for holding risky securities. It is combined with the beta and added to the risk-free rate in the following cost of capital calculation:

Cost of equity = Risk-free rate + (Beta × Market risk premium)

For example, with a risk-free rate of 9 per cent, a beta of 1.5, and a market risk premium of 4 per cent, the cost of equity would be:

9 per cent + (1.5 × 4 per cent) = 15 per cent

Betas are published for companies making this approach attractive, particularly given that estimates of the risk-free rate and the market risk premium are available in the United Kingdom. Reference to yields on government securities like long-term gilts produces a proxy risk-free rate and estimates of the market risk premium are produced by some banks and other institutions. Of course, whether such approximations are adequate will typically depend upon the purpose for which the cost of equity will be used. If it is to undertake a detailed valuation where the repercussions of an error are likely to be high, then specialist advice is really warranted.

CAPM has gained considerable acceptability in recent years and a good illustration of its use is provided in the annual report of the US-based food and toy firm, the Quaker Oats Company. It demonstrates how the cost of equity is derived using a risk-free rate comprising the sum of the expected rate of inflation and a 'real' return. The company refers to a commonly used surrogate for the risk-free rate as being the rate for US Treasury Bonds, which are unconditional obligations of that government and are intended to pay a real return above long-term inflation expectations. The company also publishes the risk premium needed to be added to this risk-free rate to compensate investors for holding Quaker's shares.

However, CAPM is not without its difficulties. Concern has been expressed as to the extent to which market-related risk can be satisfactorily captured in a single indicator, the beta. Empirical evidence has demonstrated circumstances in which investors demand a higher return from one portfolio than another when both apparently are equally risky by virtue of having a beta of one. The difference in portfolio returns cannot be due to differences in specific risk because diversification nearly eliminates such risk in large, well-balanced portfolios. And if the systematic risks of the two portfolios were truly identical, then they would be priced to yield identical expected returns in equilibrium. Otherwise, an arbitrage opportunity would exist: investors could purchase one portfolio, sell the other and reap a positive expected return on zero investment. The observed difference in returns between these two portfolios represents a difference in systematic risk that is not captured by the CAPM beta and has been taken to show that it is an incomplete measure of risk.

In an effort to improve upon CAPM an approach known as Arbitrage Pricing Theory (APT for short) has been developed. The principle which underpins APT is that two assets that have identical risk characteristics must offer the same return or an arbitrage opportunity will exist. APT attempts to measure the various dimensions of market-related risk in terms of several underlying economic factors, such as inflation, monthly production and interest rates, which systematically affect the price of all shares. In a nutshell, regression techniques are used to estimate the contribution made by each APT factor to overall risk. However, this approach is more complex than CAPM and not without some difficulties in terms of its application. In spite of being able to provide a better measure of market-related risk, APT shares some problems with CAPM. Both approaches assume that the past is a good representation of the future, a view that is clearly flawed for businesses undergoing or which have undergone a period of substantial structural change. For example, if a company goes into a new, more risky line of business, the covariance of the future cash flows will increase. Since beta is measured by regressing returns over a long period of time (usually five years), the effect of the change on the company's beta will be slow to appear. Thus, the historical beta of a company that has recently changed its exposure to risk may not be a good estimate of its future beta. Second, neither approach can be used directly for firms, divisions or other business entities that do not have publicly traded shares. This is an important issue which we deal with below.

MEASURING THE COST OF EQUITY IN UNQUOTED ENTITIES

One feature of unquoted entities is that there is no market price for their shares, thereby preventing either an earnings, dividend, CAPM, or APT cost of equity from being calculated. The question is then – how in such circumstances can a cost of equity be calculated? One approach is by determining betas using what is known as peer group analysis, whereby comparable quoted company peers are selected to form a peer group for purposes of comparison. In this way the beta approach can be applied to estimate the cost of equity relevant to the projects, divisions, and firms of business entities both with and without publicly traded equity and for businesses that have undergone substantial recent change.

Cost of debt

The second component of the cost of capital is the cost of debt which is the rate of return that debtholders require to hold debt. The value of a particular debt instrument like a bond can be found quite simply if it is irredeemable. Just as for a preference share the interest will be a perpetuity such that the yield is simply the interest divided by the market value of the instrument. Where the instrument is redeemable its yield is found by discounting its associated cash flow at an appropriate rate of interest. The discount rate that equates the present value of its promised cash flows to its current market value is the cost of debt, sometimes called the 'yield to maturity' or the 'yield' for short. Unlike dividend payments to holders of equity these promised cash flows in the form of interest payments are tax deductible, therefore, the after-tax cost of debt or interest payment is the relevant rate of return to be calculated for use in determining the cost of capital.

Typically, businesses have more than one source of debt financing in which case the overall cost of debt can be calculated by taking the weighted average of the individual instruments based upon market values, that is by multiplying the yield to maturity of each instrument by the percentage of the total market value of the portfolio that each instrument represents and summing the products.

Where the cost of debt of non-publicly traded companies or divisions of publicly traded companies is required two approaches may be used. First, peer analysis can be used in which the focus of attention is upon peer instruments as indicated by the yield to maturity provided. Second, synthetic bond rating analysis can be used in determining the cost of equity. In essence, from fundamental accounting data and a knowledge of the capital structure a model can be developed to simulate a bond rating and give an appropriate yield to maturity for that rating.

The weighted average of the costs of equity and debt

Once the cost of equity and the cost of debt have been determined the cost of capital can be calculated by combining them in a weighted average cost of capital equation as follows:

Cost of capital $=$ Per cent debt $(Kd)(1-Tm)$ $+$ Per cent equity (Ke)

where:

$$\text{Per cent debt} = \frac{\text{Debt}}{\text{Debt} + \text{Equity}}$$

based upon market, not book values.

Kd $=$ Cost of debt
Tm $=$ Marginal tax rate

$$\text{Per cent equity} = \frac{\text{Equity}}{\text{Debt} + \text{Equity}}$$

based upon market, not book values.

Market values not book values should be used in calculating percentage debt and percentage equity because in the case of debt book values represent simply the face value and not the real obligation. In the case of equity the book value reflects only the historical values of assets and these may often be substantially different from market values.

19.2 Conclusion

In our review of the calculation of the cost of capital it may appear to be more of a science than an art. However, as we have shown with reference to the cost of equity, there is more than one possible approach. Furthermore, different methods produce different results which may have a very material effect upon the outcome. We only have to consider the UK water industry to understand this. The regulatory body OFWAT has calculated the proposed cost of capital using the dividend growth model, the result being a figure of some 5 to 6 per cent. On the other hand, the companies backed by several independent experts have arrived at a figure of some 9.5 per cent using CAPM! A difference of this amount is significant and is not necessarily easy to reconcile.

So what conclusions should we draw that are of relevance to you?

– The cost of capital is vital to understand for all organizations. All organizations have to be funded, this funding representing a cost to the recipient of the funds and a return to the provider(s).
– This cost of capital is the rate at which all future cash flows should be discounted and the more significant the cash flows the more the concern should be that the 'correct' rate has been selected.
– Recognize that calculating the cost of capital with any accuracy is a difficult task. We have merely scratched the surface with reference mainly to the calculation for quoted public limited companies and we have assumed a very simple organizational environment not complicated by multiple business units, each potentially having its own cost of capital.
– If the sums involved are large seek specialist help in determining the cost of capital!

20
Valuation and business restructuring

Why don't we close down all the plants and then we'll really start to save money

C. BEACHAM

Well, it's one way of restructuring a business! However, in this chapter we will look at less drastic options, and how these can be managed.

In Chapter 18 we reviewed the use of discounted cash flow analysis within the context of business valuation with reference to shareholder value analysis (SVA). There we illustrated how using a number of interrelated value drivers a view of the underlying economic value of a share could be determined but, as we indicated, the results obtained are totally contingent upon the forecast assumptions. This raises one key point about valuing a business – value, like beauty, is in the eye of the beholder! It is quite possible, and usually quite likely, that different parties will have a totally different perception of the value of any given business. The purchase of Rowntree Macintosh by Nestlé serves as a good illustration of this, where the price finally paid per share far outweighed perceptions of value from a UK perspective. Nestlé may well have had a vastly different view of the benefits, or synergies, obtainable from a combination of the two organizations than did any other interested party. Such benefits will often result in higher cash flows which, when discounted at an unchanged discount rate, will produce a higher value. This, of course, ignores the fact that any valuation undertaken by, say, general management at Rowntree would have been reliant upon a UK-based cost of capital, while the board of directors of Nestlé might have been able to contemplate using Swiss rates which were of the order of 50 per cent lower.

Different perceptions of what can be done with a business provide a key stimulus for what has come to be known as restructuring. This is a term that can be used to capture all sorts of initiatives like mergers and acquisitions, divestments to unrelated parties, buyouts by existing management, joint ventures and strategic alliances. What we have provided you with so far is an approach which enables the dynamics of a business to be captured and expressed in financial terms in the form of shareholder value. However, these same principles can be extended and applied to evaluate restructuring opportunities, but there is one important complication. In many cases a realistic valuation can only be achieved by recognizing that many organizations comprise a number of different businesses and there is a need to be able to evaluate a portfolio of business units. To achieve this, a good understanding of the business units is required which necessitates careful analysis of the threats and opportunities faced by each. In addition, each of the business units may well be subject to different degrees of market risk, thereby necessitating the use of a different cost of capital for each. Thus, a company-wide valuation can only be built from separate valuations of business units which requires a much deeper level of analysis than that we have discussed earlier with reference to a company valuation that looks at the organization as a whole.

In this chapter we will look at business valuation and restructuring from two perspectives. First, we will review business valuation for assessing opportunities to restructure an organization by taking advantage of all conceivable value enhancements whether they are internal or external. In this review, which we will refer to as internal restructuring, we will describe how to analyse the multi-business so as to derive as much value from it as is possible. Second, we will look at business valuation and restructuring within the context of mergers and acquisitions. In both cases the need to take different value perspectives will be an important feature. Internal restructuring, like that proposed in the demerger of ICI, should never lose sight of closing potential value gaps that might be taken advantage of by an acquirer. Equally, in an acquisition, or external restructuring, there will always be a buyer and seller, and the picture may be complicated by the existence of multiple sellers.

One more complication to throw in the pot concerns the cost of capital. In the last chapter we discussed the issues important in its determination from a corporate perspective. This becomes even more complex when our attention is upon a business made up of a number of business units. Each of these may have a different required rate of return, or cost of capital, that has to be determined. This is definitely beyond the scope of this book and is more appropriately the concern of the financial specialist rather than the general manager. However, you should now be aware of the issues involved and why the determination of different rates is important.

20.1 Internal restructuring

As we have indicated, internal restructuring involves the assessment of opportunities and the taking of action to restructure an organization by means of all conceivable value enhancements, whether they are internal or external. How the financial benefits associated with a potential restructuring can be measured we will review using the following four steps:

- Step 1: Calculate current market value.
- Step 2: Calculate business 'as is'.
- Step 3: Calculate business value with internal improvements.
- Step 4: Calculate business value with external improvements.

Step 1 Current market value

The key purpose of this step is to establish the worth of a business as seen by the market and to determine a yardstick against which to measure your own valuations. As we demonstrated in Chapter 18 with reference to Glaxo Holdings plc, it is calculated for a quoted company by capitalizing the equity shares in issue. At its simplest, this can be found from the product of the number of shares in issue and the quoted market price of the share, but realistically the price used should also include an estimate of the premium that would have to be paid to gain control. It is important not to omit this premium for control because the quoted price of any share reflects only normal transactions in the stock market and not what would be required to gain control of the business.

For private companies and other organizations the process of determining current market value is even less precise. Peer group analysis of comparable quoted companies or companies with comparable characteristics may be necessary together with reference to some of the other valuation approaches we have reviewed. In any event, a number of different valuation approaches would typically be used in recognition of the uncertainty caused by there being no informed market as such.

Step 2 Business value 'as is'

This is a very difficult step if done properly. What often can make this particularly difficult is that different business activities may be associated with different levels of risk, thereby necessitating the use of a different cost of capital to establish the net present values of individual business units. Despite this and other complicating factors that we will discuss later, valuing a multi-business organization 'as is' involves the same principles as valuing a single business, and the only difference is that a number of individual valuations for each business unit are required which then have to be consolidated. Furthermore, the most useful analysis will treat corporate headquarters in the same way as individual business units. Differentiating between the business units and headquarters can be very useful, as we will show with reference to the identification of potential improvements for Step 3.

As you will see, the result of undertaking a valuation of individual business units and corporate headquarters will be a number of values which can be interrogated to provide an understanding of any potential benefits from restructuring the business.

The business units can be thought of as being contributors to total business value which can be fine-tuned via operating improvements, sold to owners who are willing to pay a premium to put them to a better alternative use or to manage them better, or combined with business units of another organization in an acquisition.

We have illustrated the benefit of the discounted cash flow approach for deriving the net present value of the business. This you will recall requires as a very minimum seven value drivers, but what makes it so much more difficult in practice is the need to undertake the analysis in the most detail possible, if the most benefit is to be gained. Typically this necessitates:

- Defining the main business activities to be measured.
- Collecting data relevant to these activities.
- Undertaking individual business activity valuations.
- Aggregating individual business activity valuations.

DEFINING BUSINESS ACTIVITIES

The first need is to define business activities to be measured. One approach is to look for the smallest practicable level of aggregation, that is the smallest collective unit that can be separated and potentially disposed of in its own right. How is this achieved? The maximum of independence between activities is the key to success and, therefore, the minimum of interdependence. A good example of this can be drawn from the field of management education.

Some management colleges and universities, like Henley Management College, have developed distance learning programmes at diploma and MBA level. Interdependence in developing such programmes can be achieved by providing management education qualifications at arm's length from conventional taught activities. Necessary management expertise can be harnessed by developing learning materials not dependent upon a physical presence. While in-house expertise will often be used, the resulting materials will be a distinct product capable of separation in value terms from the rest of the business. Of course, the achievement of complete interdependence in such circumstances is very difficult, because often in-house staff will be used to provide support to activities like workshops and marking. Nevertheless, in principle, such a business can be viewed and measured as an independent unit.

One other important issue worth raising at this point concerns the treatment of headquarters' costs which can be thought of as falling into two categories: those necessary to support business units and hence attributable to those activities; and those which relate specifically to the headquarters. Those costs attributable to business units, e.g. providing services centrally that would otherwise have to be provided by the units, should be treated as business unit costs and not as headquarters' costs. This distinction has important implications for the next step.

COLLECT BUSINESS ACTIVITY DATA

Once business units have been defined, the collection of business activity data should be relatively straightforward when conducting an internal analysis. In most cases the accounting system should be able to provide a good source of data, although it may often be necessary to reclassify that provided to correspond with the requirements of the analysis and selected business unit definitions. It must also never be forgotten that costs relevant for accounting purposes may often be totally irrelevant in a future-orientated business valuation.

UNDERTAKING BUSINESS ACTIVITY VALUATIONS

This is the most difficult part of the process and involves the following:

1. *Identifying the relevant cash flows for individual business activities*   Bearing in mind that the various business activities may supply and/or be supplied with goods, transfer pricing problems may represent a potential source of cash flow distortion. If at all possible, the transfer price should be set as closely as possible to the market price of any close substitutes. In this way the stand-alone notion is endorsed. On this point, corporate overheads must be dealt with carefully. Any overheads that would be incurred with the activity operating on a stand-alone basis must be estimated and deducted in arriving at the relevant cash flow, e.g. accounting and computer costs incurred by headquarters on behalf of business units. However, those that would not be borne if the activities were separate should not be allocated.

2. *Determining the cash flow costs and benefits of corporate headquarters*
   Those costs not allocatable to business activities are those requiring close
   scrutiny at this stage. They have to be viewed in conjunction with the
   benefits to be obtained so that a position can be reached whereby the
   corporate headquarters is not seen to be either an ineffective burden
   relative to its cost, nor too lean to perform the role required of it. As a
   rough guide some research undertaken on headquarters' costs based
   upon 22 of the 25 largest US industrial companies revealed a cost
   representing an average of 1.9 per cent of the 1986 year-end market value
   of equity.

   Headquarters benefits are typically very difficult to identify, but can be
   broadly grouped into those that are in principle quantifiable and others
   which are often very important but almost impossible to measure.
   Quantifiable benefits are tax advantages from corporate level tax
   planning and greater debt capacity because the cash flows between
   business activities are not perfectly correlated, thereby removing some
   potential financial risk. Benefits that are typically important but very
   difficult to measure include synergies that would otherwise not exist
   (consider, for example, synergies of the Nestlé-Rowntree operation, such
   as possibly being able to use both Nestlé and Rowntree outlets for selling
   the products of both operations).

3. *Determination of relevant tax rates* The relevant tax rate for valuing
   independent business activities is that which it would pay were it not
   under the corporate umbrella. In a nutshell, the procedure to follow is to
   determine the taxable income of the stand-alone entity over the
   foreseeable future and then seek specialist help to ascertain relevant
   allowances and ultimately the rate to apply. This will, of course, include
   the headquarters which we are treating as a separate entity.

4. *Determine capital structure and the relevant cost of capital* We discussed
   key issues associated with the cost of capital at length in the last chapter.
   Here we will draw upon that discussion and place it within the context of
   a multi-business valuation.

   Approaches have been developed for determining cost of capital of
   different business units that are reliant upon adjusting the overall cost of
   capital and those like peer group analysis which was reviewed briefly in
   the last chapter can be used to good effect. In simple terms, this latter
   approach would involve identifying a peer group of quoted companies
   preferably from the same industry or those exhibiting key characteristics.
   Companies for inclusion in a peer group may be difficult to identify but
   this can be overcome crudely but effectively by eliciting the help of
   management. A number of managers can often readily identify relevant

peers within their own line of business activity. Once the peer group has been identified, judgement will have to be exercised as to an appropriate beta to use in calculating the cost of equity. In so doing, as many potential distortions as possible should be omitted, such as high beta values associated with highly geared peer companies so that the cost of capital used would be that which would correspond with the view taken by the average firm in the industry.

AGGREGATION OF INDIVIDUAL BUSINESS ACTIVITY VALUATIONS

If undertaken properly, this will consist of more than just adding individual valuations together. There is enormous potential for error in undertaking the individual valuations which needs to be recognized. It is wise to undertake some cross-checking by asking the following questions:

– Does the sum of the debts for individual business units equal total corporate debt?
– Does the sum of individual business unit cash flows during the historical period approximate to corporate cash flows?

At this point you have to remember that it is all too easy to build a model that is flawed. Multi-business valuation is complex and will typically be undertaken using some sort of computer support, whether this is a spreadsheet like Lotus 1-2-3 or specialist business valuation software like Alcar Value Planner. It is wise to remember the old saying 'garbage in, garbage out' at this stage because the aggregate value represents the base case or reference point for identifying potential areas of improvement.

Step 3 Estimate business value with internal improvements

By now areas of potential improvement that can be dealt with should be apparent, the value of which needs to be estimated. For example, the potential benefits from cutting the costs of corporate headquarters is one typical source, but there may be many others which may range from fine tuning on the one hand to drastic action, such as a major reorganization, on the other.

It also cannot be ignored that your analysis might have revealed the need for the business activities to be more focused. This, of course, may have external implications which we reserve for the next section. However, for those warranting closer attention the internal business improvements may require more rather than less expenditure than previously estimated.

Step 4 Estimate business value with external improvements

As indicated, it may be all too apparent that the business value cannot be improved sufficiently from internal action alone. Disposing of parts of the business and restructuring to give a more focused approach to increase business value has become popular. A good example of the pursuit of such an approach was provided by BAT Industries in their circular to shareholders in 1989 'Building Shareholder Value' which made reference to the following measures and benefits:

(1) Concentration upon financial services and tobacco.
(2) Shareholding restructuring whereby shareholders would receive shares in two new publicly listed companies.
(3) A higher level of dividend payout.
(4) The proposal to buy back of up to 10% of BAT's shares.
(5) Sale of US retailing companies and sale of interests in some others.

In some cases, restructuring in this way helps to remove what has been referred to as 'conglomerate discount' in the share price. This is where the extent of an organization's diversification is seen as being almost a risk, the risk being that it will not be managed as effectively because of the breadth and often apparent lack of complementarity of activities.

A disposal should only be undertaken if to do so will create greater value. While an obvious point, it can sometimes be very difficult to ensure that this is so. Measurement of the value to be gained starts from the base case 'as is' which we discussed earlier. To this should be added the gain from its disposal, that is the difference between its market value as a stand-alone entity as operated by its current parent, and the market price when disposed of. From this value the tax liabilities created by its sale, and expected losses of benefits must be deducted. Some of these benefits may be difficult to measure accurately. For example, disposing of one business unit may impact upon all sorts of economies of scale previously received such as deals with suppliers and the management of operations.

It is obviously important to search for all of the benefits and if you have a clear idea of who might be the potential purchaser you should attempt a valuation from its perspective. As we have indicated with reference to the Rowntree Nestlé takeover, synergistic benefits can be very important.

Last, but by no means least, external improvements may warrant an acquisition. In this case establishing the benefits by way of synergies is crucial to success. As we will discuss later under the heading of external restructuring, the key message is to try and quantify all benefits as far as is possible using the net present value approach we have described.

Determining the optimal restructured value

Having gone through these four steps the optimal value of the business should be measurable using the approach we outlined in Chapter 18. The difference between this and the market-determined value represents what can be attained by a raider or by current management, if it has the foresight and determination to make changes in good time. The best defence against a takeover is to ensure that the value gap between existing and restructured activities is so small that no outsider could reasonably gain from taking control.

20.2 Mergers, acquisitions and external restructuring

Much of what was said in the last section about internal restructuring applies to evaluating external restructuring options like mergers and acquisitions. The objective in undertaking such options must be to add value, otherwise the exercise will be pointless. Of course, such additional value may not result immediately – it may take time to capture – which is where an approach reliant upon assessing future cash flows conveys distinctive advantages over more traditional measures that focus upon the shorter term.

How is value added in a merger or acquisition? This can best be understood if we recognize explicitly that value will be added quite simply if the present value of the benefits exceeds those relating to the costs – an obvious point, but one which is useful for focusing our thoughts.

The first source of value concerns the potential synergies that will arise. For example, in terms of the seven value drivers:

1. Sales growth may improve because of being able to use the distribution channels of each organization to sell the products of both.
2. Operating profit margins may be able to be reduced because of being able to use production facilities more efficiently.
3. Cash taxes may be saved by being able to plan the tax position of the new combined organization. This area may be particularly beneficial for certain types of cross-border deals.
4. Fixed capital requirements may be lowered by being able to use available spare capacity for providing for increased sales activity. There may also be an impact upon replacement capital requirements, a good example of this being the decision to merge by two high street clearing banks. It may be possible to provide service to both sets of customers in the new organization by cutting the number of branches.
5. Working capital requirements can be reduced if the two businesses have a

profile of cash flows opposite in effect to one another. There may also be potential benefits arising from better debtor, creditor and stock management.

6. The planning horizon may be lengthened because, for example, the new larger venture increases barriers to entry.

7. The cost of capital may fall if access is obtained to cheaper sources of finance.

A second, and very important source of value comes from stripping out activities that may be a source of potential 'conglomerate discount'. In this way the costs associated with a merger or acquisition can be substantially reduced and the real benefits drastically improved. You may remember the Hanson example from Chapter 18 where, after buying Imperial Tobacco for £2.5 billion and selling off the group's Courage and Golden Wonder businesses and other relatively small businesses for £2.3 billion, the company retained businesses worth about £1.4 billion.

Just as with an internal restructuring, there are important questions to be asked about the source of benefits as well as potential problem areas. The methodology employed should be exactly the same involving the four steps identified earlier. However, what makes the merger and acquisition trail more challenging is that obtaining good quality, robust financial information may be very difficult for the acquirer. For the organization being acquired a major difficulty may be in terms of understanding the basis for the value placed upon the organization by the outsider whose rationale might be based upon a totally different view of its future potential.

20.3 Conclusion

In this chapter we have reviewed valuation within the context of restructuring, which is a term that can be used to capture all sorts of initiatives like mergers and acquisitions, divestments to unrelated parties, buyouts by existing management, joint ventures and strategic alliances. We have shown how the valuation approach developed earlier can be used in a way which enables the dynamics of business to be captured and expressed in financial terms in the form of shareholder value, for organizations that comprise a number of different businesses. In such circumstances, there is a need to be able to evaluate a portfolio of business units for which a good understanding of the business units is required. This necessitates careful analysis of the threats and opportunities faced by each and recognition that each of the business units may well be subject to different degrees of market risk, thereby necessitating the use of a different cost of capital for each. Looking at the total business as a portfolio of business units, a company-wide valuation can be built from separate valuations of business units, but this requires a much deeper level of analysis than a valuation that looks at the organization as a whole.

As we have demonstrated, business valuation and restructuring can be looked at from two perspectives. First, for assessing opportunities to restructure an organization by taking advantage of all conceivable value enhancements whether they are internal or external. This is internal restructuring where the challenge is to analyse the multi-business so as to derive as much value from it as is possible. Second, there is external restructuring commonly associated with mergers and acquisitions. The distinction between the two may not always be crystal clear, but irrespective, the ability to take different value perspectives will be an important feature. As we indicated earlier, internal restructuring, like that proposed in the demerger of ICI, should never lose sight of closing potential value gaps that might be taken advantage of by an acquirer. Equally, in an acquisition, or external restructuring, there will always be a buyer and seller, and the picture may be complicated by the existence of multiple sellers.

The main points to remember from this chapter include the following:

- Different perceptions of what can be done with a business provide a key stimulus for business restructuring.
- The need to take different value perspectives is an important feature in business restructuring.
- Internal restructuring involves the assessment of opportunities and the taking of action to restructure an organization by means of all conceivable value enhancements.
- The financial benefits of a potential restructuring can be measured by calculating market value, business 'as is', business value with internal improvements and business value with external improvements.
- The objective of undertaking an option such as external restructuring must be to add value, although this may not result immediately but relate to future cash flow possibilities.

21
Conclusion

Our path through the world of finance has brought us to the end of the trail. We have progressed through four stages:

1. Financial principles and practices
2. Financial awareness
3. Financial management
4. Financial direction.

We have ended our journey at a most appropriate juncture – the interface between finance and strategy.

As we indicated at the outset, this book has been written with the general manager in mind and was designed so as to track the requirements of such an individual's career progression. In recognition of the demands of general management we have taken an integrative, holistic and strategic approach, but one also which recognizes that many general managers will have developed an understanding of accounting and finance based on what is known as the conventional wisdom, which focuses upon profit analysis over a relatively short-term horizon. This conventional wisdom represents the language of accounting within most of the organizations of which we have experience and cannot, therefore, be completely ignored.

We have, therefore, reviewed this conventional wisdom, discussed its shortcomings, and presented an alternative approach more appropriate to the needs of general management, the applications of which we discussed in the last chapter.

We believe that you are now equipped to understand the key issues in working with finance from a general management perspective. Doubtless there are 'i's' that need dotting and 't's' that need crossing. This we would expect because our intention was never to make you into an accountant or a finance specialist. We believe our challenge was to give you sufficient financial insight to have an overview of the subject, be able to ask the right questions of your financial specialists, and ultimately to be able to interpret and understand their comments. We sincerely hope that we have succeeded.

Glossary

Note: Words set in italic are cross-references.

A

Absorption costing (more accurately full absorption costing) Ascertaining and recording the combined fixed and variable cost of a product or service. In this system, fixed costs are absorbed into the cost of a product or service – hence 'absorption' costing.

Accounting The process used to measure and report relevant financial information about the economic activities of a business to its stakeholders, e.g. shareholders, management and employees.

Accounting conventions Principles and practices developed by the accounting profession for the construction of financial accounts. These include:

- going concerns (see Chapter 4)
- separate identity/entity
- money measurement
- timing of reports
- realization
- consistency
- prudence
- matching
- materiality, etc.

Accounting policies The interpretation of the rules applied by a company in producing its financial statements

Accounting ratio A relationship derived from the values of two pieces of accounting or financial information that can be used to draw inferences about performance which are otherwise impossible when those data are assessed separately.

Accounting standards See *Statement of standard accounting practices.*

Accounting Standards Board (ASB) The UK body responsible for producing accounting standards.

Accounts (or books): The financial records kept by a business.

Accrual Accounting The process of accounting which recognizes the incidence of income and expenditure, irrespective of the timing of associated cash flows.

Accumulated depreciation The accumulation of annual depreciation charges which, when deducted from the value of fixed assets, yields what is referred to as their 'net book value'.

Acid test An American term for the quick ratio.

Activity-Based Costing (ABC) A cost acounting approach concerned with linking costs with the activities that caused them.

Allocation (of costs) The attribution of whole items of cost to individual cost centres.

Amortization A reduction in the book value of a fixed asset over time like depreciation and normally associated with the treatment of intangible assets.

Annual report: See *Corporate report.*

Apportionment of costs The distribution of items of common cost to several cost centres on the basis of estimated benefit received.

Appropriation A term normally used to describe the division of profit generated.

Asset An item of value. Also the accounting term used to describe the items which a business owns or possesses.

Asset stripping A term associated with the acquisition of a business with a view to generate cash by disposing of assets while often retaining its core.

Asset turnover A measure of the efficiency with which the assets of a business generate their output. The ratio is:

$$\frac{\text{Sales}}{\text{Assets (net or total)}}$$

Associated company A company which has 20 per cent or more of its equity share capital owned by another company.

Audit The examination of an organization's affairs, mainly through its accounting records. It is often associated with the legal requirement for all limited liability companies to be audited externally by those qualifed to do so, but it may also be undertaken internally for achieving financial control.

Auditors' report A statutory report on the annual accounts of an organization resulting from an audit by an independent firm of accountants.

Authorized share capital The total number of/value of shares that a company can issue, as set out in its memorandum of association.

B

Balance sheet A statement showing the assets held by a company, their value and the sources of its finances at a point in time, i.e. a 'snapshot'.

Batch costing The calculation of the total expenditure attributable to a group or quantity of finished goods of similar kind.

Beta A measure of the riskiness of a share relative to the market bookkeeping. The system is associated with recording financial transactions (keeping the accounts) of borrowed capital. The finance of a company that has to be paid back to the lender.

Brand accounting A term associated with carrying brand names as intangible assets in the balance sheet.

Break-even analysis or BEA See *cost–volume–profit analysis (CVP).*

Break-even point The volume of activity or sales at which total revenue equals total cost.

Budget The expression of management's forecast short-term achievement in financial and numerical terms.

Budget centre A generic title to describe all responsibility centres. (See *Responsibility centre, Cost revenue centre, Profit centre* and *Investment centre.*)

Budgetary control A system of setting budgets, recording activity and evaluating ongoing performance.

Budgeting The process of setting budgets.

Buffer budgets Budgets for stocks, debtors, creditors and cash/bank balances; their common characteristic being to even out discontinuities between (among other items) production and sales, cash inflows and cash outflows.

Burden An American term for 'overhead' (see *Overhead cost*).

Business risk Risk to the business performance arising from foreign competition, price competition, substitute products, technological obsolescence and/or fluctuations and changes in the national economy.

C

Called-up share capital That part of issued share capital for which funds have been called up, e.g. a company that has authorized share capital of £1 million but has only issued or called up 75 per cent, or £3/4 million.

Capital When used without a qualifying adjective, this word is ambiguous. Use with caution!

Capital Asset Pricing Model (CAPM) A technique associated with deriving the cost of a business's equity from the risk-free rate, the business's beta, and the marked risk premium. The formula for its calculation is:

Cost of equity = Risk free rate + (Beta × Market risk premium)

Capital employed The funds used to finance business. Measured in 'total' or 'net' of current liabilities.

Capital expenditure The purchase of fixed assets.

Capitalization The recognition of an item of cost normally written off against periodic profit as a fixed asset carried in the balance sheet.

Capital structure The way a company has raised its long-term finance, through borrowing or equity capital.

Cash flow The amount of cash flowing into or out of a business during a prescribed period of time.

Cash flow forecast The expression of the amount of cash expected to flow into or out of a business over a prescribed period of time (e.g. 1 year) analysed by shorter time periods (weekly, monthly, daily).

Cash flow statement The financial statement required to be produced by limited liability companies for the last year and analysed by operating, financing and investing activities.

Cash limit A means of controlling costs (usually, fixed overheads) by a limit of cash payments for each budget period.

Centre for Interfirm Comparison (CIFC) A company involved in all aspects of performance measurement and improvement, particularly interfirm comparison (see *Interfirm comparison*).

Chairman's statement A review of a company's activities made by its chairman, included in the corporate/annual report.

Charge on assets Security on a loan which gives the lender priority in recovering outstanding amounts should the business fail.

Commercial loan A loan made to a business at a rate of interest which may be secured by a charge on assets, or be unsecured for the most reptuable businesses (e.g. blue chip companies).

Company A legal organization set up by registration under the Companies Act, or by Act of Parliament or by charger, and having a life independent of its members.

Companies Acts Acts of Parliament that specify legal requirements of companies on a wide range of activites, including accounting.

Company limited by shares A company where the members are liable for the company's debts only to the amount they owe on their shares.

Compounding The process of accumulating interest with the principal associated with it (see *Compound interest*).

Compound interest Interest payable on the principal sum lent and the accumulated interest on the principal.

Consistency An accounting principle meaning that the treatment of particular items should be the same from period to period.

Consolidated accounts Accounting statements where the accounts of a holding company and all its subsidiaries are amalgamated into one, as though it were a single entity.

Consolidation See *Consolidated accounts*.

Contingent liability A liability which is likely to occur soon after the balance sheet date but which is included in the accounts only by way of a note.

Contract costing Ascertaining the amount of expenditure attributable to a complete contract, e.g. the construction of a new factory.

Contribution The difference between sales revenue and marginal or variable costs.

Contribution margin per unit The difference between the selling price of a product and its unit marginal or variable cost of production and sale.

Contribution/sales ratio See *Profit/volume ratio*.

Control Monitoring performance, recording and measuring actions and evaluating results.

Convertible loan stock A loan which entitles the holder to change to ordinary shares, usually at a set time.

Corporate control The acquisition of control of a company as a result of buying up sufficient of its shares in the market.

Corporate liquidation The winding up of a company typically because of its failure due to cash flow shortages

Corporate report The annual published financial report of an organization.

Cost driver The event or forces that are the significant determinants of the cost of business activities.

Cost of capital The cost to a business of the funds actually raised from its various sources or, from the opposite perspective, the return required by the providers of funds for their investment.

Cost of debt The cost of loans to a business calculated after tax.

Cost of equity The cost to a business that is typically calculated using a dividend valuation approach or the Capital Asset Pricing Model (see *Capital Asset Pricing Model*).

Cost of sales The expenses associated with sales turnover, including overheads and the direct costs.

Cost revenue centre An area of responsibility in which the manager has control of either all costs or revenues of that area.

Cost–Volume–Profit (CVP) analysis A technique for analysing the relationship between costs, volume and profit, e.g. to determine the break-even point (see *Break-even point*).

Creative accounting The term used to describe the use of accounting principles to convey the performance of the business in the most favourable light.

Credit rating An opinion on the risk of default of a fixed income security.

Creditor (trade) A person or business to whom a trade debt is owed and (in the balance sheet) the total of such sums.

Creditor days The number of days of creditors 'held' by the business is estimated from the following ratio:

$$\frac{\text{Creditors}}{\text{Sales}} \times 360$$

Creditors – amounts due within one year The amount of money owed and payable by the business within one year, e.g. short-term loans.

Creditors – amounts due after one year The amount of money owed and payable by the business after one year, e.g. long-term loans.

Creditor turnover A measure of a firm's credit policy. The ratio is:

$$\frac{\text{Payments for goods and services}}{\text{Trade creditors}}$$

but may sometimes be expressed:

$$\frac{\text{Sales}}{\text{Trade creditors}}$$

Cumulative preference shares Shares entitling the holder to a fixed rate of dividend, before the ordinary shareholders and any arrears are made up in future years.

Current asset The assets used in a company's day-to-day trading activities all of which at some stage will become cash. Includes cash, debtors and stocks.

Current cost accounting (CCA) A method of accounting which uses current costs rather than historic costs. A system of accounting that used to be required for all companies by a UK accounting standard. While the standard has been withdrawn it is still used by some organizations. Under this system assets are included at their present-day values rather than the cost at which they were obtained. Profits are adjusted to reflect these higher values.

Current liabilities Amounts of money owed by a company which have to be paid in the near future, normally within a year; includes creditors, bank overdrafts, current tax due and dividends due.

Current ratio The ratio of current assets to current liabilities. A (crude) measure of liquidity.

D

Debentures A source of borrowing for a company, of a long-term nature and usually stating the rate of interest and when repayment is to occur.

Debt The total amount owed by a company to external providers of funds.

Debt capacity The total amount of finance a company could in theory borrow.

Debtor days The number of days debtors 'held' by the business estimated from the following ratio:

$$\frac{\text{Debtors}}{\text{Sales}} \times 360$$

Debtor (trade) An individual or organization who owes money.

Debtor turnover A measure of the credit policy of a firm. The ratio is:

$$\frac{\text{Credit sales}}{\text{Trade debtors}}$$

Depreciation The loss of the value of fixed assets over time which is normally assumed to reflect their usage.

Depreciation charge The charge for depreciation made against profit in the profit and loss account.

Deprival value The value of an asset (often equivalent to replacement value) which would be measured by the reduction in wealth of a business were it to be deprived of the asset.

Development expenditure Expenditure associated with developing a new product normally charged against profit.

Differential cost A cost which differs between two or more alternative courses of action.

Diluted earnings per share Profit after taxation divided by the weighted average of ordinary shares, after allowing for full conversion rights attaching to convertible securities and the allotment of shares under option schemes and warrants, and with a corresponding adjustment to income for interests.

Direct cost A cost directly attributable to a product or service.

Direct cost of sales The sum of materials used, direct wages and direct expenses associated with the item sold.

Directive A legal instrument issued by the EC Commission covering a wide range of issues including accounting intended for adoption by member states in their legislation.

Directors' report A report from the directors of a limited company to its shareholders, included in the corporate or annual report.

Discount rate See *Cost of capital.*

Discounted cash flow (DCF) A technique for appraising investment or financing opportunities which expresses cash flow in terms of the 'time value' of money.

Dividend The money paid out of profits to shareholders.

Dividend cover A measure of the protection against dividend variation. It can be calculated from post-tax earnings per share divided by dividend paid per share.

Dividend yield The dividend per share (gross of tax) expressed as a percentage of the market price of a share.

Double-entry bookkeeping A system of bookkeeping attributed to the Italians in the sixteenth century whereby every transaction is recorded twice in the books, once as a debit and once as a credit. This system is widely used and underpins the main financial statements produced by an organization.

E

Earnings Profit after deducting interest charges, tax, minority interests and preference dividends, but before deducting extraordinary items.

Earnings per share (EPS) Profit after taxation divided by the weighted average of ordinary shares in issue during the year. Also known as the undiluted earnings per share (see *Diluted earnings per share*).

EBIT (PBIT) Earnings before the deduction of interest and tax – used in calculating profit on capital employed (see *Profit on capital employed*).

Economic value The value of an asset which is derived from expressing all of its potential cash flows (over its lifetime) in terms of present worth.

Employee report A version of the annual report prepared for the specific needs of employees.

Equity See *Owners' equity.*

Equity capital The net worth of a business, or the capital belonging to the ordinary shareholders – includes issued share capital, reserves and profits retained in the company (see *Owners' equity*).

Exception reporting A system of variance accounting where only those major/ significant variances from standard or budget are reported.

Exceptional items Costs and revenues that relate to normal business activities and which are exceptional only in terms of their value.

Exposure A term used in relation to the risk associated with international activities, i.e. the exposure to transactions and the translation from a foreign currency into the parent company's currency.

Extraordinary items Costs and revenues that do not relate to normal business activities.

F

Financial accounting Recording the financial transactions and positions of a business principally for the benefit of external parties, e.g. shareholders.

Financial direction Direction of the organization's long-term funding and investing activities, typically the responsibility of the most senior financial specialist.

Financial management Management of all aspects of the organization's finances.

Financial model A model of a business in quantitative and financial terms.

Financial picture The view of the business provided by the profit and loss account, the balance sheet and the cash flow statement.

Financial Reporting Council The body responsible for the setting and enforcement of accounting standards in the United Kingdom.

Financial reporting standards (FRSs) The name now adopted for UK accounting standards which are required by the accounting standards boards and replace statements of standard accounting practice.

Financial risk Risk that arises from the funding of operations by sources attracting fixed-term interest payments rather than variable dividend payments. It is a risk resulting from an organization's financial structure.

Financial structure The way a company's total finances have been arranged.

Financial summary Financial status measures ratios designed to assess the financial status and riskiness of a company.

Financing costs Costs associated with servicing the capital structure of an organization.

Fixed assets The possessions of a business, not used up in the trading process nor held for resale in the normal course of trading, which it uses to carry out its activities. Includes land, buildings, machinery and vehicles.

Fixed period costs Costs which remain at a static level, or relatively unchanged within a given time period over a prescribed range of activity or volume or output or sales (see also *Period cost*).

Flexed budget A budget which assumes several levels of activity and which anticipates costs and revenues appropriate to the various levels assumed.

Forecast The most likely anticipated result, based on relevant history, research and assumptions.

Full listing Public limited companies with at least 25 per cent of their funds in the hands of the public are said to have a full listing specified in the so-called *Yellow Book*.

Funds flow statement A statement setting out where the funds to run a business have come from and where they have gone to.

G

Gearing (gearing ratio) Strictly speaking, the proportion of a company's capital that has been borrowed (sometimes called prior charge capital) in relation to its equity. Sometimes this relationship is relaxed to include preference share capital. If there is a higher proportion of prior charge capital than equity capital, the gearing is high. If the proportion is low, the gearing is low.

Generally accepted accounting principles (GAAPs) See *Accounting conventions.*

Going concern An accounting principle meaning that an organization is assumed to continue in operational existence for the foreseeable future.

Goodwill The excess price paid for a business over its book value. The difference between the value of a company as a whole and the value of its assets and liabilities taken separately – usually the result of a change in the ownership of a business.

Gross profit (turnover) Sales revenue minus the cost of sales.

H

Historical cost (accounting) The actual cost of obtaining an asset, or goods or services. The system of accounting whereby transactions are recorded in the accounts at their money values when they took place (also known as historical cost accounting).

Historical summaries Summaries of performance (after five years) found in an organization's annual report.

Hurdle rate A term taken from the sport which describes the rate of return that must be achieved or jumped, or proposed capital expenditure to be acceptable in economic terms.

I

Incremental budgeting A means of estimating future fixed overhead costs by adding a predetermined percentage to the previous accounting period's actual costs.

Incremental costing See *Marginal cost.*

Inflation accounts Financial statements which incorporate the effects of price-level changes in preference to relying upon the historic cost convention (see *Current cost accounting*).

Insolvency The inability to meet debts that are due.

Institutional shareholder A pension fund, insurance company or similar organization devoted to the professional investment of savings.

Intangible asset An asset that does not have a physical appearance but which has a value to a firm.

Interest The sum of money paid by a borrower to a lender for the use a loan.

Interest cover Profit before interest and tax divided by interest payable. A measure of income gearing. The ratio is:

$$\frac{\text{Net profit before interest and tax}}{\text{Interest payable}}$$

Interfirm comparison A cooperative activity based on detailed information provided by participants in absolute confidence from which a set of ratios relevant to a specific type of organization can be produced to identify areas of relative strength and weakness.

Interim reporting Half-yearly unaudited reports required to be produced by quoted public limited companies.

Internal rate of return The discount rate (as used in DCF) which forces the present value of a future cash flow stream to be exactly equal to the capital sum required to purchase that stream, i.e. net present value = zero.

Investment centre An area of responsibility for which the manager has control of costs, revenues and investment in fixed and other assets.

Investment measures Ratios that examine the mechanisms by which financial results relate to shareholders' funds and stock market prices.

Investments Money which is invested outside the business to earn interest, dividends or other benefits.

Issued share capital The number and amount of shares issued to ordinary shareholders.

J

Job costing Ascertaining the amount of expenditure attributable to a specific complete unit of finished output.

L

Lease An asset hired rather than bought, on which rent is paid.

Lease capitalization See *Capitalization.*

Leverage An American term for gearing.

Liabilities The financial obligations of a company represented by the financial claims of lenders and others who supply money, goods and services to a business.

Limiting factor Internal and/or external factors which may limit a firm's ability to control its future.

Liquid assets Assets that can be turned quickly into money.

Liquid ratio See *Quick ratio.*

Liquidity The ability of a business to pay its way.

Listed company See *Quoted company.*

Listing agreement Any company with publicly quoted share capital or debt is subject to a listing agreement that specifies its duties towards the various stakeholders involved.

Loan capital Finance that has been borrowed and not obtained from the shareholders.

Long-term liabilities Liabilities of a business which are not current, e.g. medium-term bank loans.

Long-term planning Assessing trends and identifying and choosing between alternative courses of action over a period of many years.

Loss The reduction in wealth occurring between the start and finish of a period of trading.

M

Management accounting The provision of information required by management in the formulation of policies, planning and controlling business activities and selecting appropriate courses of action from available opportunities.

Marginal cost The cost of producing and selling one additional unit of output.

Master budget The end result of the budgeting process expressed in terms of a profit and loss account, balance sheet, and cash flow statement.

Matching An accounting principle which ensures that costs are matched with their associated revenues.

Materiality An accounting convention meaning that the non- standard usage of an accounting practice is permissible if the effects are not material.

Medium-term planning Optimizing the use of resources over a manageable future period bearing in mind the strategies identified in long-term planning.

Memorandum of association The document that contains the basis of the legal constitution of a company.

Merger The amalgamation of organizations where no controlling interest is explicitly evident.

Money measurement A convention whereby accounting only records those events which may be described in money terms.

N

Net assets The total assets of a business minus its liabilities, i.e. equal to owners' equity.

Net assets per share A measure of the underlying asset value of a share. The ratio is:

$$\frac{\text{Net assets}}{\text{Number of ordinary shares issued}}$$

Net current assets The excess of current assets over current liabilities. Also known as working capital.

Net interest income Interest receivable *less* interest payable.

Net present value The difference between the present value (i.e. discounted value) of a future cash flow stream and the capital sum required to purchase that stream.

Net profit before tax What remains after costs, overheads *less* other income and net interest income have been deducted from sales turnover but before tax is deducted.

Net profit after tax Net profit before tax *less* tax payable.

Net realizable value The value of an asset which is equivalent to its sales proceeds minus costs of disposal.

Net worth The sum of a company's paid-up share capital and reserves (including retained profits).

Non-accrual accounting Processes focus upon receipts and payments and cash.

O

Operating gearing The risk to the business from investing in fixed assets that need to be funded by regular inflows of profit/cash to ensure business viability.

Operating profit What remains after cost of sales, administrative and distribution costs have been deducted from sales turnover.

Operation costing See *Process costing* and *Service costing*.

Opportunity cost The notional cost to be incurred from being unable to undertake the next best alternative course of action.

Option A financial instrument that enables the purchaser to minimize risk by limiting it only to the 'upside', or the potential to benefit from a transaction.

Ordinary shares Shares that attract no guaranteed return by way of a dividend – the dividend is contingent upon performance.

Overdraft A facility granted by a lending body like a bank whereby credit can be obtained, the interest payable being contingent upon the extent to which the facility is used.

Overhead cost Cost incurred other than direct costs, i.e. not charges directly applicable to the product sold. In other words, the costs of production, selling and administration of a business, other than the direct costs of producing its products or services. Also known as burden.

Overtrading Expanding business activities more quickly than the capacity of the business to finance them without exposing it to the risk of not being able to meet the demands of providers of finance.

Owners' equity The financial claims of the owners of a business, i.e. ordinary share capital plus reserves.

P

Participating preference shares Shares with a fixed dividend and the possibility of a share of remaining profits if profits are sufficient to allow this.

Payback The period required for the operating cash surpluses generated by a particular investment to equate, in aggregate, to the capital sum originally invested.

Payments Quite simply the payments in cash made by the business.

Payments in advance Sums paid out in one year for the benefit of a future period. A current asset.

Period cost A cost related to the passage of time rather than the volume of output, e.g. depreciation.

Perpetuity Investment offering a level stream of cash flows in perpetuity.

Planning Determining the direction of a business and setting suitable targets for achievement.

Political risk The risk to business profits that arises from political events, e.g. expropriation of assets and profits.

Preference shares Shares that have a fixed rate of dividend and which are paid before ordinary shareholders' entitlement.

Present value The discounted value of a future cash flow. The present value is a function of the timing of the cash flow and the rate of interest assumed to be paid or earned.

Price/earnings ratio (P/E) The current market price of a share divided by earnings per share.

Price/earnings relative (PER) A means of comparing a company's PE ratio with the market as a whole:

$$PER = \frac{PE \text{ of company}}{PE \text{ of market}}$$

Prime cost The cost of direct materials, labour and expenses incurred in producing a product.

Principal budget factor The most important limiting factor for a business.

Private company A company with at least two members which has the word 'Limited' or 'Ltd' after its name and is not a public company.

Process costing Ascertaining the amount of expenditure attributable to the production of goods by a continuous operation or process.

Productivity A measurement of the quantity of output in relation to input; often output per employee.

Product mix The mix of products of a business, usually expressed in sales volume or sales value terms.

Profit   The difference between the wealth of a business at the start of a period of trading and its greater wealth at the end of that period.

Profitability   A measure of how effectively a company has been operating.

Profit and loss account   A statement showing what profit has been made over a period and the uses to which the profit has been put.

Profit centre   An area of responsibility for which the manager has control of revenues and associated costs.

Profit margin   A measure of the profitability of sales which reflects the combination of cost and pricing structures of the business. The ratio is:

$$\frac{\text{Operating profit}}{\text{Sales}}$$

Profit on capital employed   A measure of the profitability achieved on capital employed (in the United Kingdom, often measured in terms of total assets *less* current liabilities). The ratio is:

$$\frac{\text{PBIT}}{\text{Capital employed}}$$

Profit on sales   A measure of the profit(ability) achieved.

Profit/volume ratio   The ratio of contribution per unit to selling price per unit (see also *Contribution/sales ratio*).

Prospectus   A document setting out relevant financial and other information which is issued to the public when a company wishes to raise capital from the stock market.

Prudence   An accounting convention meaning that provision should be made for all potential costs, whereas profits should not be accounted for until realized.

Public limited company (plc)   A limited liability company which has a share capital, has at least two members, and is registered under the Companies Acts and has the letters 'plc' after its name (in Wales the letters 'ccc' will be found).

Published accounts   The statutory accounts that organizations like quoted public limited liability companies are required to produce annually.

Q

Quick ratio   The ratio of debtors (accounts receivable) plus cash to current liabilities. Also known as the acid test.

Quoted company   A public limited company with a stock exchange listing and which is able to sell its equity and/or debt openly in the market.

R

Rate of return   The accounting rate of return, that is, the accounting return on profit generated from an investment ratio. The expression of one price of financial data in terms of another.

Ratio analysis   A technique used for analysing the financial statements of a business.

Receipts   Quite simply, the receipts in cash received by a business realization. A convention of accounting which recognizes only those profits which have been realized in the accounting period.

Reducing balance   A term applied to depreciating a fixed asset over time in which the annual depreciation charge decreases with every additional year.

Relevant cost   A cost which is strictly germane to a particular decision.

Relevant range   The range of output over which an analysis of costs remains valid.

Replacement value   The value of an asset derived from the cost of replacing it with an identical or similar item.

Research and development   The term applied to the costs incurred in relation to a potential product or service that is, by convention, written off against annual profits.

Reserves   Part of equity capital and consisting of retained profits, surplus values created by the revaluation of assets, and other surplus sums arising from the sale of shares. Typically the largest part of reserves is represented by accumulated profits attributable to ordinary shareholders which have not been distributed by way of dividends but which have been reinvested in the business.

Residual value   The value generated by a strategic option beyond the selected planning period.

Responsibility centre   The sphere of responsibility of an individual manager.

Retained earnings/profits   Profits after tax minus dividends paid to shareholders kept in the company after all commitments have been met and shareholders paid a dividend.

Return on assets   Profit (before or after tax) expressed as a percentage of some measure of assets, e.g. in the United States total assets and in the United Kingdom net assets (see *Return on net assets*).

Return on capital employed   Profit (before or after tax) expressed as a percentage of an appropriate measure of capital employed (see, e.g., *Return on net assets*).

Return on equity   The percentage rate of return provided to equity investors. The ratio is:

$$\frac{\text{Profit after tax attributable to ordinary shareholders}}{\text{Owners' equity}}$$

Return on net assets   Profits (usually before tax and interest payable) expressed as a percentage of net assets. A measure of the efficiency with which the net assets employed in a business generate profits. The ratio is:

$$\frac{\text{Profit before interest and tax}}{\text{Net assets employed}}$$

Return on sales   Profit (usually before tax and interest payable) expressed as a percentage of sales revenue. The ratio is:

$$\frac{\text{Profit before interest and tax}}{\text{Sales revenue}}$$

Revaluation reserve   A reserve capital created when assets are revalued.

Revenues   See *Turnover*.

Rights issue   An issue of extra shares to existing shareholders in proportion to their existing holding, often at a favourable price.

Risk   The probability that the return on an investment will not be as expected. Refers also to the probability of any future event turning out worse than anticipated.

Rolling forecast   A forecast, of prescribed duration, which extends automatically as time elapses.

Roman law   An approach adopted in continental European countries that relies upon a detailed system of laws and penalties such that there should always be a law on any matter.

S

Sales as a multiple of capital employed Sales revenue expressed as a multiple of the capital employed in the form of the assets it represents. The ratio is:

$$\frac{\text{Sales revenue}}{\text{Capital employed}}$$

Sales revenue See *Turnover*.

Scrip issue (or bonus issue) An issue of extra shares (at no cost) to existing shareholders in proportion to their existing holding. The total amount involved is transferred from reserves to issued share capital and is known as the 'capitalization of reserves'.

Secret reserves Reserves appropriated from profits, the amount of which is unknown as is the accumulated value. A practice associated with some continental European countries.

Sensitivity analysis A system of examining different assumptions when planning or budgeting, or evaluating a short- or long-term opportunity.

Separate identity (entity) An acounting convention meaning that an organization is deemed to have a separate existence from its owners.

Service costing Ascertaining the amount of expenditure attributable to the provision of a service requiring repetitive or continuous operations or processes.

Share capital The shareholders' investment in a company (see also *Issued share capital*).

Shareholder value analysis A discounted cash flow technique that enables the potential value of strategic options to be evaluated from a shareholder's perspective.

Share premium The excess paid for a share, to the company, over its nominal value.

Shareholders' funds See *Owners' equity*.

Short-term planning Detailed planning by which medium-term objectives are developed into plans which reflect immediate pressures and constraints (see *Budget*).

Solvency Having enough money to meet all pecuniary liabilities.

Specific order costing See *Job costing*, *Batch costing* and *Contract costing*.

Standard costing Ascertaining the expected standard costs of a product or process after assuming specified operating conditions.

Statement A statement showing the sources of money in a company during a period and the uses to which that money has been put. Replaced in the United Kingdom and United States with a cash flow statement.

Statement of standard accounting practice (SSAP) The accountancy bodies' recommendations for good practice in accounting matters in the United Kingdom. Now replaced by Financial reporting standards (see *Financial reporting standards*).

Stock (1) Items held for conversion at a later date into sales, including materials, finished goods, components, bought-out parts and work-in-progress. Included in current assets. (2) A fixed amount of paid-up capital held by a stockholder. Also, in the United States, the equivalent of shares.

Stock days   The number of days' stock 'held' by the business estimated from the following ratio:

$$\frac{\text{Stock}}{\text{Sales}} \times 360$$

Stock market   An association of dealers in stocks conducting business according to fixed rules.

Stock turnover   A (relatively crude) measure of the efficiency with which stocks are held to meet sales, e.g. the ratio of finished goods stock turnover is:

$$\frac{\text{Cost of sales (or sales)}}{\text{Finished goods stock}}$$

Straight-line depreciation   The writing down of an asset over its useful life using an equal amount per time period.

Strategic planning   Decision making relating to the long-term future direction of a business.

Subsidiary company   A company which has 50 per cent or more of its equity share capital owned by another (parent) company.

Surplus   The name usually given to an excess of income over expenditure in a given time period in a not-for-profit organization.

SWOT analysis   A systematic review of a firm's strengths and weaknesses, opportunities and threats.

T

Takeover   The acquisition of one company's assets by another, often corresponding with a loss of identity of the company taken over.

Tangible assets   Assets that have a physical identity, e.g. motor vehicles.

Target   The achievement required of an individual, department, etc.

Time value of money   A measure of the difference in value between a sum of money received or paid today, and the same sum received or paid at some time in the future (see also *Present value*).

Timing (of reports)   An accounting convention meaning that a time period is fixed as a basis for measurement of profit or loss.

Total assets   The sum of all of the assets of a business, i.e. fixed and current.

Trade creditors   See *Creditor (trade)*.

Trade debtors   See *Debtor (trade)*.

Trading profit   Profit from the operations of the business: gross profit *less* overhead costs.

Turnover   Revenues from the sale of goods or services, usually after deducting any sales or value added taxes and duties, trade discounts and goods returned.

U

Undiluted earnings per share   See *Earnings per share*.

Unit cost   The total cost of a given volume of output divided by its volume.

V

Value   See *Economic value, Replacement value, Net realizable value* and *Present value*.

Value added   Sales turnover minus payments to external suppliers for goods and services.

Value for money (VFM)   A means of controlling fixed overhead costs by detailed consideration of each expense item.

Variable costs   Costs which change over the relevant range of activity or volume of output or sales.

Variance accounting   The recording and reporting of actual results compared with standard or budgeted levels of performance.

Variance analysis   The analysis of variances between actual results and standard or budgeted levels of performance

W

Wealth   The value of the possessions of a business.

Work-in-progress   Items held that are not in their original state, but which have been made partly ready for sale.

Working capital   The capital available on a day-to-day basis for the operations of the business, which consists of current assets *less* current liabilities (see *Net current assets*).

Y

Yellow Book   A book which provides details of the listing agreement to which companies with a full listing or quotation on the Stock Exchange are subject.

Z

Z **scoring**   A scoring technique derived from a statistical technique known as multiple discriminant analysis that is used for predicting companies likely to fail financially.

References

Archer, S. and S. McLeay, 'European financial reporting', in *Student Financial Reporting 1991–1992: a Guide to UK Reporting Practice for Accountancy Students,* The Institute of Chartered Accountants in England and Wales, 1992.

Barron, M. and J. Lawless, 'Growth of no account', *Business Magazine,* Sept. 1988.

Coopers and Lybrand Deloitte, *Shareholder Value Analysis Survey,* 1991.

Griffith, Ian, *Creative Accounting: How to make your profits what you want them to be,* Unwin Hyman, London, 1986.

Hanson PLC Annual Report 1992.

Henry, D. and G. Smith, Letter to *The Financial Times, The Financial Times,* 27 June 1991.

Marsh, P., *Short-termism on Trial,* Institutional Fund Managers Association, 1989.

Porter, M., *Competitive Strategy,* The Free Press, 1986.

Rappaport, A., *Creating Shareholder Value – The New Standard for Business Performance,* The Free Press, 1986.

Simmonds, A. and O. Azieres, *Accounting for Europe: Success by 2000 AD?,* Touche Ross, 1989.

Smith, Terry, *Accounting for Growth: Stripping the Camouflage from Company Accounts* Century Business, London, 1992.

Thorne, P., *The New General Manager – Confronting the Key Challenge of Today's Organization,* McGraw-Hill, 1989.

UBS Phillips and Drew, *Accounting for Growth,* 1991.

Index